# About IFPRI

The International Food Policy Research Institute (IFPRI®) was established in 1975 to identify and analyze alternative national and international strategies and policies for meeting food needs of the developing world on a sustainable basis, with particular emphasis on low-income countries and on the poorer groups in those countries. Research results are disseminated to policymakers, opinion formers, administrators, policy analysts, researchers, and others concerned with national and international food and agricultural policy. IFPRI also contributes to capacity strengthening of people and institutions in developing countries that conduct research on food, agriculture, and nutrition policies.

IFPRI's research and capacity-strengthening and communications activities are made possible by its financial contributors and partners. IFPRI receives its principal funding from governments, private foundations, and international and regional organizations, most of which are members of the Consultative Group on International Agricultural Research (CGIAR). IFPRI gratefully acknowledges the generous unrestricted funding from Australia, Canada, China, Finland, France, Germany, India, Ireland, Italy, Japan, the Netherlands, Norway, South Africa, Sweden, Switzerland, the United Kingdom, the United States, and the World Bank.

# Liberalizing Foodgrains Markets

# Liberalizing Foodgrains Markets

*Experiences, Impact, and Lessons from South Asia*

**Edited by A. Ganesh-Kumar, Devesh Roy, and Ashok Gulati**

OXFORD
UNIVERSITY PRESS

# OXFORD
UNIVERSITY PRESS

YMCA Library Building, Jai Singh Road, New Delhi 110001

Oxford University Press is a department of the University of Oxford. It furthers the University's
objective of excellence in research, scholarship, and education by publishing worldwide in

Oxford New York

Auckland  Cape Town  Dar es Salaam  Hong Kong  Karachi
Kuala Lumpur  Madrid  Melbourne  Mexico City  Nairobi
New Delhi  Shanghai  Taipei  Toronto

With offices in

Argentina  Austria  Brazil  Chile  Czech Republic  France  Greece
Guatemala  Hungary  Italy  Japan  Poland  Portugal  Singapore
South Korea  Switzerland  Thailand  Turkey  Ukraine  Vietnam

Oxford is a registered trade mark of Oxford University Press
in the UK and in certain other countries

Published in India
by Oxford University Press, New Delhi

© 2010 The International Food Policy Research Institute

ISBN-13: 978-0-19-806695-8
ISBN-10: 0-19-806695-3

Printed in India at Anvi Composers, New Delhi 110 063
Published by Oxford University Press
YMCA Library Building, Jai Singh Road, New Delhi 110 001

# Contents

# Tables

# Figures

# Boxes

# Foreword

The recent food price crisis reopened the debate over whether a more open, globalized, and privatized foodgrain sector would ensure food and nutrition security for millions of the world's poor. Faced with an emergency situation, many countries reverted to interventionist and protectionist stances toward food markets, almost undoing the reforms achieved painstakingly over the course of several decades. Export bans and storage restrictions cropped up in many countries. As home to the largest number of the world's poor, South Asian countries were no exception to this agonizing trend.

With food price spikes subsiding to some extent, the time has come for a serious and informed view on whether free markets can deliver on food security in poor countries. This book focuses on this extremely important issue and considers at-border and within-border policies in relation to their implications for food security. Without adopting any prior ideological perspective, the book assesses the history of policies in South Asia, a region that offers an ideal platform for analysis because many countries started with similar initial conditions and near-identical policies but have now diverged significantly in their policy stances.

The contributors describe the dire initial situations in which these countries found themselves when they became new nations. If reforms and the right mix of policies were able to help South Asian countries overcome these earlier problems, the case against abandoning such policies in the face of food price spikes is a compelling one. In this sense, this book makes an important and timely contribution.

The book also highlights the high level of interdependence among South Asian countries, with the efficacy of one country's policies depending on the response of other countries in the region. The book's analysis clearly shows that, overlaying the benefits from regional cooperation, significant gains can be achieved by simply learning from the experience of others.

Shenggen Fan
Director General, IFPRI

# Preface

Interest in food security, especially as it pertains to basic staples such as wheat, rice, and corn, has recently been rekindled among both researchers and policymakers. Persistent or reemerging food price inflation in many countries has forced policymakers and other stakeholders in those countries, and in the G8 countries, to assess the implications of various policy packages and external environmental conditions on food security. Prominent among the factors under scrutiny is the role played by agricultural markets, both domestic and foreign. Because it is home to the largest number of poor people in the world and for various historical reasons, faith in agricultural markets has been tenuous, at best, in South Asia. Reliance on trade to achieve food security is being questioned, and most South Asian countries now want a greater degree of self-sufficiency, at least in basic staples. In addition, South Asian nations are demanding higher levels of buffer stocks to ensure that they do not have to rely significantly on trade during years of need. As a result, the process of agricultural liberalization that has been under way in much of South Asia is being reversed.

Against this backdrop of "inward movement" in grain policies, this book studies the nature, design, evolution, and effects of various reforms that were undertaken over the years with respect to both domestic and international grain markets. The outcomes are judged against the objectives set out in the food policies of individual countries. Given the state of current debate, we believe that this book will contribute significantly to an assessment of the costs and likely outcomes of reversing the process of grain market liberalization, especially in light of the unprecedented heights global staple prices reached in 2007–08, especially from March to May of 2008. This will allow policymakers to avoid acting out of panic and instead enable them to make rational decisions based on years of experience with food policies.

This book provides analysis and research-based evidence on decades of myriad food policies in South Asia. The research has been conducted by experts from the very countries studied, who understand the particular social, political, and cultural contexts of food policies within each country. The in-depth country analysis suggests that, in general, past policies aimed at self-sufficiency in grains—such as relatively closed borders and internal restrictions on private trade—had a significant negative impact on food security outcomes in South Asian countries. Policies primarily intended to improve food security outcomes actually worsened them, as corruption and inefficiencies crept into the elaborate systems created in these nations. The book does not criticize the motives behind such policies and acknowledges that the history of dramatic food insecurity in South Asian countries provided a convincing rationale for them. Nevertheless, the contributors make the case for reforming food production and delivery systems.

The research in this book is the product of intensive efforts by various authors and stakeholders who analyzed extremely complex issues. The preparation of the manuscript required several rounds of deliberation among researchers, as well as consultations with policymakers and other stakeholders. The research also benefited immensely from its presentation at a multi-stakeholder international conference that IFPRI hosted in New Delhi. The debates and validation of the data that occurred at this conference were extremely helpful in bringing the book to its present level of analysis. We are grateful to the conference participants who contributed to this process and to the peer reviewers who read the manuscript. We greatly appreciate the diligence and constructive comments of the anonymous reviewers. The book in its current form also owes a great deal to the tireless efforts of the editorial staff, who showed exemplary patience in working with the book's editors. We sincerely thank them for their positive contributions.

Last, but not least, the book would not have been possible without generous financial and institutional support from the Asian Development Bank, the Ford Foundation, the European Union, and the United States Agency for International Development, all of which funded the South Asia Initiative, under which this research was conducted. We thank these sponsors and hope this research promotes rational policy choices in South Asia and elsewhere that can ensure food security for the poor on a sustainable basis. Only then, we believe, will the sponsors' investments and researchers' labors bring high returns.

# Abbreviations and Acronyms

## General

| | |
|---|---|
| **AIDS** | almost ideal demand system |
| **CES** | constant elasticity of substitution |
| **CET** | constant elasticity of transformation |
| **CGE** | computable general equilibrium |
| **EPC** | effective protection coefficient |
| **ERP** | effective rate of protection |
| **GDP** | gross domestic product |
| **HYV** | high-yielding variety |
| **ITHC** | internal transport and handling costs |
| **IFPRI** | International Food Policy Research Institute |
| **IMF** | International Monetary Fund |
| **LC** | letter of credit |
| **MM** | multimarket |
| **MMT** | million metric tons |
| **MT** | metric ton |
| **NPC** | nominal protection coefficient |
| **NRP** | nominal rate of protection |
| **SAARC** | South Asian Association for Regional Cooperation |
| **SAM** | social accounting matrix |

| **TOT** | terms of trade |
|---|---|
| **UNDP** | United Nations Development Program |
| **WTO** | World Trade Organization |

## Bangladesh

| **BFPP** | Bangladesh Food Policy Project |
|---|---|
| **DGF** | Directorate General of Food |
| **DOF** | Department of Food |
| **EP** | Essential Priorities |
| **FPMU** | Food Policy Monitoring Unit |
| **LE** | Large Employers |
| **MOF** | Ministry of Food |
| **MP** | Millgate Purchase |
| **MR** | Modified Rationing |
| **OMS** | Open-Market Sales |
| **OP** | Other Priorities |
| **PFDS** | Public Food Distribution System |
| **PR** | Palli Rationing |
| **SR** | Statutory Rationing |
| **Tk** | taka |

## India

| **APC** | Agricultural Prices Commission |
|---|---|
| **APMC** | Agricultural Product Marketing Committee |
| **CACP** | Commission for Agricultural Costs and Prices |
| **CIP** | central issue price |
| **ECA** | Essential Commodities Act |
| **FCI** | Food Corporation of India |
| **FPS** | Fair Price Shops |

| | |
|---|---|
| **MSP** | minimum support price |
| **PDS** | public distribution system |
| **TPDS** | Targeted Public Distribution System |

## Nepal

| | |
|---|---|
| **AIC** | Agriculture Inputs Corporation |
| **APP** | Agriculture Perspective Plan |
| **APROSC** | Agricultural Projects Services Center |
| **CBS** | Central Bureau of Statistics |
| **FAC** | Food Arrangement Corporation |
| **FMC** | Food Management Corporation |
| **LDT** | local development tax |
| **NFC** | Nepal Food Corporation |
| **NPC** | National Planning Commission |
| **NSCA** | National Sample Census of Agriculture |

## Pakistan

| | |
|---|---|
| **APCOM** | Agricultural Prices Commission |
| **CEC** | Cotton Export Corporation |
| **PASSCO** | Pakistan Agricultural Storage and Supplies Corporations |
| **PFD** | provincial food department |
| **REC** | Rice Export Corporation |
| **TCP** | Trading Corporation of Pakistan |

## Sri Lanka

| | |
|---|---|
| **CWE** | Cooperative Wholesale Establishment |
| **FCD** | Food Commissioner's Department |
| **FSS** | Food Stamp Scheme |
| **GPS** | Guaranteed Price Scheme |

| | |
|---|---|
| **IPS** | Internal Purchase System |
| **MPCS** | Multipurpose Cooperative Society |
| **NCRCS** | New Comprehensive Rural Credit Scheme |
| **PMB** | Paddy Marketing Board |
| **RSS** | Rice Rationing Scheme |

# Chapter 1

# Introduction

A. Ganesh-Kumar, Devesh Roy, and Ashok Gulati

The concern for food security is as old as human civilization itself. Although most rich countries have managed to achieve a high degree of food security, for a majority of countries food security is still a serious issue. For South Asia, home to the largest concentration of poor and undernourished people in the world, food security continues to be a major concern.[1]

This concern was heightened during 2007/08 as global prices of basic foodgrains (wheat, rice, and maize) reached new peaks in world markets (Figure 1.1). Several countries in the developing world—more than 40 by August 2008—faced political protests, some violent, and certain governments reacted in panic.

South Asia was no exception. In Bangladesh the wholesale price of coarse rice increased almost 88 percent between January 2007 and July 2008 (from Tk 17/kilogram to Tk 32/kilogram).[2] In Pakistan the wholesale price of wheat went up more than 50 percent from January 2007 to May 2008, and that of IR-6 rice more than 100 percent over the same period. In Sri Lanka the retail price of samba rice went up by almost 100 percent between January 2007 and March 2008. India was the sole exception, with wholesale prices of rice and wheat increasing less than 10 percent from January 2007 to May 2008.

These drastic price increases for staple cereals drew a comprehensive policy response from the governments of the countries in this region, addressing both supply and demand for foodgrains. India, the largest economy in the region, reacted by banning exports of common rice, wheat, and corn and by suspending futures trading in these commodities, to ensure adequate supplies in the domestic market at affordable prices. India also launched a National Food Security Mission in 2007, announc-

**Figure 1.1   Spike in the global rice price, 2005–09**

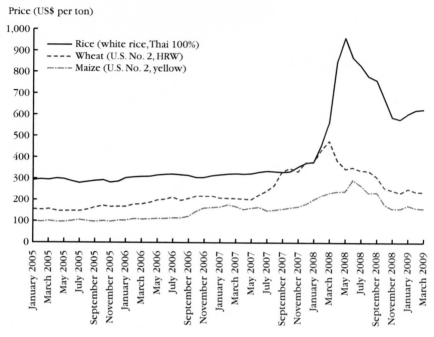

Source: FAO (2009).

ing a special agricultural package (Rashtriya Krishi Vikas Yojana), to the tune of roughly US$6 billion, to rejuvenate its agriculture.

This experience and the policy responses must be viewed within the longer-term perspective of the evolution of national food policies. The major countries of South Asia—Bangladesh, India, Nepal, Pakistan, and Sri Lanka—present historic similarities as well as contrasts in their food policies. Beginning in the 1950s with a nearly uniform policy stance—protectionist at the border and interventionist at home—the countries' policies have diverged over time. Against a backdrop of food scarcity, their peoples often plagued with famines and dependent on food aid, governments placed a premium on national self-sufficiency. Several policy interventions were aimed at creating incentives for farmers to expand production. These included both external policies, such as trade barriers, and within-border policies, such as support prices and input subsidies, with a corollary emphasis on agricultural infrastructure and research expenditures to promote productivity. There was a certain degree of uniformity among the South Asian countries on this front—understandably, given a widely shared colonial heritage as well as the commonality of the problem. The larger countries, especially India, also imposed zoning restrictions to control movement of foodgrains within the country, as a way of limiting arbitrage opportunities and the resulting hoarding and artificial scarcities.

As food self-sufficiency began to improve, policymakers in many South Asian countries also began to recognize the drawbacks of interventionist policies, prompting a gradual change in food policies. Certain commitments relating to international treaties, such as membership in the World Trade Organization (WTO), and the requirements of international donors also induced policy changes in the direction of liberalization, away from central government control and trade restriction.

But these changes have not been uniform: for whatever reason, we now see a distinct policy divergence from the initial common base. India and Pakistan continue to have a conservative stand toward food markets, while countries like Bangladesh, Nepal, and Sri Lanka have embraced reforms to a much greater degree.

The broad policy approach of market liberalization has been to enhance the role of the markets while deploying supplementary safety nets to ensure food security. What have been the consequences of these policy changes in the foodgrains markets in these countries? This book addresses this question for each of the five major countries of the region, based on country case studies, and draws broader lessons that cut across individual country experiences.

## Foodgrains Policies in South Asia

The history of government intervention in food markets in most parts of South Asia can be traced to the policies of the colonial government during World War II, when food rationing was introduced in major urban centers as a response to spiraling prices. At the end of the colonial era, the independent governments of the region, faced with continuing food shortages and haunted by the experience of the Bengal Famine of 1943, maintained this interventionist policy stance. Governments in many countries in fact scaled up the mechanisms of state intervention that they had inherited from the colonial era.

Broadly, to protect farmers' incentives and thus promote domestic production, competition from imports was limited through restrictive trade policies. Further, to reduce market risks, domestic prices were stabilized through public procurement and buffer stocks. These procurement and stocking policies were in turn facilitated by specific controls on domestic trade in foodgrains. These included, for example, compulsory sales to the government, licensing requirements, internal movement and storage restrictions, and restrictions on loans to traders and processors (within the formal financial system). Governments simultaneously tried to balance the needs of consumers —especially poor households—through safety-net programs centering on public distribution of select foodgrains at subsidized prices.

As discussed later, this policy package improved food availability. Over time, however, critics pointed to the spiraling costs, the systemic inefficiencies, and endemic leakages and corruption, questioning the efficacy of and sometimes the justification for such government interventions. Governments of the region began to liberalize their food policies, sometimes voluntarily, in recognition of the system's drawbacks, and more often because of international commitments and pressures from donors.

Such reforms started at different times in different countries, and they varied enormously in scope and detail. The rest of this chapter provides a snapshot of the key policy elements in Bangladesh, India, Nepal, Pakistan, and Sri Lanka with regard to public procurement, storage, and distribution; international trade; and domestic trade. The country chapters that follow discuss the policy regimes of the countries in greater detail.

## Public Procurement, Storage, and Distribution

At the core of government intervention in food markets in South Asia is the elaborate system of public procurement, storage, and distribution created by a set of laws and institutions largely inherited from the colonial government. All the South Asian countries had such systems, though they varied in their scope, their size, and the specific crops covered. The system had several objectives:

- to provide incentives for producers by assuring them a market for their products at preannounced prices;

- to stabilize market prices and thereby reduce risks faced by farmers; and

- to provide grains to consumers, especially the poor, at subsidized prices to enhance their food security.

Restrictive trade policies and domestic marketing policies were designed to facilitate this system.

Public procurement was carried out by parastatal agencies such as the Food Corporation of India (FCI), Nepal Food Corporation (NFC), and Pakistan Agricultural Storage and Supplies Corporations (PASSCO). Multiple state agencies might also be involved in public procurement. Procurement typically took place at an administratively fixed (preannounced) purchase price. The procurement price would be set by specialized government agencies or departments—such as India's Commission for

Costs and Prices or Pakistan's Agricultural Prices Commission—based on the cost of production as well as the competing policy objectives of boosting domestic production and controlling inflation. Typically, procurement combined an element of compulsory sales (such as a minimum percentage of government sales by farmers and grain millers) with an element of voluntary sales by farmers (open-ended procurement at minimum support prices). The grains procured by the state supplied the governments' safety-net programs—mainly the system of public distribution at subsidized (administratively fixed) prices—and also provided a buffer stock for price stabilization.

Over time, the public intervention system has been substantially rolled back in Bangladesh, Nepal, and Sri Lanka in all its dimensions—procurement, storage, and distribution. Sri Lanka was the early starter in this reform process: in 1979 it replaced the system of universal rationing with a food stamp plan that, while providing a subsidy to consumers, enabled the rollback of public procurement and storage. Starting in the late 1980s, Bangladesh has more or less done away with the system of rationing; public distribution is now limited largely to the military, the police force, and public servants. Nepal, too, has restructured its food policies since 1998, as part of its Structural Adjustment Program, funded by the World Bank and the Asian Development Bank. It has downsized the NFC significantly through closure of depots and branch offices (mostly in accessible rather than remote areas), and it has started placing greater reliance on open-market operations.

India and Pakistan, however, stand in contrast to this trend. Both countries maintain elaborate systems of public intervention in various aspects of grain marketing. The system of public procurement, storage, and distribution in India is probably the largest in the world.

### International Trade Policies

Policies relating to international trade in foodgrains were similarly designed, initially, to facilitate government intervention in grain markets. All the countries in the region at some time maintained inward-looking trade policies that severely restricted imports and exports of foodgrains.[3] These restrictions took various forms: monopoly rights for parastatal trading bodies, licensing requirements (if not prohibitions) for private-sector imports and exports, and high tariffs and quantitative restrictions. Import controls were aimed at cutting off competition in domestic markets, while export controls were intended to ensure higher availability and thus low domestic prices. The consequence of these policies for farmers was, often, to disprotect or penalize them, in the sense that the price they received was often less than the prevailing international price.

This was in fact generally the norm for developing countries during the 1950s, the 1960s, and most of the 1970s. The wave of trade reforms that has taken hold in the developing countries since the 1970s also affected South Asia, with Sri Lanka in the vanguard. In 1977 the government liberalized its trade policies in general, including those affecting the food sector, removing import controls in order to increase the availability of food. In 1993 the government gave up its monopoly over rice imports, and it delicensed rice imports in 1996. Substantial liberalization of the agriculture sector had taken place in Sri Lanka even before the adoption of the WTO Agreement on Agriculture.

Nepal and Bangladesh followed. Following a balance of payments crisis, Nepal started liberalizing its trade policies and in 1988 adopted a broad structural adjustment program that required the elimination of all quantitative restrictions, along with the reduction and rationalization of all tariffs. In 2002 Nepal had the lowest agricultural tariffs in the region, with zero tariffs on staples. In Bangladesh liberalization of foodgrains trade took place in 1993, following the legalization of private international trade in wheat and rice at modest tariff rates. Notably Nepal and, to a lesser extent, Bangladesh both have a rather porous border with India—a major producer of foodgrains in the region and globally—across which significant unrecorded trade takes place. This unofficial trade may have an even greater effect than the official trade on the availability of grains in Nepal and Bangladesh.

Although substantial reforms have taken place in India and Pakistan, their trade regimes are far more restrictive than those of Bangladesh, Nepal, and Sri Lanka. Both India and Pakistan have allowed private trade in grains, removed several export controls and licensing requirements, and replaced quantitative import restrictions with tariffs. These tariffs, however, are higher than those of their smaller neighbors; in fact, India's tariff rates are among the highest in the world. Moreover, in 2007/08 India restored export controls in response to high international food prices.

The applied tariff rates in all five countries are substantially lower than the "bound rates" allowed under the WTO. This permits them to raise their applied rates in response to changes in domestic supply-demand conditions, as India and Sri Lanka have frequently done. Even so, the trade regime in all five countries is currently far more liberal than what it was in the period prior to reforms—though that of India remains quite restrictive by world standards.

### Domestic Trade Policies

Elaborate controls over domestic trade provided the underpinning for extensive government interventions in international foodgrains markets, preventing private traders from undercutting government policies on procurement, storage, and distribution. Specifically, the government required farmers and millers to sell adequate quantities to government agencies as a first priority, to meet the government's supply targets. In addition to minimum compulsory government sales required of farmers and millers, stocking limits were imposed on private traders to restrict nongovernment supplies. Additionally zoning laws and intracountry movement restrictions were imposed, depressing the market price in grain-producing regions so that farmers had little alternative but to sell to the government. These policies prevailed in one form or another in almost all the countries of South Asia, but especially in India and Pakistan.

With the onset of liberalization in international grain markets, governments began slowly liberalizing domestic trade as well. In Bangladesh and Sri Lanka phasing out the rationing system obviated the need for large-scale government procurement and thus the need for certain domestic regulations. In 1994, for example, Bangladesh put into abeyance the 50-year-old anti-hoarding act that had imposed stocking limits on private traders.

The situation in India is somewhat mixed: certain controls were removed or relaxed, while others continue to exist. Restrictions on intracountry movement have been more or less removed, while compulsory procurement of rice from millers (known as "levy" rice) continues. With regard to storage, controls were again relaxed, though the government threatens to reimpose them when domestic prices rise sharply (as in 2007/08, when it reimposed stocking limits). In Pakistan, although the government monopoly on rice procurement and distribution was phased out and private trade was allowed, large-scale government interventions and controls continue to prevail in wheat, the main staple.

## Evolution of Food Security in South Asia: A Quantitative Assessment

The 1950s and 1960s are widely regarded as an era of serious food scarcity in South Asia. Domestic production during this period was often grossly inadequate to satisfy domestic consumption needs. Moreover, in most countries the food deficit could not be bridged through commercial imports, as countries had severely limited their foreign exchange reserves. Reliance on food aid was consequently high, no doubt imposing significant noneconomic costs in the form of political pressure. Faced with severe food scarcity and the political costs of excessive reliance on food aid, most governments aggressively pursued food self-reliance. The early 1970s started to show the results of these efforts, with sharp increases in domestic production following the Green Revolution.

Trends in the production, availability, and consumption of cereals in the five countries of the region, for the period 1961–2002, are detailed in Appendix Table A1.1. During those four decades cereal production more than doubled in all countries, with Pakistan recording the highest increase (3.75 times baseline production). In most cases growth was highest from the late 1960s to the early 1980s; the period since the late 1990s has seen a distinct slowing in the rate of growth in all five countries.

Growth in domestic production has had limited effects on *availability* and *consumption*. Only Bangladesh, India, and Nepal have seen an increase in per capita availability and per capita consumption of cereals. There has been little per capita change in Pakistan since the 1970s and in Sri Lanka since the mid-1960s, suggesting that the production, availability, and consumption of cereals has barely kept pace with the growth in population. Even in Bangladesh, India, and Nepal, the increase in per capita consumption is unimpressive over the 42-year period: it is highest in Nepal at 22 percent, followed by India at just 9 percent and Bangladesh at 7 percent.

A decline in cereal consumption per capita does not necessarily imply a worsening of economic access to food: it may reflect consumption diversification (from food to nonfood items, and from cereals to higher-value foods)—a trend that occurs naturally with rising incomes, which all these countries have witnessed. In Sri Lanka, for example, the highest per capita income group has the lowest per capita consumption of cereals (and has shown no growth). Nepal, in contrast, had much higher per capita consumption of cereals, in spite of much lower per capita income than Sri Lanka. Nevertheless, as poverty measures are indexed to access to cereals, we continue to use the somewhat misleading term "food security" to refer to cereals.

Underlying the differential rates of growth of production, availability, and consumption across these countries is the variation in stocks and trade. Except in Nepal, significant stock accumulation has taken place in all five countries. Stock changes reflect government intervention in domestic markets for cereals, through price supports and buffer stocking plans that are essentially an incentive for boosting domestic production. As seen earlier, India and Pakistan continue to pursue such policies fairly vigorously, which could explain the stock buildup in these two countries. Nepal had only a notional buffer stock policy, and in Bangladesh the importance of such interventionist domestic policies waned over time.

The evolution of cereal trade flows in these countries also presents interesting contrasts. With the exception of Sri Lanka, international trade in grains plays a relatively minor (or even insignificant) role in determining availability. Only Sri Lanka has a high degree of dependence on imports, though even here the share of net imports in cereals availability has declined significantly over time.[4] India became a net exporter of cereals in the 1990s, as did Pakistan more recently.

Bangladesh and Nepal stand in contrast to this trend of growing self-sufficiency. Net imports of cereals, as a percentage of availability, remained more or less stable over time in Bangladesh. Nepal alone has gone from a net exporter of cereals in the

1960s and 1970s to a net importer since the 1980s, although the share of net imports in availability is a mere 1 percent.

In sum, India, Pakistan, and Sri Lanka (for its main staple, rice) have been fairly successful in their pursuit of self-sufficiency in food, and in cereals in particular. In the case of Bangladesh and Nepal, those governments seem to have been less aggressive in pushing self-sufficiency and more tolerant of food imports.

Clearly, however, attaining a greater degree of food security at the national level, whether through domestic production or through imports, does not guarantee greater food security at the household level. The Bengal Famine in pre-independence India and the Bangladesh famine in 1974 both highlight the importance of distribution in ensuring household-level food security. In the case of Bengal, there had been no significant fall in production; in Bangladesh, food production was actually above normal. The extent of poverty—not the availability of food at the national level—determines the degree of household-level food security.

Widespread household-level food insecurity prevails in areas that have a high incidence of poverty, such as South Asia and Sub-Saharan Africa. Though global poverty has declined significantly, reflecting sharp reductions in Asia as a whole (Figure 1.2), in 2005 about 879 million people were living on less than US$1.00 a day, mainly in Asia and Sub-Saharan Africa (Chen and Ravallion 2008). Chen and Ravallion argue for adopting a higher poverty index, at $1.25 per day; at that level nearly 1,400 million people were below the poverty line in 2005, 595 million of them in South Asia.

In South Asia poverty (as measured by a poverty line of US$1.00 a day) has come down by about 18 percentage points between 1981 and 2005. Nevertheless about 350 million people still live in poverty in South Asia—about 40 percent of the total number of poor in the world (Figure 1.3), and more than the number of poor in all of Sub-Saharan Africa. Household-level food insecurity is indeed a major concern in this part of the world.

A direct consequence of household-level food insecurity is undernourishment. In South Asia nearly 22 percent of the population was malnourished in 2001–03 (FAO 2006). Indeed the region accounts for about 36 percent of the undernourished population in the world (Figure 1.4a); within the region 71 percent of the undernourished live in India (Figure 1.4b). There are significant differences in the household-level food security within the region, especially in the extent of malnourishment and its evolution over time. In 2001–03, the greatest proportion of the undernourished population of South Asia was in Bangladesh, at 30 percent, while the lowest was in Nepal, at 17 percent.

Why have the impressive achievements in national-level food security not translated into household-level food security? What explains the differences in

**Figure 1.2 Trends in world poverty (US$1.00 a day), 1981–2005**

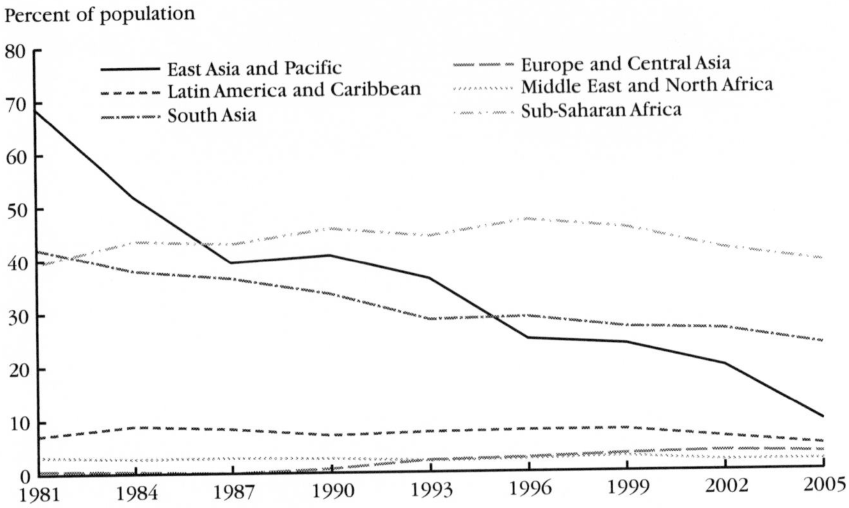

Percent of population
80
70
60
50
40
30
20
10
0
East Asia and Pacific
Latin America and Caribbean
South Asia
Europe and Central Asia
Middle East and North Africa
Sub-Saharan Africa
1981
1984
1987
1990
1993
1996
1999
2002
2005

Source: Chen and Ravallion (2008).

**Figure 1.3 Distribution of poverty (US$1.00 a day) across the world, 2005**

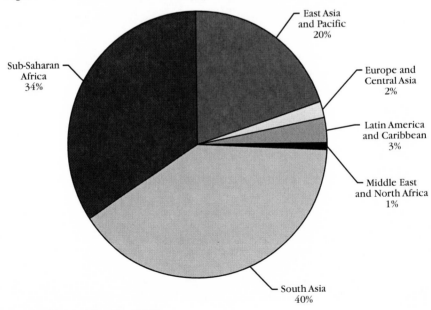

East Asia and Pacific 20%
Europe and Central Asia 2%
Latin America and Caribbean 3%
Middle East and North Africa 1%
South Asia 40%
Sub-Saharan Africa 34%

Source: Chen and Ravallion (2008).

**Figure 1.4   Distribution of malnourishment, 2001–03**

a. Distribution across the world

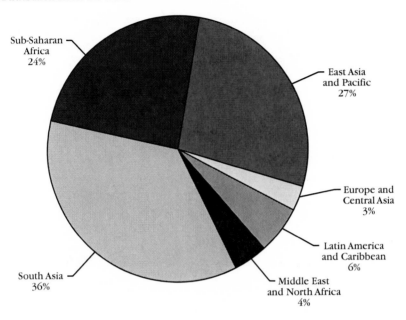

b. Distribution across South Asia

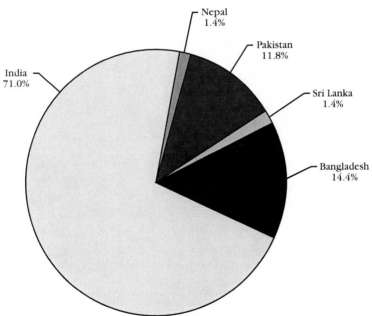

Source: FAO (2006).

household-level food security outcomes between different countries of South Asia? What have been the consequences of the attempts at liberalizing international and domestic trade in foodgrains in these countries? These questions frame the core motivation for this book. In the next section we outline the analytical framework that links border reforms and domestic market reforms with food security at the household level.

## The Analytical Framework and the Country Case Studies

A household can be considered food insecure if its food consumption is low or inadequate in relation to its dietary needs for an active and healthy life. Inadequate food consumption is often a direct consequence of inadequate purchasing power (Figure 1.5).[5] A household's low purchasing power may reflect either low income level or high retail prices for food—or both. Note that from the consumption viewpoint, the relevant food price is the *retail price* paid by households, which differs from the price paid to the farmer (the *farmgate price*). The distinction between the producer or farmgate price and the consumer or retail price is critical to understanding the role of domestic and international trade in affecting food security.

A host of factors affect the income of households and the retail price of food, including

- distributional issues,

- domestic supply issues,

- international trade issues, and

- domestic trade issues.

These factors and their complex interactions make the formulation and implementation of food policies extraordinarily difficult. The hypothesis of this book is that—although food insecurity at the household level is negatively affected by food insecurity at the national level (through a consequent rise in food prices)—*it is not necessarily alleviated* by national-level food security (due to the interplay of these four sets of issues). The analytical framework presented here outlines the linkages between all four sets of issues with household-level food security. Nevertheless the book will focus particularly on the role of international trade issues and domestic trade issues in shaping outcomes at the household level.

**Figure 1.5    Food security at the household level**

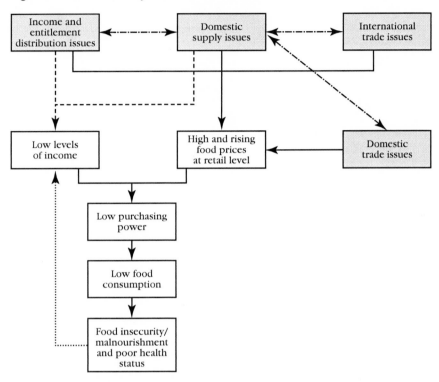

### Distributional Issues

Poverty is often the root cause of food insecurity of households: typically it is poor households with little or no assets that suffer from inadequate food consumption. Thus the variation in the degree of food security across households correlates with the pattern of inequality in the distribution of income and assets across households. Equitable economic growth is the only durable solution for increasing the incomes of the poor. In the short run, however, effective policy interventions would include methods of improving the income levels of the poor, such as safety-net programs (including employment generation) and income transfer mechanisms (including consumption subsidies). All the South Asian countries have safety-net programs in one form or another, including food consumption subsidies provided through public distribution systems. These programs have undergone changes over time; in some cases, they have been completely disbanded. While analysis of the impacts of safety-net programs is beyond the scope of this book, available evidence (notably for India) suggests that they are grossly inadequate in relation to the needs of the poor and riddled with problems of coverage, targeting, and inefficiency (see, for example, Dev et al. 2004).

### Domestic Supply Issues

While inadequate income is an important factor behind food insecurity, high food price is the other determinant. High food prices are often a reflection of national-level food insecurity. The food security of a nation is threatened if its food supply is insufficient to meet the needs of a growing population. A host of domestic supply issues lie behind the shortages in domestic food production, pertaining to the economy as a whole and specifically to the agricultural sector. Concerted policies to augment domestic food production are often the preferred strategy, as in India's Green Revolution and similar programs elsewhere in South Asia. These policies have in general had a positive impact in improving the availability of cereals.

### International Trade Issues

Inadequate domestic food production by itself should not be a reason for high food prices—if the country is able to import food. While the availability of foreign exchange is often a severe constraint, the nature of the country's trade policy (especially relating to foodgrains) also plays a major role in affecting food availability. A restrictive trade regime that hinders food imports during periods of supply shortages limits availability and results in rapid price increases; a liberal trade regime that allows easy imports can help avert such a situation.

Trade liberalization corrects distortions in the relative prices and profitability of different commodities. Theoretically, liberal imports bring down the domestic price of those commodities in which the country has a comparative disadvantage.[6] Conversely a rise in exports of commodities in which a country has a comparative advantage results in a rise in domestic prices. These sector-specific interventions can have spillover effects in other sector prices.

However, the impact of trade liberalization on food security is not so straightforward. If a country had a comparative advantage in food crops whose exports rise following liberalization, then the domestic price of food would increase. This would impair the food security of net purchasers of food—primarily urban consumers and rural landless households. However, farmers and farm workers producing those crops would witness a rise in income and an *improvement* in their food security. The converse holds for a country that is a net food importer. In other words, the net effect is country and commodity specific.

As seen earlier, all the South Asian countries had very restrictive trade regimes in the past, but over time they have liberalized their trade policies, either in recognition of the futility of restrictions or in keeping with international agreements. The country case studies that follow this chapter examine the impacts of changes in trade policy regime—particularly regarding the major cereals in the country's consumption basket (rice and wheat)—on poverty, food security, and welfare.

### Domestic Market Issues

Food prices at the retail level (as distinct from farmgate prices) can be high even when sufficient food is available in the country. Distortions in the domestic markets can cause both high domestic trade margins and high storage and transport costs; both tend to increase the price differential between the farm and the retail levels. Domestic market distortions in developing countries can be traced to weak institutional structure or restrictive government policies or both. Typical distortions include

- barriers to entry in domestic trading services,

- barriers to intracountry commodity movements,

- state intervention in the markets, and

- inadequate marketing and transport infrastructure.

South Asian countries suffer from all four problems to varying degrees. The first three factors give rise to high domestic trade margins and spatially unintegrated markets, while the last factor causes high storage and transport costs.

High domestic trade margins arise when trading services are dominated by a few traders, who act as price makers in the food market. In such a highly concentrated trading sector, transactions between traders and farmers (who are numerous and fragmented) can be described as monopsonistic—exchanges in which the traders can effectively dictate the price.[7] Similarly transactions between traders and the (numerous) final consumers can be described as monopolistic—again with traders as the price makers. Consequently it is quite common to find a very low farmgate price and a high retail price for the same commodity. A low farmgate price is a disincentive to the farmers (discouraging supply), while high retail prices hurt consumers (inhibiting demand).

The institutional inequities in the agricultural markets affect not just the price that farmers receive for their produce but also the way in which price risk is shared between traders and farmers. During times of supply shortages (that is, high prices), traders reap high profits that they do not pass on to the farmers; during times of glut (low prices), however, traders are indeed likely to pass on the adverse price shock to the farmers. Such a distribution of value, by limiting the farmers' upside revenue, acts as a major disincentive for investing in modern farm techniques and farm inputs. Consequently farmers often choose to produce for their subsistence rather than for the market, restricting their income and diminishing supply.

The market power and high margins enjoyed by the traders reflect market distortions due, first, to entry barriers in the domestic trading services sector, including institutional legacies as well as policy effects. For example, markets for several agricultural commodities in developing countries have historically been dominated by tightly knit communities with their own codes of practice. Governmental regulations often reinforce these institutional barriers to entry into domestic trade.

The second source of distortions in domestic trade is the lack of marketing infrastructure. Thus large-scale markets involving several agents are rare in developing countries. This infrastructure barrier perpetuates dominance by a few large traders and fosters spatial isolation of markets, dominated by localized monopolies or monopsonies.

Spatial isolation can also arise due to governmental regulations that restrict the movement of commodities across different parts of the country. Such movement restrictions can take the form of outright bans or fiscal measures—usually differential tax rates imposed by subnational governments. The lack of transport and storage facilities can also contribute to spatial isolation.

Another form of distortion commonly observed in developing countries is direct state intervention in markets, through parastatal marketing agencies or commodity boards. Parastatal agencies may be granted monopoly powers by law; in any case, their large size and fiscal resources tend to make them dominant players, liable to heavily distort commodity markets. Thus when international trade liberalization opens up opportunities for growth in these commodities, the parastatal agencies often prevent effective transmission of price signals to the local markets, keeping prices artificially low and perpetuating farmers' disincentives.[8]

The chapters on Bangladesh, India, and Sri Lanka emphasize the importance of domestic trading structures and the removal of policy-induced barriers to domestic market integration. The chapter on India also attempts to quantify the welfare impacts of transport sector inefficiencies. The chapter on Nepal brings out the spatial dimension of inadequate infrastructure.

## Organization of the Book

The country case studies—Bangladesh (Chapter 2), India (Chapter 3), Nepal (Chapter 4), Pakistan (Chapter 5), and Sri Lanka (Chapter 6)—describe in detail the evolution of the food sector and the policies affecting it, focusing on the staple cereal(s). For Bangladesh, Nepal, and Sri Lanka the focus is on rice; for India and

Pakistan it is on rice and wheat, with greater stress on wheat in Pakistan. Food policy includes policies relating to production, stocks, trade, and consumption, as well as an examination of the respective roles of the public and private sectors in the domestic market. Each country case study goes on to evaluate the impacts of these policies in terms of food security outcomes and the cost effectiveness of public-sector institutions in comparison to the private sector. Finally each chapter assesses the impact of border trade reforms on food security, through reduction in trade protection. That assessment is based on an evaluation of actual data or on empirical models (or both), in either the partial or the general equilibrium framework.

The chapters on India and Sri Lanka also examine two important domestic market issues that could affect food security outcomes. The chapter on India discusses the importance of spatial integration in determining food security outcomes in different parts of the country, and specifically the impacts of removing intracountry movement restrictions and improving the transport sector. The chapter on Sri Lanka looks at the impact of domestic market structures on food security. Specifically it attempts to quantify the impact of the monopsony power of the rice trader vis-à-vis farmers, using a partial equilibrium model of market structure. The chapters on Bangladesh and Nepal present some empirical evidence of the impact of government zoning policies and infrastructure development in bringing about spatial integration of markets.

Table 1.1 presents a snapshot of the different issues addressed by each of the country case studies. Even though the country studies evolve around a few common themes, they vary in their methodology and emphasis, depending upon the relevance of each question. A variety of models are used in these studies: a computable general equilibrium model (India, Nepal, and Pakistan), a spatial equilibrium model (India), an econometrically estimated partial equilibrium model (Sri Lanka), and a multimarket model (Bangladesh). The choice of methodology is dictated primarily by the research question and by data availability.[9] The final chapter summarizes the main messages emerging from these studies and goes on to discuss the implications of these results for government policy changes and for intraregional trade and policy coordination.

Table 1.1    Questions addressed by the country case studies

| Country | Border reforms | Spatial integration | Public procurement | Domestic market reforms |
|---------|:---:|:---:|:---:|:---:|
| Bangladesh | ✓ | ✓ | ✓ | ✓ |
| India | | ✓ | ✓ | ✓ |
| Nepal | ✓ | ✓ | ✓ | |
| Pakistan | ✓ | | ✓ | |
| Sri Lanka | ✓ | | ✓ | ✓ |

**Appendix Table A1.1   Production, availability, and consumption of cereals in South Asia, 1961–2002**

| Period/year | Production (thousand tons) | Imports (thousand tons) | Stock change (thousand tons)a | Exports (thousand tons) | Availability (thousand tons) | Consumption (thousand tons) | Net imports percent of availability | Availability per capita per year (kg) | Consumption per capita per year (kg) |
|---|---|---|---|---|---|---|---|---|---|
| Bangladesh | | | | | | | | | |
| 1961–65 | 10,127 | 759 | –314 | 0 | 10,573 | 9,734 | 7.2 | 189.8 | 174.7 |
| 1966–70 | 11,200 | 1,167 | –690 | 0 | 11,678 | 10,746 | 10.0 | 184.9 | 170.1 |
| 1971–75 | 11,380 | 2,036 | –924 | 0 | 12,492 | 11,512 | 16.3 | 174.6 | 160.9 |
| 1976–80 | 13,371 | 1,398 | –381 | 0 | 14,388 | 13,300 | 9.7 | 177.6 | 164.2 |
| 1981–85 | 15,668 | 1,854 | –688 | 4 | 16,829 | 15,597 | 11.0 | 183.1 | 169.7 |
| 1986–90 | 17,532 | 2,018 | 177 | 0 | 19,726 | 18,306 | 10.2 | 189.2 | 175.6 |
| 1991–95 | 18,948 | 1,472 | 1,354 | 0 | 21,774 | 20,025 | 6.8 | 185.1 | 170.2 |
| 1996–2000 | 22,833 | 2,660 | –331 | 0 | 25,161 | 23,096 | 10.6 | 190.2 | 174.6 |
| 2001 | 25,936 | 2,908 | –1,025 | 2 | 27,818 | 25,493 | 10.4 | 197.5 | 181.0 |
| 2002 | 26,924 | 2,826 | –460 | 1 | 29,289 | 26,912 | 9.6 | 203.7 | 187.1 |
| India | | | | | | | | | |
| 1961–65 | 70,123 | 5,512 | 1,327 | 3 | 76,959 | 68,826 | 7.2 | 162.5 | 145.3 |
| 1966–70 | 80,620 | 7,130 | –2,538 | 16 | 85,196 | 75,760 | 8.3 | 160.4 | 142.6 |
| 1971–75 | 93,739 | 3,960 | –1,116 | 160 | 96,423 | 85,293 | 3.9 | 162.4 | 143.6 |
| 1976–80 | 109,517 | 1,850 | –2,166 | 526 | 108,674 | 95,871 | 1.2 | 164.3 | 144.9 |
| 1981–85 | 127,882 | 1,560 | –3,285 | 529 | 125,628 | 111,248 | 0.8 | 171.3 | 151.7 |
| 1986–90 | 146,066 | 823 | 401 | 507 | 146,784 | 130,849 | 0.2 | 180.4 | 160.9 |
| 1991–95 | 166,434 | 431 | 388 | 2,067 | 165,186 | 144,765 | –1.0 | 184.1 | 161.4 |
| 1996–2000 | 186,096 | 1,166 | –6,607 | 3,350 | 177,305 | 154,244 | –1.2 | 180.5 | 157.0 |
| 2001 | 196,267 | 43 | –8,056 | 5,379 | 182,875 | 157,980 | –2.9 | 177.0 | 152.9 |
| 2002 | 174,655 | 54 | 23,826 | 9,485 | 189,051 | 165,662 | –5.0 | 180.1 | 157.8 |
| Nepal | | | | | | | | | |
| 1961–65 | 2,513 | 1 | –117 | 307 | 2,091 | 1,693 | –14.6 | 197.8 | 160.2 |
| 1966–70 | 2,589 | 1 | –34 | 290 | 2,265 | 1,857 | –12.8 | 194.5 | 159.4 |
| 1971–75 | 2,809 | 4 | –156 | 166 | 2,491 | 2,029 | –6.5 | 193.7 | 157.8 |
| 1976–80 | 2,812 | 14 | –66 | 60 | 2,700 | 2,272 | –1.7 | 189.2 | 159.3 |

| | | | | | | | | |
|---|---|---|---|---|---|---|---|---|
| 1981–85 | 3,186 | 50 | −20 | 45 | 3,171 | 2,701 | 0.1 | 199.4 | 169.9 |
| 1986–90 | 4,083 | 41 | −3 | 10 | 4,111 | 3,422 | 0.7 | 230.6 | 192.0 |
| 1991–95 | 4,478 | 45 | −5 | 2 | 4,516 | 3,805 | 0.9 | 226.1 | 190.6 |
| 1996–2000 | 5,361 | 89 | −135 | 23 | 5,292 | 4,198 | 1.3 | 235.5 | 186.7 |
| 2001 | 5,733 | 55 | 11 | 12 | 5,787 | 4,662 | 0.7 | 240.5 | 193.8 |
| 2002 | 5,839 | 38 | 57 | 10 | 5,924 | 4,773 | 0.5 | 240.7 | 193.9 |

Pakistan

| | | | | | | | | |
|---|---|---|---|---|---|---|---|---|
| 1961–65 | 6,655 | 987 | 137 | 242 | 7,537 | 6,698 | 9.9 | 143.9 | 127.8 |
| 1966–70 | 9,033 | 763 | 177 | 374 | 9,599 | 8,502 | 4.1 | 162.5 | 143.9 |
| 1971–75 | 11,106 | 1,020 | 235 | 484 | 11,877 | 10,584 | 4.5 | 177.9 | 158.6 |
| 1976–80 | 13,976 | 1,117 | −703 | 963 | 13,427 | 11,469 | 1.2 | 176.0 | 150.3 |
| 1981–85 | 16,484 | 468 | −713 | 1,127 | 15,112 | 12,849 | −4.4 | 169.5 | 144.1 |
| 1986–90 | 18,463 | 1,423 | −1,397 | 1,078 | 17,410 | 15,018 | 2.0 | 166.1 | 143.2 |
| 1991–95 | 21,126 | 2,107 | −1,241 | 1,316 | 20,677 | 17,996 | 3.8 | 173.0 | 150.6 |
| 1996–2000 | 25,046 | 2,263 | −1,458 | 1,846 | 24,005 | 21,004 | 1.7 | 177.3 | 155.1 |
| 2001 | 25,109 | 170 | 3,277 | 3,260 | 25,295 | 22,287 | −12.2 | 172.9 | 152.4 |
| 2002 | 24,936 | 287 | 3,818 | 2,965 | 26,076 | 23,099 | −10.3 | 173.9 | 154.1 |

Sri Lanka

| | | | | | | | | |
|---|---|---|---|---|---|---|---|---|
| 1961–65 | 675 | 791 | −36 | 0 | 1,430 | 1,358 | 55.3 | 136.2 | 129.3 |
| 1966–70 | 897 | 978 | −76 | 0 | 1,798 | 1,708 | 54.4 | 152.6 | 145.0 |
| 1971–75 | 945 | 938 | 112 | 2 | 1,992 | 1,898 | 47.0 | 152.9 | 145.7 |
| 1976–80 | 1,226 | 1,078 | −75 | 6 | 2,223 | 2,106 | 48.2 | 157.5 | 149.2 |
| 1981–85 | 1,635 | 731 | −7 | 1 | 2,360 | 2,205 | 31.0 | 155.4 | 145.3 |
| 1986–90 | 1,618 | 884 | 72 | 0 | 2,575 | 2,384 | 34.3 | 157.5 | 145.9 |
| 1991–95 | 1,745 | 1,025 | −37 | 16 | 2,718 | 2,509 | 37.1 | 155.9 | 143.9 |
| 1996–2000 | 1,731 | 1,206 | −28 | 3 | 2,907 | 2,622 | 41.4 | 159.0 | 143.4 |
| 2001 | 1,831 | 952 | 249 | 5 | 3,026 | 2,722 | 31.3 | 161.4 | 145.2 |
| 2002 | 1,938 | 1,306 | −252 | 10 | 2,982 | 2,745 | 43.5 | 157.7 | 145.2 |

Source: FAO (2007).
aNegative figures indicate stock depletion; positive figures indicate addition to stocks.

## Notes

1. South Asia accounted for about 40 percent of the people living on less than US$1.00 per day in the world in 2005 (Chen and Ravallion 2008) and 36 percent of the undernourished population in the world in 2001–03 (FAO 2006).

2. The taka (Tk) is the unit of currency of Bangladesh.

3. In fact these inward-looking trade policies covered all commodities, not just foodgrains.

4. In fact, in the case of rice, the main staple in Sri Lanka, domestic production in 2002 accounts for nearly 96 percent of domestic consumption, up from 60 percent in 1961 (Weerahewa 2004). Wheat imports (at around 0.7–1 million tons) now constitute a major portion of cereal imports in Sri Lanka.

5. Disruptions in supplies due to natural and human calamities may sometimes affect the food security of even the rich. In normal times, however, well-off households manage to meet their needs even when there is a countrywide shortage of food. Food insecurity is an issue mainly for poorer households.

6. It is of course possible that international prices are distorted by subsidies provided by other countries and do not accurately reflect differences in comparative advantages across countries.

7. Traders in developing countries often supply credit to the farmers as well. Such bundling of services increases the dependence of the farmers on the traders and correspondingly increases the market power of the traders to set the price.

8. Numerous agency problems plaguing the parastatals (such as incentive problems, job security for the employees without performance monitoring, lack of accountability, and corruption) only reinforce this domestic market distortion.

9. Some of the models used are proprietary to the authors of the country case studies. In some cases impact assessments are based on a review of the relevant literature.

## References

Chen, S., and M. Ravallion. 2008. *The developing world is poorer than we thought, but no less successful in the fight against poverty.* Policy Research Working Paper 4703. Washington, D.C.: World Bank.

Dev, S. M., C. Ravi, B. Viswanathan, A. Gulati, and S. Ramachander. 2004. *Economic liberalisation, targeted programmes and household food security.* MTID Discussion Paper 68. Washington, D.C.: International Food Policy Research Institute.

Food and Agriculture Organization of the United Nations (FAO). 2006. *The state of food insecurity in the world 2006.* Rome.

———. 2007. FAOstat. http://faostat.fao.org/. Accessed January 4, 2010.

———. 2009. *Rice Market Monitor* 12 (3).

Weerahewa, J. 2004. *Impacts of trade liberalization and market reforms on the paddy/rice sector in Sri Lanka.* MTID Discussion Paper 70. Washington, D.C.: International Food Policy Research Institute.

# Chapter 2

# Food Market Liberalization in Bangladesh: How Well Did the Government and the Markets Deliver?

Nuimuddin Chowdhury, Nasir Farid, and Devesh Roy

The common perception is that Bangladesh always seems to be in the news for the wrong reason: for yet another natural disaster, for example, or its high ranking on the list of corrupt countries. Despite these perceptions, Bangladesh has done quite well by some important measures—in particular, in managing its food and agricultural policies over the past quarter of a century. The policies—especially those pertaining to liberalization, agricultural research, and development of physical infrastructure—have created notable gains, resulting in one of the highest growth rates in the size of foodgrains markets in South Asia.

Government interventions in foodgrains markets in South Asia took shape against the backdrop of the infamous Bengal Famine of 1943, in which millions died (Bangladesh was then part of Bengal, in British India). The policy mindset was also conditioned by certain structural factors characterizing foodgrains markets:

- a low production base, consisting of rain-fed, fragile monocrop staples;

- fragmented infrastructure, financial, and information networks;

- thin market supplies; and

- high prices, large seasonal spreads in prices, and susceptibility to sudden price spikes.

In 1950/51 Bangladesh's rice production per capita stood at only 60 percent of the 2000 level, and the seasonal spread in rice price was greater than 40 percent. Scarcities were rife and crop failures contributed to dreadful political fallouts. Agricultural interventions thus reflected a scarcity syndrome, predating the Green Revolution. Conceived by bureaucrats and politicians, with the backing of traders, the public distribution system was expansive, expensive, hugely loss-making—and yet politically untouchable.

The technologies, infrastructure, and markets in Bangladesh have come a long way since those shadows of famine and starvation (Ahmed, Haggblade, and Chowdhury 2000). Those successes are in part due to the program of market reforms undertaken beginning in the 1980s. (Other contributing factors include the acceleration of plant-breeding research and infrastructure development throughout the 1970s and 1980s.)

During the second half of the 1980s, and especially during the last two years of that decade, Bangladesh substantially reformed the markets for two farm inputs of critical importance: fertilizer and minor irrigation equipment. Beginning in the early 1990s the country began to liberalize the foodgrains markets themselves; this process included easing import restrictions. Private imports of fertilizer and both rice and wheat were legalized in 1993; afterwards, the anti-hoarding act was put in abeyance and private traders were now allowed to seek institutional credit for carrying inventory. Border protections on manufactured goods have been continually lowered, especially since the early 1990s, increasing the economy's overall openness. Furthermore the government substantially refrained from direct foodgrains distribution, with transforming effects on the dynamics, seasonality, and spatial integration of rice prices.

Price dynamics, seasonality, and spatial integration are important determinants of foodgrains production and consumption. In order to assess food security outcomes, we will therefore examine the behavior of rice and wheat prices—their interyear and seasonal variability and long-term trends.

Liberalization has also significantly enlarged the role of the private sector vis-à-vis the public sector, in market share and shares in stocks. How has the private sector performed relative to the public sector? This chapter gives a comparative analysis of the performance of public and private sectors as reflected in marketing margins.[1]

Finally we assess the prospective impact of the now-stalled Doha Round of the World Trade Organization (WTO) trade negotiations. With its food markets already significantly liberalized, Bangladesh could experience significant effects on them—and hence on real incomes and food security—arising from liberalization elsewhere. Taking the Doha Round outcomes as a plausible scenario, we present a counterfactual exercise regarding the potential impact of such liberalization if it were to occur.

The chapter is organized into six sections. The next section describes the food-grains economy in Bangladesh and the response of the public and private sectors to the changing policy regime. The third section presents a brief assessment of the public food distribution system following the reforms. The fourth section looks at some indicators of food security, focusing only on cereals. The fifth section presents the results from a partial equilibrium multimarket model that estimates the effect of Doha Round multilateral liberalization on rice and wheat sectors in Bangladesh. It also summarizes the results from an existing computable general equilibrium study on Bangladesh for comparison. The sixth section concludes with a summary and suggestions for the way forward for food policy in Bangladesh.

## Bangladesh's Foodgrains Economy and Policy Changes over Time

Bangladesh shows elements of pro-poor economic growth and an active Green Revolution, led by high-yielding varieties (HYVs) of rice, large investments in physical infrastructure (including irrigation), and ready availability of fertilizer. In these respects the country is similar to Indonesia (Timmer 2004).

Policy reforms in Bangladesh food markets consist of two main elements: legalizing or liberalizing private imports of wheat and rice (and some inputs) and downsizing the role of the government in domestic food markets (procurement as well as distribution). Between the mid-1980s and the mid-2000s, the share of public distribution in market supply shrank from 13 percent to 5.2 percent. Table 2.1 shows the transition in government food and agricultural policies.

As Table 2.1 shows, the food distribution system accounts for between 3 and 4 percent of total public expenditure. All public supply of foodgrains is handled by the Public Food Distribution System (PFDS). The overriding objectives of the PFDS are supplying food through priority channels, stabilizing prices, implementing targeted interventions for poverty reduction, and maintaining security stocks.

The value of subsidies as a percent of the government budget can be compared over time, based on preliberalization estimates from Ahmed (1988). The numbers for three fiscal years—1977/78, 1978/79, and 1979/80—indicate subsidy shares of 3.4, 8.5, and 3.4 percent, respectively, if we include food aid; the subsidy shares rise to 10, 8, and 11 percent, respectively, when we exclude food aid. On average subsidies have decreased since liberalization.

On the disbursement side, public distribution involves two kinds of channels—sales and nonmonetized. Nonmonetized distribution provides no financial return into government accounts. Sales distribution is further categorized into Essential Priorities (EP), Other Priorities (OP), Open-Market Sales (OMS), and Large Employers

Table 2.1    Food subsidies relative to expenditures, 1999–2004 (billions of Tk)

| Year | Gross domestic product | Revenue expenditure | Development expenditure | Total public expenditure | Food subsidy per government accounts | Food subsidy[a] | Food subsidy as a percentage of public expenditure in Bangladesh | Food subsidy as a percentage of public expenditure in India |
|---|---|---|---|---|---|---|---|---|
| 1999–2000 | 2,370 | 181.95 | 152.21 | 344.6 | 3.69 | n.a. | n.a. | 3.03 |
| 2000–01 | 2,535 | 205.36 | 159.01 | 374.0 | 3.34 | 8.25 | 4.0 | 2.88 |
| 2001–02 | 2,732 | 227.0 | 150.5 | 407.6 | 3.35 | 9.47 | 4.2 | 4.41 |
| 2002–03 | 3,006 | 253.07 | 169 | 439.04 | 4.64 | n.a. | n.a. | n.a. |
| 2003–04 | 3,326 | 289.69 | 203 | 519.8 | 3.03 | 8.77 | 3.0 | n.a. |

Sources: Bangladeshi numbers are from the Ministry of Finance (various years); Indian numbers are from Government of India (2002).

Note: n.a., not available.

[a]All valuations are based on market prices.

(LE).[2] EP provides for public employees in the armed forces, paramilitary border forces, police, and "Ansars" (a parapolice cadre of armed security forces). These public servants are treated as a special case; the issue price for this category has not been revised during the past 10 years.[3] EP accounts for most of the food subsidy each year. OP provides for the employees of the civil defense forces and other strategically influential agencies. Through LE the government allots grains to large registered manufacturing enterprises (those with more than 100 employees) in the Statutory Rationing areas.

Bangladesh has partly reformed its PFDS over the years. In the 1980s and early 1990s policy work exposed inequities in several channels: Statutory Rationing (SR), Modified Rationing (MR), and OP (Beacon Consultants 1986; Chowdhury 1988; Ahmed 1992). Two of these inequitable channels, SR and MR, were phased out in 1990–91 and 1991–92.

The government has since been pushing rice into food-for-work programs. From one-tenth of total rice distribution in the 1980s, these channels have accounted for more than three-fifths of all public rice distribution since 1997.

Table 2.2 summarizes the transition of food policy between 1977 and 2008. The private sector has responded to these policy changes in several ways, affecting production, marketing, stocking behavior, and spatial integration of markets. It is not possible, however, to isolate the contribution of market reforms from the effects of such co-occurring factors as technology and infrastructure development.

### Outcomes: Foodgrains Production and Supply

The liberalization of the markets for fertilizer and minor irrigation equipment during 1988–92 had a concentrated impact, expanding the area under irrigation during the dry season and resulting in increased rice output.[4] The growth rate for rice production was substantially higher in the postliberalization period (assuming 1992–93 as the starting period for liberalization) (Figure 2.1)—and indeed growth in rice production outstripped population growth. The share of boro rice in the total has grown rapidly, while the share of aman rice has declined (Table 2.3). Thus the postliberalization period has witnessed significant acceleration in the growth of Bangladesh's rice supply.

### Outcomes: Marketable Surplus and Private Stocks

The favorable supply performance was accompanied by a dramatic increase in the proportion of rice output that was marketed, leading to a fairly rapid expansion in the size of the market (Table 2.3). Between 1980 and 2003 the rice markets grew by about 10 million metric tons (MMT). During the same period the nominal price per ton had risen by Tk 6,110. As a rough approximation, then, the market had grown by Tk 61.1 billion. With an estimated 13 million farms in 2003, this translates to a

**Table 2.2    Milestones in agricultural and food policy transitions, 1979–2004**

| Date | Milestone |
|------|-----------|
| September 1979 | The World Bank produced an important document, *Food Policy Issues* (World Bank 1979), that framed all the major policy and analytical issues in managing Bangladesh's food sector. The report cited optimal national stocks as equal to 1.5 MMT as of July 1 of every year and 1.2 MMT as of November 15 of every year. Security stocks equal to 600,000 MT were considered "appropriate." |
| 1981 | With the launch of the country's Second Five-Year Plan, the government adopted an ambitious long-term plan for accelerating the growth of rice production. |
| 1982 | The FPMU was established based on a recommendation in *Food Policy Issues*. |
| 1986 | A study led by Beacon Consultants—the first-ever evaluation of the welfare effects of both SR and MR—demonstrated the inequities in the operation of both channels. |
| 1988 | Pursuant to PL Title III (signed in 1988), OMS came into existence. In the event the market price exceeded a meaningful threshold, OMS grains would be disproportionately distributed in poor neighborhoods. In July 1988 the government waived the standardization requirement for imported irrigation equipment, allowing cheap imports from China and South Korea that contributed to the growth of rice production. |
| 1989 | MR was replaced by PR, under which rice was no longer distributed in rural areas but wheat would be distributed to small milling units. Each licensed mill would receive about 500 kg of wheat per month: it would then sell the atta (flour) to villagers at a preset price. The government instituted PR to distribute foodgrains (subsidized at 25 percent) to eligible households in rural areas. PR soon became the single most important public distribution channel for rice, distributing rice all year, including at harvest time; however, it was poorly targeted (Ahmed 1992). |
| March 1989 | Direct sales of urea by parastatal fertilizer factories to private traders were allowed for the first time, enabling a rapidly increasing number of private traders to move large quantities of urea across the country (Samad, Haque, and Sidhu 1989). Previously wholesale urea trade had been a parastatal monopoly. |
|  | The government started a new procurement program called Millgate Purchase (MP). The idea was to procure milled rice from prequalified contractor mills on a cost-plus basis, pivoted around the procurement price . For a marketing agent, access to an MP contract implied secured access to implicit credit subsidies (Chowdhury 1994). The procurement price easily exceeded the going price during procurement season, due to such generous provisions as a highly favorable milling ratio. MP was also lucrative for mill owners who qualified.[a] |
| 1989–90 | The government procured record quantities of rice during both aman and boro seasons. MP, highly profitable to contractors, distorted incentives in milling and trade. Previously all millers and traders had competed in one national rice market; MP created incentives for local rent seeking. |
| 1991 | The government suspended PR, causing public rice stocks to swell. The procurement price was nevertheless raised to Tk 240, even though the single most important distribution channel had been terminated. |
| 1992 | SR, which entitled each cardholder to weekly grains from licensed dealers within the limits of six SR cities, was abolished. The absence of public outcry indicated widespread awareness of mistargeting. Private imports of fertilizer of all types were legalized for the first time. |
| 1993 | The importing of wheat by private mills was legalized. Imports of foundation seeds and power tillers were liberalized. |
|  | Private wheat imports (by licensed large mills) and private rice imports were legalized. |

*(continued)*

**Table 2.2    Continued**

| Date | Milestone |
|------|-----------|
| 1994 | The 50-year-old anti-hoarding act was suspended. The act had barred merchants from keeping inventories exceeding 1 week or working stocks without a statutory license from the Food Department. |
| 1996 | Bangladesh implemented the Uruguay Round Agreement on Agriculture. Tariff rates were bound at a much higher level relative to that applied. Bangladesh's aggregate measure of support was far below the de minimis level set by WTO rules. |
| 1998 | Rice prices peaked significantly during severe monsoon flooding, creating pressure on the Ministry of Food to control hoarding (Dorosh, del Ninno, and Shahabuddin 2004). To the credit of the government, those pressures were resisted; private traders delivered a stunning 2.4 MMT tons of imported rice over a nine-month period. In 1999–2000, rice production rose from 19 MMT (during the five years ending the previous year) to 23–25 MMT. |
| 2000–08 | Private importing of hybrid seeds for rice, maize, and vegetables was legalized, prodded by growing demand and the widespread realization of the importance of raising productivity. Within five years, the major proportion of maize was sourced from hybrid seeds. For several commercially important crops, the proportion of hybrid seeds in use is now 15–20 percent, with smaller increases for rice. The government promotes the agricultural use of sulfur, zinc, and boron as a way to reduce erosion of micronutrients in the soil; it also promotes the use of organic fertilizer. |

Note: FPMU, Food Policy Monitoring Unit; MMT, million metric tons; MR, Modified Rationing; OMS, Open-Market Sales; PR, Palli Rationing; SR, Statutory Rationing; WTO, World Trade Organization.
[a]Rice procurement rose to record levels between 1989–90 and 1991–92.

per-farm expansion equal to Tk 6,000 (at average price levels prevailing during the past 20 years). This expansion was bound to provide a powerful stimulus toward commercialization of rice.

Chowdhury (1992) and Dorosh, del Ninno, and Shahabuddin (2004) attribute this pressure for commercialization to a rising share of irrigated rice, which is more intensive in purchased inputs, and to the resulting increased business confidence on the part of farmers. Chowdhury (1994) showed that the seasonality of rice production changed from being single-humped in the interval November–January to double-humped, with a second peak in May–July. The production stabilization resulting from two such humps further increased farmers' economic confidence (Dorosh, del Ninno, and Shahabuddin 2004).

From less than 15 percent in the early 1970s, the share of overall rice output harvested during the boro season (May–September) rose to more than 65 percent in the 1990s. As the boro season HYVs are very cash intensive, they result in a greater share of the surplus being marketed.

During the five years ending in 1969–70, 62 percent of the annual rice output was harvested in December–January, and the next sizable rice crop was harvested in September. Rice prices were lowest in December and highest in August–October. Three decades later, owing to the diffusion of boro-season HYVs, the December

**Figure 2.1    Some summary food security indicators: Pre- and postliberalization-period growth rates**

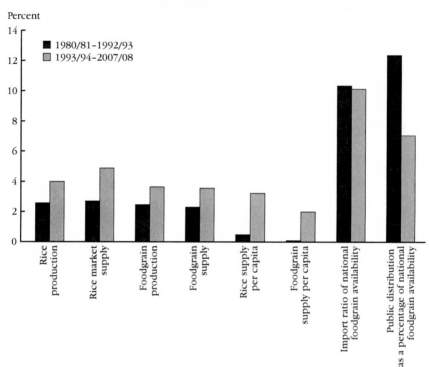

Sources: Department of Agricultural Marketing and Food Policy Monitoring Unit.
Note: Import ratio of national foodgrain availability is not a growth rate.

harvest share has shrunk to under two-fifths; nearly 50 percent of rice is now harvested between May and August. The August–September period used to be the hungry season, with seasonally high rice prices and high incidences of malnutrition (Chen, Chowdhury, and Huffman 1979; Clay 1981). Thanks to the large and increasing boro harvests, that hungry season has been transformed into a benign harvest season.

Price seasonality has now become bimodal, with one peak in March–April and another in September–October. As seasonal price spreads have fallen through the late 1980s and 1990s until today, storing rice for intertemporal arbitrage—that is, to buy low and sell high—has become less and less profitable. The typical storage period has fallen significantly, from about four months in the late 1960s to about one month in 1989–90 (Farruk 1972; Chowdhury 1992). With storage of shorter duration, finance becomes a less important factor and the competitiveness of smaller farmers is enhanced.

Table 2.3    Broad changes in Bangladesh rice markets, 1960s–2003

| Dimension | 1960s | 1970s | 1980s | 1990s | 2003 |
|---|---|---|---|---|---|
| Aspects of output | | | | | |
| Level (MMT) | 10 | 12 | 15 | 18 | 23 |
| Boro share (%) | 7 | 18 | 26 | 38 | 52 |
| HYV share (%) | 1 | 23 | 36 | 63 | 80 |
| Quantity marketed | | | | | |
| Level (MMT) | 1 | 3 | 5 | 9 | 15 |
| Percentage share in output (%) | 12 | 27 | 34 | 49 | 60 |
| Per capita (kg) | 20 | 41 | 51 | 76 | 109 |
| Public share of rice supply (%) | 30 | 15 | 11 | 7 | 6 |
| Share sold on the farm itself (%) | 28 | n.a. | n.a. | 66 | >66 |
| Number of marketing agents | | | | | |
| Number of traders | 4,000 | n.a. | n.a. | 48,000 | >48,000 |
| Millers | | | | | |
| Automatic | 0 | 3 | 66 | 88 | n.a. |
| Major | 106 | 152 | 251 | 480 | n.a. |
| Husking mills | 6,049 | 11,437 | 43,374 | 50,300 | n.a. |
| Total | 6,155 | 11,592 | 43,691 | 50,868 | n.a. |
| Private rice stocks | | | | | |
| Number of months of consumption needs | 1 | n.a. | n.a. | 3 | n.a. |
| Average storage time for trader stocks (months) | 4 | n.a. | n.a. | 1 | n.a. |
| Typical distance of spatial arbitrage (miles) | 50 | n.a. | n.a. | 100 | n.a. |

Sources: Chowdhury (1992); Ahmed, Haggblade, and Chowdhury (2000); Ministry of Food and Food Policy Monitoring Unit data; authors' calculations.

Note: HYV, high-yielding variety; MMT, million metric tons. n.a., no recent survey data are available.

Greater surplus has also meant that private stocks have ballooned in relation to public stocks. Chowdhury (1992) showed that per capita private rice stocks roughly doubled between the 1960s and early 1990s. In absolute terms, private rice stocks have grown even faster, particularly since the late 1980s. In the lean season, just before the aman harvest, private rice stocks typically exceeded those held in government godowns (warehouses) by about a factor of three. In the postharvest months of January and June, private rice stocks alone exceeded *total* government foodgrains stocks by a factor of five.

Among private holdings, farm-held stocks dominate trade stocks. On-farm stocks account for about 75 percent of all holdings, and trade stocks account for the remainder (Chowdhury 1992). Overall private stocks rose during 1989–94, both in absolute terms and relative to total estimated stocks, for each peak season: October, the end of the kharif (rainy) season; January, the end of the aman harvest season; and June, the peak of the boro harvest season. In the late 1960s private stocks supplied, on average, one month of the country's foodgrains requirements; in 1994 private stocks supplied more than three months of those requirements.[5]

All these developments occurred *prior* to liberalization of food markets. The increased supply and decreased seasonal variation—reflecting the combined effects of the Green Revolution and liberalization of certain agriculture-related markets—created favorable initial conditions for the liberalization policies that followed.

For example, the growing farm surpluses and private stocks created a new breed of traders to channel the produce to market. Back in 1990 Chowdhury (1992) found that farmers sold two-thirds of their marketed output at the farmgate, through marketing agents. These agents, operating with little capital (Ahmed, Haggblade, and Chowdhury 2000), probably represented one of the most labor-intensive rice trading regimes in Asia. The increased prominence of arbitrage across space (rather than time) put a premium on transportation rather than storage; that, along with improved supporting infrastructure, enhanced the competitiveness of labor relative to capital and favored not only small farmers but also small traders.

Effective transportation costs were reduced by the development of transportation infrastructure. Satellite population centers sprang up outside two megacities, Chittagong and Dhaka. In this changed scenario, the marketing advantage lay in possessing information about sources and destinations—as well as the ability to physically negotiate the distance. Labor could now compete more equally with capital.

Hence, by 1990, the marketing of rice showed a fairly even distribution, across classes of farms and across months (Table 2.4). Table 2.4 also suggests the absence of distress selling by farmers; distress selling would be indicated by sharp declines in the percentages sold by small and marginal farmers in nonharvest months compared with the months closer to harvests. Growing rice in Bangladesh had become a profitable business, and marginal and small farmers shared in this propitious development.[6]

The uniformity in the seasonal pattern of marketing can be seen in Table 2.5. Given widespread HYV adoption by farms of all sizes, a large proportion of even marginal farms (up to 0.2 hectare of land) had become net sellers of paddy in good harvest years. After good aman and boro harvests during the 1989/90 crop year, an estimated 70 percent of all farms were net sellers of rice (Chowdhury 1994).

All these changes—increasing production of grains, an improving infrastructure, and rising farmer confidence in marketing—engendered seasonal smoothing and moreover created a basis for spatial integration of markets.

### Outcomes: Spatial Integration of Markets

Beginning in the late 1980s, as technological change fostered greater commercialization, trade-related infrastructure (roads and communication networks) improved significantly. The marketing costs of suppliers at each level fell as a result. For instance, in 1990 a long-distance call from Thakurgaon in the northwest to Chittagong, an important terminal market, would cost Tk 30 per minute. In 2002 such a call was only Tk 6 per minute.

Table 2.4    Farm marketing of paddy over seasons, year through November 1990 (percent of quantity marketed)

| Farm size class | November | December | January | February | March | April | May | June | July | August | September | October | Total |
|---|---|---|---|---|---|---|---|---|---|---|---|---|---|
| Marginal farms | 11.29 | 11.94 | 7.79 | 12.0 | 2.51 | 15.6 | 15.31 | 8.4 | 8.61 | 3.85 | 1.6 | 0.8 | 100 |
| Small farms | 9.41 | 6.13 | 6.15 | 10.6 | 7.09 | 11.1 | 14.11 | 7.1 | 6.65 | 14.1 | 3.9 | 3.2 | 100 |
| Medium farms | 9.35 | 5.98 | 5.28 | 11.0 | 10.26 | 9.85 | 15.42 | 9.8 | 5.78 | 5.36 | 6.2 | 5.5 | 100 |
| Large farms | 8.67 | 7.00 | 5.76 | 11.5 | 10.42 | 9.45 | 16.94 | 8.0 | 4.67 | 6.79 | 5.0 | 5.6 | 100 |
| All farms | 8.92 | 6.69 | 5.67 | 11.3 | 10.09 | 9.72 | 16.32 | 8.4 | 5.13 | 6.92 | 5.2 | 5.4 | 100 |

Source: Bangladesh Food Policy Project farm survey conducted by the International Food Policy Research Institute, 1989–94.

Table 2.5    Coarse rice and seasonality of farm rice marketing, 1990

| | Marketing per farmer by month by grade (all milled rice) | | |
|---|---|---|---|
| Month | Coarse rice (kg) | Noncoarse rice (kg) | Percent of coarse rice in total marketing |
| November | 417 | 156 | 72.7 |
| December | 294 | 135 | 68.5 |
| January | 219 | 145 | 60.1 |
| February | 246 | 126 | 66.1 |
| March | 219 | 150 | 59.4 |
| April | 420 | 202 | 67.5 |
| May | 915 | 134 | 87.2 |
| June | 469 | 74 | 86.3 |
| July–August | 591 | 136 | 81.3 |
| September–October | 506 | 141 | 78.1 |
| All months | 4,315 | 1,399 | 76.0 |

Source: Bangladesh Food Policy Project farm survey conducted by the International Food Policy Research Institute, 1989–94.

Note: kg, kilogram.

For any long-distance trade, if the price in the importing market equals the price in the exporting market plus transport costs (to a reasonable approximation), then the two markets are considered spatially integrated (the "law of one price").

The spatial integration of markets is a function of both infrastructure development and a broad-based rise in marketing surpluses. Empirical evidence tends to support the hypothesis that food markets in Bangladesh are spatially integrated. There is also evidence that integration has improved since the advent of market liberalization.

Dawson and Dey (2002) test for long-run spatial market integration in rice using a dynamic vector autoregressive model and co-integration. Their paper uses monthly prices on wholesale rice markets in Bangladesh since 1992. Following Ravallion (1986), Dawson and Dey assume a radial market structure, with a group of local, regional markets surrounding a central market in Dhaka. The regional markets are Bogra, Comilla, Faridpur, Jessore, Khulna, Kustia, Mymensingh, Noakhali, Pabna, Rajshahi, and Tangail. All these regional markets are within about 170 miles by road and ferry. Although trade between regional markets does exist, trade with the central market dominates price formation. Accordingly Dawson and Dey examine 11 pairwise relationships between prices in Dhaka and those in regional markets. For perfect market integration, a price increase in one market would produce an equivalent effect in another.

Previous studies of rice market integration in Bangladesh examined the preliberalization period prior to 1992 and found limited integration (Ahmed and Bernard 1989; Goletti 1994). Hence the preliberalization levels of infrastructure and marketed surplus appear to be insufficient to effect significant integration.

Dawson and Dey (2002) find that since liberalization, in contrast, the law of one price holds between rice prices in Dhaka and each regional market; moreover, this spatial integration is perfect, so that a price change in one market is mirrored elsewhere. In its relationships with near markets, Dhaka is dominant; in its relationships with more distant markets, however, regional markets dominate.

The IDS report (1998), "The Spatial Integration and Pricing Efficiency of the Private Sector Grain Trade in Bangladesh," arrived at a similar conclusion, including wheat markets as well. Along with rice, wheat markets were also found to be spatially well integrated, with the extent of integration improving since 1992. The study attributes this spatial integration to grain market liberalization, combined with investments in roads and telecommunications. Millers and wholesalers in the procurement regions were found increasingly to bypass traditional marketing intermediaries and sell directly to wholesalers in terminal markets. Shortening the marketing chain in this way has important implications for spatial integration of the markets.

### Private Sector Response to Opportunities from International Trade

In legalizing private imports the government crossed a major psychological barrier. And when given the opportunity to take advantage of international trade, the private sector delivered. Two years (1995–96 and 1998–99) experienced large production shortfalls, with flood-induced losses of standing crops and seedbeds during the aman season. On both occasions, price increases raised expected profits to importers, prompting them to open letters of credit (LCs) for fairly small quantities of rice. The result was that large quantities of rice were imported within a very short period of time.[7]

In the wake of the disastrous flood in 1998, within a period of nine months 2.4 MMT of rice were imported by the private sector. Ironically, less than one year after the floods of 1998 and consequent food shortages and high prices, short-term food policy debates throughout 1999–2000 focused on the problem of *low* rice prices.

Since private imports were legalized, private importers and the government and donors have switched their market shares. From a one-third share of imports in the mid-1990s, private imports have become the mainstay of imports, with India emerging as a primary source of supply. A next-door neighbor, India had a large and growing public foodgrains stock and was a major producer of parboiled rice, the variety preferred in Bangladesh. Between 1998 and 2004, although the percentage of public imports in both rice and wheat fell sharply, India remained a major source of imports. According to Dorosh and Murshid (2004), the Indian rice enjoyed an advantage (in terms of import parity price) of 10–16 percent over the nearest competitor in the period after the 1998 flood.

## Assessment of the Cost Effectiveness of the PFDS following Reforms

Cost effectiveness refers to efficacy relative to input. How much does it cost to transfer one unit of income to target groups? In the case of foodgrains interventions, this has been assessed in two ways. First, studies carried out by IFPRI during 1993 produced estimates of the cost effectiveness of income transfers from various targeted interventions (Working Group on Targeted Food Intervention 1994). In a variation implemented by Ahmed (1993), the following question was posed to measure effectiveness: do beneficiaries of targeted interventions have a higher marginal propensity to consume out of a dollar received as wheat ration than out of a dollar received as cash income? If they do, this would make a food-based program more effective in providing nutritional support than an equivalent payment in cash (Ahmed 1993).

We build on this framework and extend it further to measure cost effectiveness. In effect we determine the net *social welfare gain* from the operations by the Department of Food (DOF), whether from procuring grains domestically or distributing domestically procured grain among various channels, including food-for-work activities and vulnerable-group development programs.

In our estimate we use distributional weights in assessing program benefits. In order to use distributional weights, we obtained data on the average incomes of all kinds of program beneficiaries. The weights are inversely proportional to the per capita incomes of households in each beneficiary class. Based on our estimates, the cost effectiveness of the existing PFDS has improved from the mid-1980s by 40 percentage points. The movement toward targeted channels (in place of the openly inequitable sales channels) has contributed to this extremely positive development.

### Components of Cost Effectiveness: Evolution of the Cost of Marketing

For comparing public- and private-sector efficiency in food marketing we use data on (1) the unit transportation cost, based on a benchmark grid of marketing routes; (2) the cost of transit and storage loss; and (3) the marketing margin, adjusted for marketing life cycles. The construction of the benchmark grid is based on the movement program drawn up by the DOF for rice each year, before the onset of the procurement season. The cost data are based on the actual movement of grains during 2002. We consolidate data from actual shipments involving a total of 35 marketing routes. We also aggregate Local Supply Depot data to the level of new districts.

The most important routes for DOF marketing originate from the rice surplus districts in the northwest: Bogra, Dinajpur, Rajshahi, and Rangpur. From these districts the rice is shipped mainly to the rice-deficit districts. With the exception of greater Sylhet and Comilla, the deficit districts are in the south: Barisal, Chittagong, Khulna, and Noakhali. These 35 routes accounted for nearly 75 percent of all rice procurement during 2002. The unit (quantity-weighted) transportation cost was calculated based on actual fares, incorporating data on losses, financing costs, and fixed costs in distribution. For the PFDS as a whole, the distribution cost of rice on a full-cost basis is 21 percent of the cost of procurement.

There are notable similarities in the public- and private-sector marketing grids for rice. Bogra and Rajshahi are the grain arteries for both the public and the private sector, allowing us to compare marketing spreads between the two sectors. For the private sector, marketing margins range between Tk 2,020 and Tk 2,620 per ton. For the public sector, the corresponding number was Tk 2,450 on average (in 2002). The last two columns of Table 2.6 compare the percentage marketing spreads between the private and public sectors. As a percentage of farmgate prices, the marketing margin for private trade is slightly higher, at 21.7 percent compared to 20.8 percent for public-sector marketing, but those margins have fallen over time. The opening of the Jamuna Bridge in 1999 cut travel time by more than 40 percent between procurement and destination points; moreover, private traders face growing competition, reflected in a rising number of merchants.

Why is the marketing margin for the public sector only slightly smaller? First, the public sector is still much larger, in terms of capitalization, scale of operations, and geographic spread of operations. It also enjoys a more favorable regime of input prices. The scale for the Directorate General of Food (DGF) is much larger than that for a representative private trader, maintaining stocks equal to five to seven months' anticipated requirements. The rice stocks of the entire private sector are equal to no more than two to five *weeks'* requirements. In addition public institutions have an insider's advantage in dealing with regulatory and donor institutions.[8] The DGF also has a favored place at the lending windows of state-owned banks.

Table 2.6    Comparative marketing spreads of private trade and the Directorate General of Food

| Terminal market | Retail price, 2002 (Tk/ton) | Private-sector marketing spread for rice, 2002 (Tk/ton) | Marketing spread (% of farmgate price) | |
|---|---|---|---|---|
| | | | Private trade | Directorate General of Food |
| Barisal | 13,290 | 2,430 | 22.38 | 21.1 |
| Chittagong | 13,540 | 2,620 | 20.69 | 22.0 |
| Comilla | 13,060 | 2,470 | 23.32 | 20.1 |
| Dhaka | 13,220 | 2,100 | 18.88 | 19.5 |
| Faridpur | 13,240 | 2,260 | 20.58 | 19.3 |
| Khulna | 13,000 | 2,260 | 21.04 | 19.8 |
| Mymensingh | 12,950 | 2,020 | 18.48 | 19.3 |
| Noakhali | 13,460 | 2,450 | 22.25 | 20.9 |
| Sylhet | 13,080 | 2,620 | 25.04 | 25.1 |
| All | 13,240 | 2,360 | 21.69 | 20.8 |

Source: Authors' calculations.

Note: Tk, taka.

## Overall Costs and Benefits of the PFDS Operation

Because 94 percent of consumer demand is met by the market, subsidies must be calculated on the basis of market prices (as opposed to administered prices). On that basis consumer subsidies during 2003–04 can be re-estimated at Tk 7.3 billion. This level is about 30 percent higher than the figure for 2001, reflecting higher market prices during 2003–04—even though administered prices were not raised during that period.[9] The *producer* subsidy for that period, however, is estimated at a mere Tk 1.4 billion—only 64 percent of the level in 2001. This reflects the fact that, despite its best attempts, the government was virtually unable to procure wheat in 2003–04.

Recent research by IFPRI shows that, even within current pricing and distributional outcomes, the government could run the system at a lower cost. When net stock increases to 0.8 MMT, keeping the distribution level identical to the base scenario, the amount of old stock increases from 332 MT to 908 MT. This led to a loss, with a benefit-cost ratio equal to −14 percent. With the closure of the Food for Education program (about 0.35 MMT) and downsizing of the PFDS operation—for example, eliminating the Food for Work program (more than 0.2 MMT) in 2002—the ideal PFDS stock level and distribution level should be 0.6 and 1.35 MMT, respectively.

Ahmed et al. (2004) reported that the benefit-cost ratio of managing 0.6 MMT of foodgrains could be as high as 74 percent, as against a negative benefit-cost ratio of −14 percent cited previously. The implicit cost of holding greater stock is substantially higher, about US$15 million at 2002 exchange rates.

## Evolution of Indicators of Food Security

### Transition in Price of Foodgrains in Bangladesh

This section looks at different aspects of foodgrains prices: their levels, year-to-year variability, and range of seasonal variation—and how these indicators changed with liberalization. These price indicators are closely (negatively) related to economic access to cereals; the other factor is of course the level of income. (In estimating real cereal prices, the deflator is the consumer price index for nonfood goods in Dhaka.)

For both rice and wheat, annual price variability has clearly fallen: both real prices display statistically significant negative trends. For rice the negative time trend for the period 1981–2003 is 2.57 percent per year; for wheat it is 1.76 percent. Dorosh (2001) also found a distinct negative trend in *nominal* prices of rice following liberalization of imports in 1994. The nominal prices (based on Dhaka wholesale prices) continued to decline overall until 1998, when prices spiked owing to massive flooding.[10] Importantly, large imports by the private sector quickly brought prices back to the level of import parity prices.

A total of six months during the postliberalization period show positive trend deviations, that is, prices rising above the trend line, compared to only four months during the preliberalization period. There is some clustering of positive price shocks for coarse rice in the run-up to the boro planting season (between February and May). However, both intra- and interyear fluctuations in rice prices diminished in the 1980s—and still further in the 1990s—compared to the 1970s. The standard error of estimate around a simple time trend for the years 1973–93 based on nominal rice price is 0.5, only one-third of that in the later period. The intrayear range between the highest and lowest rice prices shows the following results: 1973–80, 29.2 percent; 1981–93, 17.4 percent; and 1994–2003, 14.8 percent. The instability in rice prices has thus diminished remarkably over the decades.

### Effect on Cereal Availability

The per capita availability of all grains has increased following liberalization. Availability may not translate into consumption, because of either lack of economic access or a shift in preferences. During the entire period, rice and wheat consumption per capita has averaged 147.2 and 18 kilograms, respectively. Overall per capita foodgrains consumption has averaged 165.2 kilograms—meeting the government's targeted norm of 165 kilograms per year. In the preliberalization period, per capita foodgrains availability was only 158 kilograms.

For assessing household-level consumption of cereals, we use the foodgrains intake data (by income deciles) from Household Income and Expenditure Surveys for four years: 1985, 1988, 1992, and 2000 (Table 2.7). Per capita consumption of all

Table 2.7   Rice and cereal intake by Bangladeshi households by bottom and top quintiles, 1988–2000

| | Rice | | | | All cereals | | | |
|---|---|---|---|---|---|---|---|---|
| Year | Bottom 40% of consumers[a] | Middle 40% of consumers | Top 20% of consumers | Average level | Bottom 40% of consumers | Middle 40% of consumers | Top 20% of consumers | Average level |
| 1988–89 | 143.36 | 167.74 | 184.68 | 165.26 | 169.18 | 190.68 | 206.0 | 188.6 |
| 1991–92 | 143.4 | 182.3 | 185.8 | 170.5 | 158.6 | 199.2 | 211.05 | 189.6 |
| 1995–96 | 148.1 | 167.4 | 164.4 | 159.96 | 164.1 | 182.6 | 184.6 | 177.1 |
| 1999–2000 | 156.8 | 167.4 | 164.2 | 162.8 | 161.9 | 173.4 | 181.15 | 172.1 |

Source: Bangladesh Bureau of Statistics (various years).
[a]By income.

cereals shows a declining trend between 1992 and 2000, from 185 to 170 kilograms.[11] Per capita consumption of rice, however, is largely unchanged. Since per capita incomes during the same time grew at a rate of 3 percent, with shrinking inequality in income, the fall in average foodgrains consumption is probably due to nonincome factors, such as shifting dietary preferences. The distribution of rice consumption has indeed improved between 1992 and 2000: the bottom 40 percent of consumers (by income) raised their intake, while the top 20 percent reduced theirs. The Gini coefficient of cereals consumption fell from 0.08 in 1992 to 0.04 in 2000.

## Assessing the Effect of Multilateral Trade Liberalization on Food Security in Bangladesh

### Results from a Multimarket Model

This section assesses the likely impact of the stalled Doha Round—if it were to be successfully concluded—on the rice and wheat sector in Bangladesh. A multimarket (MM) model distinguishing several household types is used to study the potential impacts on real incomes and food consumption of the poor in Bangladesh, arising from anticipated changes in world prices of rice and wheat resulting from multilateral trade liberalization under the Doha Round.

The MM model that we use was originally developed in 1994 (Dorosh 1994; Dorosh and Haggblade 1995). This model distinguishes 13 commodities: rice, wheat, pulses, fruits and vegetables, potatoes, onions, fish, meat, milk, oils, sugar, other food, and nonfoods. It also distinguishes five household types: urban poor, urban nonpoor, rural landless, rural small farm, and rural large farm. A notable feature of this categorization is that it differentiates net producers (large farmers) from net consumers, to identify differential consumption responses to price shocks.

The demand side for each market distinguishes between in-kind consumption and consumption out of cash income, with elasticities taken from Ahmed (1993) and Goletti (1993). On the supply side, the model allows endogenous production responses to output price, using supply elasticities estimated by Rahman and Yunus (1993). Price formation in the model differs for traded and nontraded commodities. For traded commodities, the cost insurance freight import price sets the domestic price level, with net imports adjusting to clear the market. For nontraded commodities, prices adjust to equilibrate domestic production, consumption, and changes in stocks. For details about the model structure and the baseline, see Goletti (1993), Dorosh (1994), and Dorosh and Haggblade (1995).

We use the same set of elasticities as in the original model, after updating the vector of exogenous variables to the year 2000–01, the new base year for the model. (Exogenous variables include, for example, the per capita incomes of the five household classes.) We run simulations in which the world prices of rice and wheat are shocked to reflect the effect of multilateral trade reforms.

A pertinent issue here is the extent to which the world prices of rice and wheat are expected to change following multilateral trade reforms. A recent study by the United States Department of Agriculture, using global computable general equilibrium (CGE) models, analyzed the effect of reforms under the Doha Round that would eliminate three major policy distortions in international trade: agricultural import barriers (tariff equivalents), agricultural export subsidies throughout the world, and domestic support in developed countries. The study found that the world prices would likely change by 10.1 percent for rice and 18.1 percent for wheat (Diao, Somwaru, and Roe 2001). But these substantial values are based on a model structure that does not admit of a positive supply response to initial price increases and a negative aggregate-demand response, and they may well represent an upper bound. It is conceivable that there is a lower bound: there is an imperative need to carry out alternative sets of model simulations, based on both the upper and the lower bounds.[12]

Accordingly we shock the MM model of Bangladesh with both upper and lower bounds of the estimates of the effect of multilateral trade liberalization on world prices.[13] Table 2.8 reports the results of the effects of price increases on real incomes and foodgrains consumption of rural and urban poor in Bangladesh, measured in kcal/day.[14]

Real incomes fall except for the most well-off rural income class, across all the simulations. At the upper bound increases in the world prices of both rice and wheat (simulation 5), real incomes of rural large farm households rise by close to 1.5 percent, while the urban poor and rural landless lose nearly 2 percent of their real incomes. Large farmers are net producers, for whom the increase in the domestic price (in line with the movement in world prices) increases their revenues. All other household

Table 2.8    Simulations 1–6, higher world grain prices with liberalized trade

| Outcome | Simulation 1 | Simulation 2 | Simulation 3 | Simulation 4 | Simulation 5 | Simulation 6 |
|---|---|---|---|---|---|---|
| Real incomes | | | | | | |
| Urban poor | −0.922 | −0.45 | −1.544 | −0.62 | −1.977 | −0.93 |
| Urban nonpoor | −0.4655 | −0.225 | −1.08 | −0.29 | −1.25 | −0.61 |
| Rural landless | −0.79 | −0.38 | −1.357 | −0.53 | −1.836 | −0.89 |
| Rural small farm | −0.17 | −0.09 | −0.506 | −0.22 | −0.576 | −0.29 |
| Rural large farm | 0.91 | 0.48 | 0.987 | 0.25 | 1.47 | 0.73 |
| Calories (absolute change per capita, kcal/day) | | | | | | |
| Urban poor | −13.7 | −7.0 | −51.8 | −0.23 | −65.1 | −27.0 |
| Urban nonpoor | −7.84 | −4.0 | 0.0 | 0.0 | −7.84 | −0.39 |
| Rural landless | −13.0 | −7.2 | −28.1 | −0.12 | −40.2 | −21.5 |
| Rural small farm | −8.16 | −3.80 | 7.5 | 3.0 | −1.1 | −0.57 |
| Rural large farm | −9.215 | −4.4 | −20.07 | −9.1 | −28.8 | −11.0 |

Notes: Simulation 1 reflects a 10 percent increase in the world price of rice. Simulation 2: 5 percent increase in the world price of rice. Simulation 3: 18 percent increase in the world price of wheat. Simulation 4: 7 percent increase in the world price of wheat. Simulation 5: 10 percent and 18 percent increases in the world prices of rice and wheat, respectively. Simulation 6: 5 percent and 7 percent increases in the world prices of rice and wheat, respectively.

types in the model are net consumers, for whom an increase in the price of these two cereals lowers their purchasing power. The increase in the world price of wheat has much larger effect on real incomes than the increase in the world price of rice (simulations 1 and 3). These changes (rise or loss) in the real income across household types are roughly halved when the increases in the world prices are at their lower bound (simulation 6). In calorie intake, however, this minimal estimated price increase results in reduced consumption for all households.

Not surprisingly that decline in consumption is highest among urban poor and rural landless, by 65 and 40 kcal/day per capita, respectively. Much of this decline is due to the rise in wheat prices following trade liberalization. But for large farmers, as net sellers, there is also an increase in income, so the decline in their calorie intake at first seems surprising. Yet wheat is considered an inferior good, so the rise in incomes results in lower intake; rice intake, in contrast, goes up for big farm households in the same scenario. (IFPRI's estimates of income elasticities were −0.19 and 0.03 for wheat and rice, respectively [Dorosh 1994].) For other food items—particularly high-value products like fish, fruits and vegetables, meat, and milk—consumption goes up with a rise in incomes. The disparity in overall nutrition (both macro- and micronutrients) across income classes would have worsened in this scenario.

Hence multilateral trade liberalization that results in an increase in world (and hence domestic) prices for rice and wheat is likely to have adverse income distributional effects in Bangladesh: only the rural large farmers benefit, while all other sections of the population suffer income losses.

## Results from a CGE Analysis

The results from the MM model capture the impact of trade liberalization for only rice and wheat. The Doha Round trade negotiations had a more ambitious agenda, however, covering all of agriculture as well as non-agriculture, including services. The MM model cannot capture the impact of more widespread trade reforms, either national or international. An analytical framework typically used for such analysis is the CGE framework. Annabi et al. (2005) have examined the impacts of trade liberalization on poverty in Bangladesh using a CGE model.

The study by Annabi et al. (2005) uses a sequential dynamic CGE model based on the social accounting matrix of Bangladesh for the year 1999–2000. The model, solved over a 20-period time horizon, generates "steady-state" paths that help in quantifying both short-run impacts (mainly allocative effects) and long-run impacts (both allocative and factor accumulation effects). The study finds that trade liberalization could have different, and often opposite, impacts in the short run versus the long run, clearly demonstrating the need to analyze these effects within a dynamic framework.

The model distinguishes nine household categories: five are rural, based on occupation and landownership status (landless, marginal farmer, small farmer, large farmer, non-agricultural); four are urban, based on education level (illiterate, low-educated, medium-educated, high-educated). The other agents in the model are firms (one representative firm per sector), the government, and the rest of the world. The model further distinguishes four types of primary production factors: skilled labor, unskilled labor, agricultural capital, and non-agricultural capital; and it assumes full mobility for both skilled and unskilled labor throughout the 15 commodity-producing sectors in the model.

Annabi et al. (2005) study the impact of trade liberalization, either unilaterally by Bangladesh or as part of a larger process of multilateral trade liberalization. The main findings relating to food security are as follows:

- Import competition forces a reduction in domestic prices, producing a fall in overall consumer prices for both rural and urban households (ranging between 5.5 and 24.6 percent in the long run).

- Over time, non-agricultural capital and labor shift toward the textiles-garments sector and away from other manufacturing sectors (although there is relatively little movement within the agricultural sector). As a result, impacts (positive or negative) on imports, exports, and output will be stronger in the long run than in the short run.

- The decline in product prices results in a decline in factor prices as well (5.2–27.8 percent in the long run), with diminishing impact in the long run. The returns to capital fall more than returns to labor, reflecting the contraction of several industrial sectors. Within labor, the wage rate for unskilled labor declines less than that for skilled labor, due to the expansion of the labor-intensive textile-garments sector.

- The decline in factor returns results in a fall in the nominal income of households (5.2–6.8 percent in the long run, and more in the short run). The decline is smallest among the poorest households (urban illiterate, urban low-educated, rural landless, and rural marginal), whose income consists mostly of unskilled wages. The biggest losers are households whose income comes from skilled labor and non-agricultural capital (medium- and high-educated urban households and non-agricultural rural households).

- In real consumption, all households suffer a decline in the short run (0.1–0.7 percent), as nominal income falls more than consumer prices. In the long run, however, all households gain (0.6–1.8 percent), with the poorest households emerging as the biggest winners.

- As anticipated, all measures of poverty show that, although unilateral trade liberalization *increases* poverty in the short run, in the long run poverty *decreases* for all household types.

    Given that poverty will decline over the long run for all households, the overall effect of unilateral trade liberalization on food security is postulated to be positive.

## Summary and Conclusions

Bangladesh's success with food security following liberalization represents the outcome of three major interrelated factors: technology (the spread of HYVs of rice), infrastructure development (development of roads and waterways), and liberalization policies, both on the domestic front and at the border (in both inputs and output markets).

    On the food policy front there were far-reaching changes. To begin with, the inequitable foodgrains distribution channels were abandoned, and the dissolution of those channels was properly marketed to the public: the government faced no backlash as a result of its belt tightening. In the reformed public distribution process, more than three-quarters of the foodgrains distributed accrue to the poor.

    Following this policy watershed, the government overcame another major psychological barrier by legalizing private imports of fertilizer in 1992 and of foodgrains in 1993. As the government transformed the environment with infrastructure investments and policy reforms, markets swung into action. Irrigated acreage rose sharply. Foodgrains production and availability per capita rose as well, along with absolute yields. The import dependency for foodgrains fell from 12 percent in 1980 to 5.5 percent in 2004.

The public sector also responded to the policy transition. Statutory foodgrains subsidies were abolished. The proportion of market supply sourced from the PFDS fell from 12 percent in the early 1980s to 6 percent in the early 2000s. The broader prioritization of poverty reduction led to a significant pro-poor focus at the PFDS.

When we look at indicators related to economic access to foodgrains, we see that, for both grains, real prices (nominal price relative to the price index) fell markedly following liberalization. Seasonal price fluctuations have also diminished. Secondary evidence also shows greater spatial integration of markets postliberalization.

However, some issues remain. First, the government's rice stocks policy tends to defeat its own pricing policy. High government stocks produce lower expected prices and possibly depress current prices as well. In the long run prices can be sustained more effectively by a rise in incomes than by a procurement strategy. Any time the government raises either its procurement price or the target procurement amount, it runs the risk of an overaccumulation of public stocks; but any effort to cut back on the procurement program leads to uneconomic public stocks (by eliminating economies of scale) and lowers the operational efficiency of the PFDS.

Second, government subsidies continue to be extremely large. The official estimates of food subsidies do not reflect either market prices or the quality of grains distributed. Estimated at market prices, government subsidies are much higher. And as the market prices of grains rise from the atypical lows of 2000 and 2001, budgetary costs will also grow.

The third issue relates to the impending trade liberalization. Partial equilibrium MM analysis shows adverse distributional impacts in Bangladesh from multilateral liberalization in rice and wheat, arising from an increase in world and domestic prices of both grains. Taking a more general equilibrium view, Annabi et al. (2005) look at the impact on poverty from unilateral as well as multilateral liberalization in Bangladesh. The initial impact on poverty is adverse; but in the long run poverty declines for all households, due to efficiency gains.

In conclusion, the experience of Bangladesh in unilaterally liberalizing its food markets has had several positive impacts on the food security situation in the country. Some concerns remain with regard to the potential impacts of multilateral liberalization and especially its impact in the short run. With adequate safety nets, however, the overall long-run impact will be favorable. This outcome is made more likely by the improved cost effectiveness of Bangladesh's safety nets, made possible through improved targeting strategies.

## Notes

1. Marketing margins are defined as the difference between the retail price and the farmgate price, expressed as a percentage of the retail price.

2. The monetized channels of rationing, consisting of Statutory Rationing (SR), Modified Rationing (MR), and Palli Rationing (PR), have been abolished.

3. The subsidy to EP recipients is classified information but is assumed to be high. Since 1992, when SR was abolished, EP is the only channel in which grains are shipped by the Directorate General of Food (DGF) at a fraction (between 10 and 20 percent) of what the DGF sets as the economic price of the grain.

4. This phenomenon has been widely documented; see Hossain (1988); Ahmed, Haggblade, and Chowdhury (2000); and Dorosh, del Ninno, and Shahabuddin (2004).

5. Even though the private sector has risen in importance in production, trade, and stocks, there remains scope for improvement. The unit cost of rice production in Bangladesh is high compared with that in other countries in the region: 62 percent higher than in Thailand in the dry season (boro) and 18 percent in the wet season (aman), and 25 and 36 percent higher, respectively, than in Vietnam. Compared to the Indian states of Punjab and Andhra Pradesh, production cost is 26–81 percent higher in Bangladesh (Deb and Hossain 2003).

6. Similar conclusions have been reached using more recent data. Dorosh, del Ninno, and Shahabuddin (2004, 17) write: "All farm size-classes sell at least a half of their rice output. The price of rice during the harvest season is therefore a major determinant of farmers' incomes."

7. The Bangladesh Food Policy Project of the International Food Policy Research Institute (IFPRI) showed that a large proportion of the LCs opened by private importers were for less than 500 MT. The numbers of LCs opened during both 1994 and 1998 suggest a large number of imports. The average quantity of rice imported per consignment fell between 1994 and 1998. The 10 largest traders imported 142,369 MT or 16 percent of the total. The structure of the rice import trade was atomistic, with little real possibility of price collusion among so many importers.

8. In 2001 the DGF implemented construction of modern storage depots throughout the country, mostly funded by food aid donors. These may have lowered storage costs for the DGF, while leaving the costs of private storage unaffected.

9. Rice prices globally were rising during 2003 and 2004, rebounding from the historic lows reached during 2000 and 2001. Thus for instance the price of benchmark Thai 100% white rice in 2003 and 2004 reached, respectively, US$240 and $280 per MT, compared to $180 and $195 in 2000 and 2001. Global stocks also achieved a marked increase during 2003/04 compared with 2000/01. Unsurprisingly prices in Bangladesh too were much higher in 2003/04 than in either of the earlier years.

10. There were some deviations from trend based on seasonality.

11. While comparison of average foodgrains availability pre- and postliberalization points to growth, data from household surveys is vague regarding growth in consumption levels. There is no doubt, however, that the poorest 40 percent of the population have increased their consumption of rice.

12. All the more so because WTO bound tariffs will offer considerable flexibility, even under the total multilateral liberalization.

13. For the lower bound we use a 5 percent and a 7 percent increase in the world price of rice and wheat, respectively, as suggested by an anonymous referee who reviewed an earlier version of this chapter.

14. Due to space limitations, we present only the findings about the impact on real incomes and consumption of foodgrains. For more detailed findings see Chowdhury and Farid (2005).

## References

Ahmed, A. U. 1992. *Operational performance of the rural rationing program in Bangladesh.* Food Policy in Bangladesh Working Paper 5. Washington, D.C.: International Food Policy Research Institute.

———. 1993. *Food consumption and nutritional effects of targeted food interventions in Bangladesh.* Bangladesh Food Policy Project Manuscript 31. Washington, D.C.: International Food Policy Research Institute.

Ahmed, A. U., S. Rashid, M. Sharma, and S. Zohir. 2004. *Food aid distribution in Bangladesh: Leakage and operational performance.* Food Consumption and Nutrition Division Discussion Paper 173. Washington, D.C.: International Food Policy Research Institute.

Ahmed, R. 1988. Structure, costs, and benefits of food subsidies in Bangladesh. In *Food Subsidies in Developing Countries,* ed. P. Pinstrup-Andersen. Baltimore, Md., U.S.A.: Johns Hopkins University Press.

Ahmed, R., and A. Bernard. 1989. *Rice price fluctuation and an approach to price stabilization in Bangladesh.* Research Report 72. Washington, D.C.: International Food Policy Research Institute.

Ahmed, R., S. Haggblade, and T. E. Chowdhury (eds.). 2000. *Out of the shadow of famine: Evolving food markets and food policy in Bangladesh.* Baltimore, Md., U.S.A.: Johns Hopkins University Press.

Annabi, N., H. K. Bazlul, S. Raihan, J. Cockburn, and B. Decaluwe. 2005. *Implications of WTO agreements and domestic trade policy reforms for poverty in Bangladesh: Short vs. long run.* Modeling and Impact Analysis Working Paper 2005-02. Available at SSRN: http://ssrn.com/abstract=985622.

Bangladesh Bureau of Statistics. Various years. *Household expenditure survey.* Dhaka: Bangladesh Bureau of Statistics.

Beacon Consultants. 1986. *The existing system of public foodgrain distribution in Bangladesh and proposals for restructuring.* Report prepared for the Ministry of Food, Government of Bangladesh, and funded by United States Agency for International Development (USAID).

Chen, L., A. K. M. A. Chowdhury, and S. L. Huffman. 1979. Seasonal dimensions of energy-protein malnutrition in rural Bangladesh: The role of agriculture, dietary practices and infection. *Ecology of Food and Nutrition* 8: 175–187.

Chowdhury, N. 1988. Where the poor come last: The case of modified rationing in Bangladesh. *Bangladesh Development Studies* 16 (1): 27–54.

———. 1992. *Rice markets in Bangladesh: A study in structure, conduct and performance.* Bangladesh Food Policy Project Manuscript 22. Washington, D.C.: International Food Policy Research Institute.

———. 1994. *Credit and Bangladesh's foodgrain market: New evidence on commercialization, credit relations and effects of credit access.* Bangladesh Food Policy Project Manuscript 64. Washington, D.C.: International Food Policy Research Institute.

Chowdhury, N., and N. Farid. 2005. *Liberalization, adjustment and food security in Bangladesh, 1981–2004: Prognosis for the future.* Project Report. Washington, D.C.: International Food Policy Research Institute.

Clay, E. 1981. Seasonal patterns of agricultural employment in Bangladesh. In *Seasonal dimensions to rural poverty,* ed. R. Chambers, R. Longhurst, and A. Pacey. London: Frances Pinter.

Dawson, P. J., and P. K. Dey. 2002. Testing for the law of one price: Rice market integration in Bangladesh. *Journal of International Development* 14: 473–484.

Deb, U. K., and M. Hossain. 2003. Liberalization of rice trade: Can Bangladesh withstand regional competition? Paper presented at the South Asia Initiative Workshop on Analysis of Trade Liberalization for Poverty Alleviation, held at Colombo, Ceylon, April 21–25.

Diao, X., A. Somwaru, and T. Roe. 2001. A global analysis of agricultural reform in WTO member countries. In *Agricultural policy reform in the WTO: The road ahead,* ed. M. E. Burfisher. Market and Trade Economics Division, ERS/USDA Agricultural Economic Report 802. Washington, D.C.: Economic Research Service, United States Department of Agriculture.

Dorosh, P. A. 1994. *Food policy, external shocks and income distribution in Bangladesh: A multi-market analysis.* Bangladesh Food Project Manuscript 60. Dhaka: International Food Policy Research Institute.

———. 2001. Trade liberalization and national food security: Rice trade between Bangladesh and India. *World Development* 29 (4): 673–689.

Dorosh, P. A., C. del Ninno, and Q. Shahabuddin. 2004. *The 1998 floods and beyond: Towards comprehensive food security in Bangladesh.* Washington, D.C.: University Press Limited and International Food Policy Research Institute.

Dorosh, P. A., and S. Haggblade. 1995. Filling the gaps: Consolidating evidence on the design of alternative targeted food programmes in Bangladesh. *Bangladesh Development Studies* 23 (3–4): 47–80.

Dorosh, P. A., and K. A. S. Murshid. 2004. Trade liberalization and national food security: Rice trade between Bangladesh and India. In *The 1998 floods and beyond: Towards comprehensive food security in Bangladesh,* ed. P. A. Dorosh, C. del Ninno, and Q. Shahabuddin. Washington, D.C.: University Press Limited and International Food Policy Research Institute.

Farruk, M. O. 1972. *The structure and performance of the rice marketing system in East Pakistan.* Special Publication. Ithaca, N.Y., U.S.A.: Cornell University.

Goletti, F. 1993. *Food consumption parameters in Bangladesh.* Bangladesh Food Policy Project Manuscript 29. Dhaka: International Food Policy Research Institute.

———. 1994. *The changing public role in a rice economy approaching self-sufficiency: The case of Bangladesh.* Research Report 98. Washington, D.C.: International Food Policy Research Institute.

Government of India (GOI). 2002. *The report of the high-level committee on long-term grain policy.* New Delhi.

Hossain, M. 1988. *Nature and impact of green revolution in Bangladesh.* Research Report 67. Washington, D.C.: International Food Policy Research Institute.

Institute of Development Studies (IDS). 1998. *The spatial integration and pricing efficiency of the private sector grain trade in Bangladesh.* Phase II Report. Sussex, UK.

Rahman, S. H., and M. Yunus. 1993. *Price responsiveness of supply of major crops in Bangladesh.* Bangladesh Food Policy Project Manuscript 19. Dhaka: International Food Policy Research Institute and Bangladesh Institute of Development Studies.

Ravallion, M. 1986. Testing market integration. *American Journal of Agricultural Economics* 68: 102–109.

Samad, A., A. Haque, and S. S. Sidhu. 1989. *Low cost intervention study for the fertilizer market of Bangladesh.* Dhaka: International Center for Soil Fertility and Agricultural Development.

Timmer, C. P. 2004. *Food security in Indonesia: Current challenges and the long-run outlook.* Working Paper 48. Washington, D.C.: Center for Global Development.

Working Group on Targeted Food Intervention (WGTFI). 1994. *Options for targeting food interventions in Bangladesh.* Washington, D.C.: International Food Policy Research Institute.

World Bank. 1979. *Bangladesh: Food policy issues.* Washington, D.C.

# Chapter 3

# Achieving Food Security in a Cost-Effective Way: Implications of Domestic Deregulation and Liberalized Trade in India

Shikha Jha, P. V. Srinivasan, and A. Ganesh-Kumar

The foodgrains market in India has been characterized by a dominant government presence in pricing, procurement, stocking, transport, and distribution. Two implicit but important objectives of the Indian food policy have been to stabilize foodgrains supplies and prices, both *over time* (through stock policies) and *across regions* (by procuring grains from surplus areas to supply deficit areas). These policies have their origin in the food shortages of the 1950s and 1960s, when dependence on foodgrains imports was high. Highly restrictive controls on international and domestic trade in foodgrains made it possible for the government to achieve a dominant position in foodgrains marketing.

On the foreign trade front, severe restrictions were placed on exports and imports of most agricultural products, including foodgrains. For the most part, trade was channeled through government agencies, with the private sector allowed almost no role. On the domestic trade front, restrictions were imposed on storage of grains, both through policies such as the Essential Commodities Act (ECA) and through *zoning* restrictions that regulate or prohibit private trade in foodgrains across broad zones within the country. The government's control was based on the belief that "speculative" activities by private operators can be destabilizing and that legal restrictions on collusive and manipulative practices may be inadequate. In addition private operators faced problems arising from inordinate delays at checkposts, bad roads, and inadequate infrastructure.

Government intervention in foodgrains markets did seem to have a positive effect in the early years of the Green Revolution, assisting the spread of hybrid varieties. The country transformed itself from a chronic state of food deficit in the 1950s and 1960s to self-sufficiency by the 1970s and 1980s—and it has been a net exporter since the 1990s. However, over time the restrictions on international trade had the effect of disprotecting poor farmers, while the restrictions on domestic trade led to significant regional price variations as well as high expenditures on public operations in foodgrains marketing.

The 1990s witnessed some small steps at reforming the food policies of the government. Export controls on foodgrains were removed, and quantitative restrictions were replaced with tariffs, though at levels that remained among the highest in the world. On the domestic front, the government has more or less removed the restrictions on interstate movement of commodities. It has proposed to do away with the ECA and replace it with an emergency act that can be applied by notification, for a limited time, to a specified commodity in a specified region. The state governments are expected to introduce appropriate laws to remove restrictions, enabling farmers and companies to jointly promote domestic and foreign trade.

In spite of the government's expressed intention to carry out these reforms, in reality most of the restrictive policies on domestic trade remain unchanged. In general the government maintains high tariff rates on most agricultural commodities, unless domestic shortages of specific commodities warrant a tariff reduction to improve their availability in domestic markets. On the export side, the government has not shied away from bringing back export controls (as it did recently for foodgrains, including common-variety rice), if, in its assessment, the prevailing price and supply-demand situation appear to threaten food security. Thus we see strong reluctance on the part of policymakers to lift all restrictions on imports and exports and to allow the private sector to operate freely in the grain markets. The key to resolving the policymakers' fears is to assess realistically the likely impacts of liberalizing foreign and domestic trade in foodgrains.

The logic for domestic trade reforms is that freer domestic trade could reduce the need for protecting farmers' prices: regional exports out of surplus areas would have the effect of raising the local prices there and reducing them in deficit regions. Decentralized procurement and allowing a greater role for the private sector would moreover be likely to reduce overall costs and improve efficiency in the foodgrains markets. Simultaneously easing international trade would enable traders in border states such as West Bengal to export more easily to Bhutan, Bangladesh, or other neighboring countries. Similarly, during shortages, they could import from those countries rather than depend on central government stocks. In short, domestic market efficiency and domestic welfare could be increased through larger private-sector participation and a gradual reduction in the level of government intervention.

This chapter addresses several questions related to both international trade and domestic market deregulation. Many studies have assessed the impacts of international trade liberalization on India, but little has been done to examine the impacts of domestic market deregulation. Here, after reviewing the literature on international trade liberalization, we look at the issues of domestic market deregulation in greater detail. Specifically we examine the possible impacts on food security of removing all domestic controls on grain marketing, including movement restrictions; centralized procurement, including levies on rice millers; and stocking limits on traders. We use a multimarket spatial equilibrium model of the rice and wheat markets across the states of India.

The following section gives an overview of the foodgrains policies of the Indian government, with discussions of international trade, pricing, the procurement system, and domestic trade. The third section provides a brief assessment of the performance of the public procurement system. In the fourth section, we review the literature on the ex ante impacts of border trade liberalization, especially with regard to the welfare of the poor, and compare it with the actual experiences of the Indian economy. In this context we also discuss the incompatibility of the existing domestic system—that is, government intervention in foodgrains markets at administratively fixed prices—with a relatively liberal international trade regime.

The fifth section presents a spatial model of the rice and wheat markets in India, to analyze the impacts of domestic market reforms addressing interstate barriers to movement of foodgrains. The next section describes the scenarios studied using this spatial model; it is followed by a discussion of the simulation results. The final section provides a summary of the findings of this study.

## Policy Environment

The chronology of India's food policies is presented in Table 3.1. Indian food policy has its origins during World War II and the Bengal Famine of 1943, when a series of food-price control conferences was held by the colonial British administration, in response to shortages in foodgrains supply and a sharp rise in prices. The early 1950s saw a brief period when the government more or less withdrew from foodgrains markets.

From the mid-1950s onward, however, government intervention has been increasing steadily. The experiences of the droughts of 1965/66 and 1966/67 necessitated massive emergency food-aid imports. That experience, coupled with the government's commitment to promote high-yielding hybrid varieties (the Green Revolution), led to the creation of a policy package centering on public procure-

**Table 3.1  Chronology of government policies on foodgrains**

| Date | Major policy initiatives |
|------|--------------------------|
| 1942 | Colonial government introduces food price controls and food rationing in selected cities. |
|      | Department of Food established to (1) import, procure, and maintain foodgrain reserves; (2) regulate food prices and control interstate movement of foodgrains; and (3) construct and rent storage facilities. |
| 1952 | Forward Contracts (Regulation) Act prohibits all types of futures trading in most agricultural commodities, including foodgrains. |
| 1952–54 | Gradual relaxation of controls by independent government, reduction and eventual abolition of rationing, and abolition of procurement; full free trade in foodgrains. |
| 1955 | Reintroduction of food controls and PDS in urban areas in response to price rise. |
|      | ECA governing domestic trade (including storage and internal movement) in several commodities, including foodgrains. |
| 1957 | Foodgrains Enquiry Committee recommends establishment of a "foodgrains price stabilization organization," taking over the role of the Department of Food and operating as a food trader. |
| 1965 | Establishment of APC and FCI. |
|      | APC (later called the CACP) responsible for recommending procurement prices for wheat and paddy, and levy price for rice. |
|      | FCI (and other state agencies) responsible for procurement, imports, storage, and distribution of foodgrains. FCI operations supported by monopoly controls over international trade in grains, extensive controls over private storage and internal movement of grains, credit controls on private traders, and cheap credit and transport (railway) concessions for FCI. |
| Mid-1960s | Introduction of high-yielding variety seeds to expand domestic output (Green Revolution), supported by input subsidies (fertilizer, irrigation, and power) and public procurement at preannounced prices. |
| Mid-1980s | Revamped PDS, extending coverage to all rural areas to remove "urban bias"; coverage becomes universal. |
| 1991 | Broad-based economic reforms following macroeconomic crisis. |
|      | Attempts to rationalize fertilizer subsidy. |
| 1994/95 | Opening of export of common rice and subsequently wheat. |
| 1995 | India becomes a signatory to the WTO Agreements and announces high bound tariffs for agricultural commodities as a step toward tariffication of quantitative restrictions on imports. |
| 1997 | Introduction of TPDS to improve delivery of consumption subsidy to the poor. |
| Late 1990s onward | Frequent changes in trade policies: removal and reimposition of export controls, frequent changes in applied tariffs in response to domestic supply situation. |
| 2000 | National Policy on Handling, Storage, and Transportation of Foodgrains to minimize storage and transportation costs, improve grain storage practices, and develop infrastructure through public-private partnerships. |
| 2001 | India eliminates all quantitative restrictions on imports. |
| 2002/03 | Amendments of the ECA, removing licensing requirements for storage, transportation, and distribution by private traders; but controls can be imposed by the central government on specific commodities, including foodgrains, if the need arises |
|      | Amendments to Forward Contracts (Regulation) Act (1952) allowing futures trading in agricultural commodities, including foodgrains. |
|      | Model Act on Agricultural Marketing passed by central government as a model for reforming state-level APMC acts. Allows direct marketing of all agricultural products by farmers, including contract farming. |
|      | By January 31, 2007, only 12 states have amended their APMCs per the model act. |
| 2007/08 | Futures trading in grains banned. |
|      | Export controls imposed on grains, including common-variety rice, in response to rise in global prices. |

Note: APC, Agricultural Prices Commission; APMC, Agricultural Product Marketing Committee; CACP, Commission for Agricultural Costs and Prices; ECA, Essential Commodities Act; FCI, Food Corporation of India; PDS, public distribution system; TPDS, Targeted Public Distribution System.

ment of grain at so-called procurement or support prices. This package no doubt helped the dissemination of Green Revolution varieties, and there has accordingly been a significant improvement in foodgrains self-sufficiency. By the end of the 1970s India was more or less self-sufficient in foodgrains, and it has even been a net exporter since the 1990s.

Foodgrains policies in India since the mid-1960s have had four overall objectives (GOI 1965):

- ensure a reasonable price that will induce farmers to adopt improved methods of cultivation for increasing production;

- ensure that consumer prices do not rise unduly;

- avoid excessive price fluctuations and reduce price disparities between states; and

- build up sizable buffer stocks of wheat and rice from imports and internal procurement.

To achieve these objectives the government intervenes, and indeed dominates, in all the basic aspects of grain marketing—procurement, storage, transport, and distribution. All these operations are carried out by the Food Corporation of India (FCI) and other state agencies. Figures 3.1 and 3.2 show the marketing channels for wheat and for paddy and rice in India.

The FCI procures the foodgrains in the form of wheat and paddy directly from farmers and in the form of (milled) rice from rice millers. The price at which FCI procures is called the procurement price (wheat and paddy) or the levy price (rice). It is essentially a system of open-ended procurement: the FCI is obligated to buy all the grains that farmers offer to sell at the prescribed procurement price, as long as the grains meet a certain quality standard.

Public procurement has increased significantly over the past 40 years (Table 3.2). Compared to the early years of the Green Revolution, public procurement of both rice and wheat has expanded severalfold. The degree of market intervention is more pronounced in the surplus states. For instance, according to records of the Food and Supplies Department of Punjab, private traders' market share has consistently been low: less than 10 percent in the case of wheat and about 20–40 percent in the case of paddy (Ganesh-Kumar, Gulati, and Cummings 2007). Even these numbers, however, understate the full degree of public intervention, because a significant proportion of production is used for home consumption. Expressed as a percentage of *marketed surplus,* we find the following ratios for public procurement, storage, and

**Figure 3.1   Wheat-marketing channels in India**

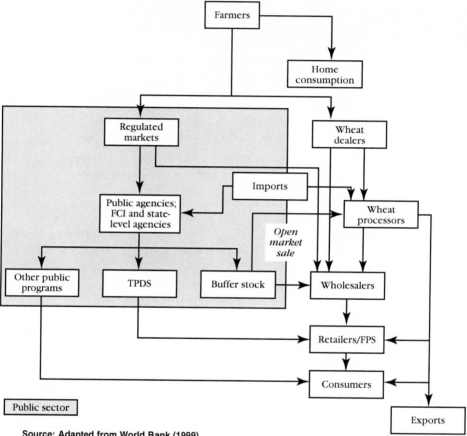

Source: Adapted from World Bank (1999).
Note: FCI, Food Corporation of India; FPS, Fair Price Shops; TPDS, Targeted Public Distribution System.

distribution for the country as a whole in 2001/02: for wheat, 41, 83, and 12 percent, respectively; and for rice, 29, 32, and 14 percent, respectively.

This massive public intervention in grain markets, however, does not occur throughout the country—although, in principle, the system of open-ended procurement is applicable to the country as a whole. The system operates primarily in a few surplus states, such as Andhra Pradesh, Haryana, Punjab, and Uttar Pradesh, where the procurement price becomes in effect a support price, below which market prices usually do not fall. With regard to rice, millers are obligated to sell a certain fraction of their product to the FCI at the levy price, making it essentially a tax on the millers.

**Figure 3.2    Paddy- and rice-marketing channels in India**

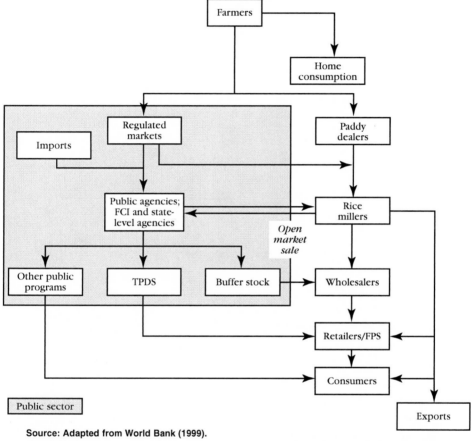

Source: Adapted from World Bank (1999).
Note: FCI, Food Corporation of India; FPS, Fair Price Shops; TPDS, Targeted Public Distribution System.

The operation of the FCI is aided by an array of self-serving legislation, rules, and guidelines. The most important are the extensive controls over international trade in foodgrains, and the internal movement and storage restrictions on private traders.[1] International controls insulate the government from movements in world prices and allow it to pursue a rather autonomous domestic price policy. Domestic regulation leaves farmers with very few options, enabling the FCI to procure grains in the surplus states. The grains so procured are used by the government to maintain a buffer stock and to meet the needs of the public distribution system (PDS) and its various other welfare programs. The PDS involves a network of more than 485,000

Table 3.2    Public procurement as a percentage of
production, selected years, 1967–2006

| Period[a] | Wheat | Rice |
|---|---|---|
| 1967/68 | 4.04 | 8.99 |
| 1973/74 | 20.10 | 7.69 |
| 1976/77 | 15.42 | 11.17 |
| 1982/83 | 17.13 | 13.14 |
| 1985/86 | 20.45 | 15.07 |
| 1988/89 | 16.46 | 13.27 |
| 1995/96 | 19.70 | 15.50 |
| 2001/02 | 24.60 | 21.55 |
| 2002/03 | 28.9 | 26.5 |
| 2003/04 | 21.9 | 23.5 |
| 2004/05 | 24.5 | 28.9 |
| 2005/06 | 21.3 | 29.5 |

Source: Rashid, Gulati, and Dev (2008).
[a]Three years ending.

Fair Price Shops (FPS), through which grains (and a few other commodities) are sold at a subsidized price. The FCI is responsible for storing, transporting, and distributing the grains to the FPS.

The objectives and key elements of this policy package have remained more or less intact over the past four decades, albeit with some changes. Following a series of studies critical of India's foodgrains policies, some reforms were attempted.[2] Limited reforms were implemented in the 1980s, including some state-level modifications of movement controls and a restructuring of the PDS to extend distribution to areas with a high incidence of poverty.

The macroeconomic crisis of the early 1990s, together with India's participation in the World Trade Organization (WTO) Agreement on Agriculture in 1995, set the stage for reforms in international trade in agriculture. The following sections give a brief overview of the critical elements of the policy regime: international trade policy, support price policy, procurement machinery, domestic trade and marketing policies, and the periodization followed in this analysis.

### International Trade Policy

For nearly four decades, from the mid-1950s to the early 1990s, government intervention in foodgrains markets went hand-in-hand with a government monopoly in international trade. International trade controls reflected the overall inward-looking economic policies of India during this period and were justified as being necessary to maintain administrative control over the use of scarce foreign currency reserves and to realize economies of scale (government as a natural monopoly).

Beginning in 1994/95 the government cautiously made room for the private exporting of rice and subsequently wheat. The initial export successes were accompanied by a rise in domestic prices, especially of wheat—highlighting the challenge of maintaining a balance between consumer interest in low food prices and producer interest in higher returns. Confronted with this dilemma, the policy reaction since the mid-1990s has been a series of flip-flops in the imposition and relaxation of export controls. On the import side, since 2001 the government has replaced quantitative restrictions on all agricultural products with tariffs.

### Support Price Policy

A key component of the government's procurement operations is setting the procurement or support price. Since the early 1990s the government has followed a minimum support price (MSP) policy for 24 major crops, including paddy and wheat. The Commission for Agricultural Costs and Prices (CACP) recommends the MSP levels, taking into account the cost of cultivation (including a "fair" return to the land and family labor of the farmers), the overall availability of grains (as reflected by the trend in wholesale prices), and the need to check inflation. The commission incorporates regional variations by including cost estimates provided by the states.

In reality, however, the MSP announced at the beginning of the sowing season is based on various noneconomic factors, such as the political influence of state governments and farm lobbies (Rao 2001). Such pressures have sometimes resulted in the MSP reaching the level of the market price, especially for wheat, as witnessed in the early 2000s. Several committees and researchers have recommended that the MSP be made a true "minimum" support price by including in it only the variable costs, that is, the costs of material inputs and labor (Expenditure Reforms Commission 2001; GOI 2001, 2002; Parikh, Ganesh-Kumar, and Darbha 2003; Ganesh-Kumar, Gulati, and Cummings 2007). These recommendations, however, have yet to be implemented by the government.

### Procurement Machinery

The Department of Public Distribution in the Ministry of Consumer Affairs and Public Distribution has primary responsibility for the formulation and implementation of national food policies. These policies cover a range of operations: procurement, import, and export; movement, storage, and distribution of foodgrains; administration of subsidies, buffer stocking, provision of storage facilities, and promotion of scientific storage techniques; and quality control and specification of foodgrains. The department is assisted by two public-sector entities, the FCI and the Central Warehousing Corporation and its subordinate offices, the Save Grain Campaign and the Indian Grain Management Research Institute, with its five field stations.

Established in 1964, the FCI operates through a countrywide network of about 60,000 employees, five zonal offices, 23 Regional Offices in almost all state capitals, one Port Operation Office, 165 District Offices, and over 1,470 depots (as of 2009). Its board of directors is responsible for general superintendence, direction, and management of the affairs of the corporation. FCI enjoys significant autonomy in several functions relating to storage, movement, mode of transport, field operations pertaining to procurement, estimation of its credit requirements, and negotiations with the Reserve Bank of India.

In the immediate postharvest season, FCI and state government agencies establish about 8,000 centers for wheat and 4,000 centers for paddy, to facilitate purchase of foodgrains at assured prices. The centers are selected so that farmers do not have to travel more than 10 km to reach them. In 2002 the total FCI capacity for storage of foodgrains was about 36 million metric tons (MMT), including more than 20 MMT of rented storage. Grain is stored in silos and godowns, as well as with the "cover and plinth" system of open storage in stacks covered by specially fabricated polyethylene. On average the FCI moves about 25 MMT of foodgrains from surplus to deficit areas each year, over an average distance of 1,500 km. On a daily basis this amounts to about 12 million sacks (of 50 kilograms each) transported by rail, road, and inland waterways (FCI 2009).

The "food subsidy," paid by the government to the FCI, is determined by the gap between FCI's "economic costs" of procurement, storage, transport, and distribution and its revenue from grain sales to government welfare programs at the central issue price (CIP) as fixed by the government. Food subsidies as a percentage of gross domestic product (GDP) have more than doubled over the past decade and a half (Figure 3.3). (See the section "Costs and Performance of the Public Procurement System" for a discussion of those aspects of the FCI.)

### Domestic Trade and Marketing Policies

The imposition of internal trade restrictions is common in developing countries: see Krishna and Raychaudhuri (1980) and Jha (2002) for India; Kherallah et al. (2000) for Egypt; Ellis, Senanayake, and Smith (1997) for Sri Lanka; Minot and Goletti (2000) for Vietnam; and Drèze and Sen (1993) for several countries in Africa and Asia. The rationale behind internal trade restrictions has been to prevent destabilizing speculative activities by private operators—on the assumption that legal restrictions against speculation may not succeed.

In line with such policies, grain markets in India have faced several storage and movement controls, including policies such as the ECA and zoning that prohibits private trade in grains across broad zones (Box 3.1).[3] Furthermore several state-level trade and storage restrictions prevail, notably limits on grain stocking. (Bengal, for

**Figure 3.3    Food subsidy at 1993/94 prices**

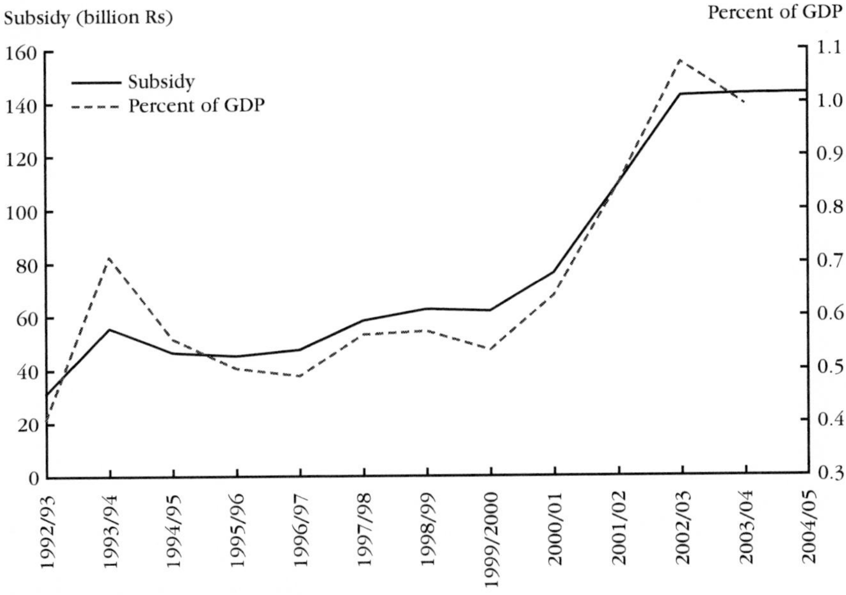

Subsidy (billion Rs)                                                    Percent of GDP

Source: Government of India (2006).
Note: GDP, gross domestic product.

example, caps storage at 750 quintals for rice and 400 quintals for wheat.) States may impose trade restrictions, such as requiring permits for farmers to sell directly outside the state (Table 3.3). The main rationale for movement restrictions was to help procurement. The government procured grain at below-market price and distributed it across the country through the PDS, at subsidized prices. Zoning policies, however, systematically increase rather than reduce interstate food price discrepancies, thus worsening the situation for deficit households in deficit states (Krishna and Raychaudhuri 1980).

Wheat production is concentrated in a few states; Haryana, Madhya Pradesh, Punjab, Rajasthan, and Uttar Pradesh contribute close to 90 percent of the country's production. Although rice is produced almost everywhere, just six states—Andhra Pradesh, Bihar, Punjab, Tamil Nadu, Uttar Pradesh, and West Bengal—account for about 75 percent of the country's output. Given this concentration, there is wide scope for private traders to move grains from surplus to deficit areas (Table 3.4). For arbitrage, private traders can buy grains at low prices in peak seasons or from surplus areas, thus lifting prices in source areas. They can sell them when prices are high during the lean season or in deficit areas, thus bringing down peak prices. This

**Box 3.1    Barriers to interstate trade and commerce**

*Constitutional provisions.* Article 301 allows state legislatures "throughout the territory of India" to "impose such reasonable restrictions on the freedom of trade, commerce or intercourse with or within the State as may be required in the public interest." Article 304 allows a state to impose, by law, any tax on goods imported from other states that is also imposed on goods produced in the state concerned.

*Interstate and national permits.* Vehicles operating within a state must have a permit, obtained by paying the motor vehicle tax of the state. There are two categories for vehicles operating in more than one state: (1) counter-signature permits and permits under reciprocal agreements (the operator pays the tax of both the home state and the other state), and (2) national permits, introduced by the government of India in 1975 for movement between the home state and three or more other states (the operator pays the tax for the home state and a composite tax for each of the other states).

*Road infrastructure.* National highway networks are designed for long-distance traffic, shifting local traffic to side roads. Commercial vehicles carrying twice the permissible load (in connivance with road transport authorities) annually involve corruption worth an estimated Rs 200 billion and reduce the life of pavements by 30–60 percent—in turn reducing average speeds by 20–30 km/hour, amounting to a further annual loss of Rs 200–300 billion.

*Detention of vehicles at checkpoints.* This practice results in lost time, high fuel consumption owing to idling of vehicles, and resulting underutilization of capacity and lower operational viability. Nevertheless the practice continues at regional transport offices and police checkpoints (for checking documents, maintaining driving and traffic safety, and so on); at goods-related checkpoints (for levying of taxes, including octrois [local-level entry taxes], sales taxes, entry permits, and tolls); and through other forms of monitoring (spot checks by flying squads to control the movement of essential commodities, as well as other checks by local authorities). These checkpoints do not contribute significantly to stopping tax evasion, but they do contribute to wastage through stoppage of traffic. For example, paper clearance and checkpoint delays account for 12 percent of total trip time between Delhi and Mumbai.

*Other barriers to trucking operation.* Burdensome paperwork requirements include 58 forms required under the Central Motor Vehicles Rules of 1989. The complex paperwork procedures are illustrated by Entry Permit—Form 32,

(*continued*)

required for goods entering a state. The form, to be filled in by the buyer, requires such information as the nature of the commodity, name and address of the seller, total amount of goods (quantity and value), name of the transporter, registration number of the truck, and date of dispatch. As some of these details are only available at different stages of the transport chain (seller–transporter–driver–booking agent–buyer), the form is likely to remain incomplete, ultimately entailing a "dispute resolution" process at the buying state's border.

Source: Debroy and Kaushik (2002).

Table 3.3   Indian states: Prevalence of storage and trade restrictions

| State | Limits on storage | | Limits: Stocks or time period |
| | Commodities | Agents | |
| --- | --- | --- | --- |
| Andhra Pradesh | Pulses and oils | | 1 month |
| | Raw materials | | 1 month |
| | Finished goods | | 15 days |
| Assam | | Wholesale dealers | 10 quintals |
| Gujarat | Pulses | Licenseholders | 25 quintals |
| | | Others | 9 quintals |
| Kerala | Sugar | | 250 bags |
| Maharashtra | | Wholesale dealers | 15 days |
| Punjab | Rice | | 250 quintals |
| Uttar Pradesh | | Wholesale dealers | 1,000 quintals |
| West Bengal | Rice | Wholesale dealers | 750 quintals |
| | Wheat | Wholesale dealers | 400 quintals |

| State | Trade restrictions | |
| | Agents | Restrictions |
| --- | --- | --- |
| Andhra Pradesh | Farmers | Permit required for direct sales outside state |
| Maharashtra | | Control on movement of cotton |
| Tamil Nadu | Farmers | Permit required for direct sales outside state |
| Tanjore district | Farmers | Control on movement of paddy out of district |

Source: Government of India (2001).

complementary role of the private sector has not been fully appreciated in India, and the government's policy of maintaining narrow price bands, or even panseasonal and panterritorial pricing, reduces the incentives for arbitrage.

In the late 1990s and early 2000s the government of India took steps toward deregulation of both domestic and international trade in agricultural commodities. State governments were expected to respond with appropriate follow-up legislation.

Table 3.4    Surplus or deficit states in India, 1996–99

| | Wheat | | Rice | |
|---|---|---|---|---|
| State | Per capita monthly surplus (kg) | Total consumption (kg/year) | Per capita monthly surplus (kg) | Total consumption (kg/ year) |
| Andhra Pradesh | −0.21 | 0.22 | −0.88 | 10.84 |
| Assam | −0.32 | 0.62 | −3.17 | 11.92 |
| Bihar | −1.93 | 5.26 | −2.29 | 7.59 |
| Gujarat | −1.79 | 4.22 | −0.35 | 1.95 |
| Jammu and Kashmir | −3.95 | 7.06 | −0.41 | 4.69 |
| Karnataka | −0.48 | 0.74 | −0.63 | 5.55 |
| Kerala | −0.43 | 0.43 | −7.19 | 8.97 |
| Maharashtra | −2.00 | 2.83 | −0.82 | 2.91 |
| Madhya Pradesh | 1.54 | 5.88 | −0.14 | 5.32 |
| Orissa | −0.45 | 0.46 | −2.91 | 14.14 |
| Tamil Nadu | −0.33 | 0.33 | −1.36 | 9.88 |
| Goa | −1.93 | 1.93 | 2.00 | 6.64 |
| West Bengal | −0.74 | 1.49 | 1.11 | 11.34 |
| Himachal Pradesh | 1.55 | 5.96 | −2.16 | 3.64 |
| Rajasthan | 0.35 | 9.19 | −0.03 | 0.3 |
| Haryana | 20.22 | 9.76 | 8.65 | 0.94 |
| Punjab | 34.20 | 8.98 | 24.37 | 0.79 |
| Uttar Pradesh | 1.84 | 8.68 | 1.86 | 3.63 |

Source: Chand (2002).

Note: Per capita monthly surplus equals per capita production less per capita demand.

In March 1993 the central government decided to treat the entire country as a single food zone. However, some states (such as Jammu and Kashmir and West Bengal) continue to restrict intrastate movement of paddy and rice, in order to maximize procurement or to prevent smuggling across the international border. Some states also impose informal restrictions on outside movement of grains for some part of the year. Stock limits are placed on rice in Andhra Pradesh, Jammu and Kashmir, and Tamil Nadu. Most states have no stock limits on wheat, although they are directed by the government of India to impose stock limits if the situation warrants.

Many restrictions are simply verbal instructions, the documentation for which is difficult to obtain. GOI (2001) argued for strengthening the role of private trade in storage and distribution by removing restrictions and giving tax concessions as an incentive for investment in grain handling. The Department of Consumer Affairs accordingly issued a central order to facilitate free trade and movement of foodgrains, allowing any dealer to buy, stock, sell, transport, distribute, dispose of, acquire, use, or consume any quantity of wheat, paddy and rice, coarse grains, sugar, edible oilseeds, and edible oils without any license or permit. This liberalizing order overrides any requirement of a state government.

Apart from restrictions on interstate trading, private trade has also suffered in its marketing. ECA alone requires a large number of permits and licenses, periodic submission of returns, and submitting to inspections. The government is currently adopting several measures to improve agricultural marketing—for example, establishing regulated markets and constructing warehouses. It has also advised state governments to enact marketing legislation to provide for competitive and transparent transactions, to protect the interests of farmers. These regulations now cover almost all wholesale markets.

Only 15 percent of the nearly 28,000 rural periodic markets (markets that function regularly on fixed days of the week at fixed locations) function under similar regulations, safeguarding producers and sellers at the wholesale level. Despite these reforms, however, there is no scope under existing law for direct marketing by farmers. Commission agents, traders, processors, weigh men (those who weigh goods), surveyors, and brokers all have to obtain market licenses, a process involving lengthy procedures and extensive documentation. However, as a part of the government of India's initiative to encourage private traders, the Department of Consumer Affairs issued a central order removing licensing requirements, storage limits, and movement restrictions on specified foodstuffs (under Section 3 of the ECA, dated February 15, 2002).

The government is also initiating steps to encourage private participation in grain storage and handling. The role of the FCI would be restricted to ensuring timely sales and purchases, maintaining stability in food prices, and regulating exports and imports of foodgrains when required. But more needs to be done. The National Policy on Handling and Storage of Foodgrains (July 2000) envisages encouraging the private sector to build storage capacity to be rented by government agencies, as well as developing infrastructure for integrated bulk handling, storage, and transportation of foodgrains.

On the international trade front, too, some restrictions were relaxed in the early 2000s, due to mounting government stocks as well as market access requirements imposed by the WTO agreement. Elimination of price distortions could induce farmers to shift to crops offering higher prices than rice and wheat. Nevertheless in recent years—with food prices rising in international markets—the government has responded by bringing back many of the export controls on foodgrains.

### Periodization

The year 1991 is generally considered the watershed in India's economic policies, as the country undertook major economic reforms following the 1991 macroeconomic crisis. The first set of reform measures focused on the exchange rate, industrial licensing and industrial trade policies, and agricultural inputs subsidies (especially a fertilizer subsidy).

Although changes in agricultural trade policies came about only some years later, the reform measures of 1991 did have direct and indirect impacts on agriculture. In an effort to reduce the fertilizer subsidy, the government raised fertilizer prices in 1991 by 30 percent, with substantial impact on agricultural costs; the government followed this initiative in 1992 with decontrol of phosphatic and potassic fertilizer prices. Changes in the exchange rate regime also affected the overall competitiveness of Indian agriculture. Similarly changes in industrial policies affected the domestic terms of trade between agriculture and non-agriculture. The early measures to liberalize imports of capital goods did reduce capital goods prices and helped improve real investment rates relative to the nominal investment rate. Considering all these direct and indirect impacts on agriculture, we consider the period before 1991 as the prereform period and that after 1991 as the postreform period.

## Costs and Performance of the Public Procurement System

The functioning and costs of the FCI have been analyzed extensively (GOI 1991, 2002; Gulati, Kahkonen, and Sharma 2000; ASCI 2001). Its costs fall into two categories: policy-induced costs and operational costs. The policy-induced costs relate to MSP, CIP, specification of grain quality, buffer stock norms, railway freight, procurement incidentals, and so forth; they make up close to 70 percent of the economic cost of the FCI. This component can be reduced by reforming such policies as MSP and levy prices. The remaining 30 percent of the costs reflect overhead and operational inefficiencies. An analysis of recent trends in these components indicates that procurement incidentals and distribution, administrative, and carrying costs together form a high percentage of the actual purchase cost of grain. The high operating costs of FCI result in a high cost-benefit ratio for the PDS (Jha and Srinivasan 2001). Gulati, Kahkonen, and Sharma (2000), moreover, demonstrate a widening gap between the costs and revenues of the FCI, leading to spiraling government subsidies. The lack of accountability within the FCI, and the knowledge that the government will cover any costs, are responsible for this inefficiency.

Many studies that have assessed the relative efficiency of the FCI and private agents have found that, in spite of the array of formal and informal barriers, private agents operate at lower costs for both storage and trade. (Informal barriers include harassment by officials and accompanying corruption and bribery, impeding domestic trading, storage, and interstate movement of agricultural produce.) (See, for example, studies by Tyagi 1990; World Bank 1999; Gulati, Kahkonen, and Sharma 2000; Acharya 2001; and Jha and Srinivasan 2001.) Chand (2002) provides a recent estimate of private marketing costs and margins. Figure 3.4 shows a break-down of private costs and marketing margins vis-à-vis those of the FCI. Clearly labor, interest, and administrative costs make up a significant component of FCI costs. (The lower transport costs for FCI reflect the unknown amount of the subsidy it receives on

**Figure 3.4   Trading costs and wholesale marketing margins of private traders and FCI, 2000/01**

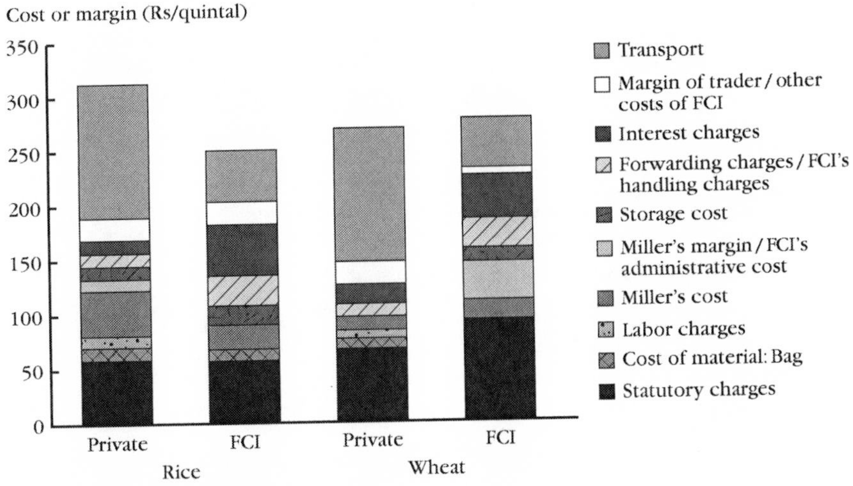

Cost or margin (Rs/quintal)

Legend:
- Transport
- Margin of trader / other costs of FCI
- Interest charges
- Forwarding charges / FCI's handling charges
- Storage cost
- Miller's margin / FCI's administrative cost
- Miller's cost
- Labor charges
- Cost of material: Bag
- Statutory charges

Sources: Chand (2002) and GOI (2002).

Notes: FCI's transport costs (by rail) are subsidized, though the extent of the subsidy is not readily known. FCI, Food Corporation of India; Rs, rupees.

railway freight.) Interestingly FCI also shows diseconomies of scale—despite its large scale of operation—and it moves its stocks several times between warehouses.

There are several reasons for the lower operating costs in the private sector. Traders avoid *mandi* (marketplace) charges by buying directly from farmers, reuse gunny sacks several times (unlike the FCI), move grains by truck (a mode of transport more readily available than railway wagons), and have lower transit losses.[4] Note that it is perfectly legal for private traders to buy directly from farmers: they *avoid* rather than *evade* mandi charges.[5]

In order to cover their losses due to levy sales to the FCI, rice millers apparently sell their lower-quality product to the FCI and their better-quality product in the open market. Even though the FCI receives subsidized rail freight and credit rates, and is not subject to the government's Selective Credit Control policies, the ECA, and zoning regulations, it incurs much higher operational costs. In comparing FCI margins with those of private traders, however, we note that some of the higher costs of the FCI do not reflect inefficiency: for example, the FCI must transport grains over longer distances to meet procurement and PDS requirements. The FCI also pays statutory and nonstatutory fees to state governments and their agencies.

Using an estimated relationship between public storage costs and capacity utilization (assuming higher capacity utilization for private agents and lower labor and establishment costs), Jha and Srinivasan (2001) estimate private storage costs at 70 percent of FCI storage costs in 1999/2000. Figure 3.5 presents the estimated private and observed FCI costs. The slope of the observed cost curve is much steeper in the 1990s than in the early 1980s, and it is also steeper than that of the private cost curve; the annual average observed costs are rising faster than in the past and faster than the current private costs. However, it is likely that private storage can play only a complementary role and cannot replace public storage. Jha and Srinivasan (1997), using a dynamic stochastic simulation model, find that private storage leads to price stabilization to only a limited extent.

Despite evidence of lower trading margins and storage costs for private traders, the government continues to maintain several restrictions on them. The stringent rules and declining credibility of regulated markets have resulted in a decline in the share of produce sold through these markets (Chand 2003). Sales through informal markets also allow traders to avoid market charges and taxes. The low level of private trade in regulated markets thus leads to higher public storage and associated costs.

**Figure 3.5    Unit public and private storage costs**

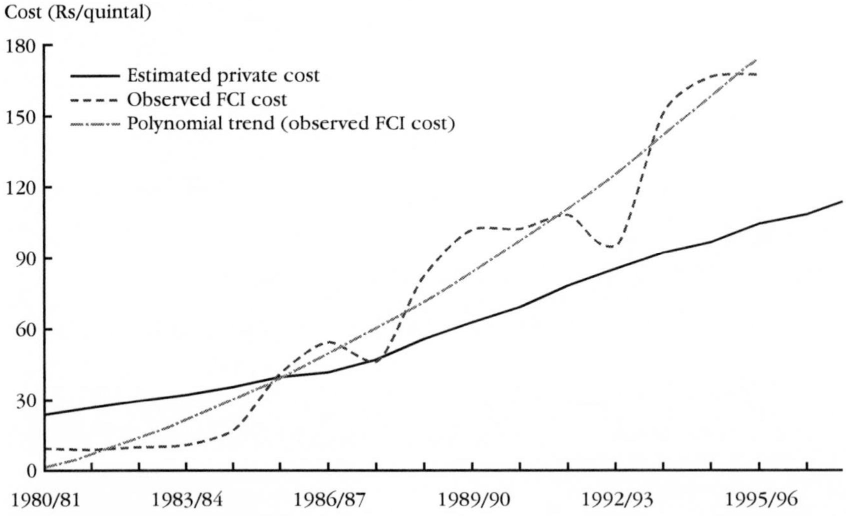

Source: Jha and Srinivasan (2001).
Note: FCI, Food Corporation of India; Rs, rupees.

## Border Reform and Its Impacts

The effects of trade liberalization have been analyzed using computable general equilibrium models by Parikh et al. (1995, 1997) and Panda and Quizon (2001). These two studies found that, prior to the reforms, the agricultural sector was typically disprotected and the manufacturing sector protected. Consequently domestic prices of agricultural goods remained below world prices while domestic prices of industrial goods remained above world prices. Thus trade liberalization would lead to higher agricultural prices and lower industrial prices.

In the short run, trade liberalization adversely affects both growth and equity. In the medium and long run, it helps to accelerate growth by bringing about more efficient allocation of resources across sectors—and in the process helps to reduce poverty. The growth-enhancing effect of liberalization operates through an increase in the real investment rate: a constant nominal investment rate translates into a higher real investment rate, as the relative price of investment goods falls (as a result of the removal of protection on capital goods). Industrial trade liberalization helps to increase the real income of all classes in the medium and long run—rich as well as poor, in both rural and urban sectors. But agricultural trade liberalization benefits only *some* types of households in rural areas, while it adversely affects *all* classes in the urban sector.

Within agriculture, liberalization of the rice sector increases both rice exports and rice prices, as the preliberalization domestic price is lower than the world price. This hurts the welfare of all sections of the population except the rural rich. Since India is a major producer of rice, and the world trade in rice is thin compared with public stocks of rice in India, an increase in Indian exports could in fact depress the world price of rice.[6] To guard against this, an export tax on rice would help both growth and equity. The simulations also show that the welfare of the poor can be protected by safety nets such as additional public employment programs. Thus trade liberalization coupled with safety-net mechanisms could lead to a Pareto improvement, in which *all* classes gain with liberalization.

The actual Indian experience during the 1990s has been along the lines predicted by the counterfactual simulation results from these studies. Table 3.5 provides some relevant indicators on growth and poverty. After an initial drop in the crisis year 1991/92, overall GDP growth rose to an average of 6.1 percent per annum in the postreform period (1992/93 onward) compared with 5.6 percent in the prereform period (up to 1990/91). This increase in the growth rate was driven mostly by the non-agricultural sector, while agriculture witnessed a marginal decline. In fact the economy achieved a growth rate exceeding 7.3 percent for the three consecutive years 1994/95 to 1996/97, with another high-growth phase (exceeding 7 percent) from 2003/04 onward.

Table 3.5    Economic growth and incidence of poverty in India, 1981–2005

| Year | Real GDP growth rate (%) | | | Poverty: Head count ratio[a] (%) | | |
|---|---|---|---|---|---|---|
| | Total | Agriculture | Non-agriculture | Rural | Urban | All India |
| 1981/82 | 6.0 | 5.3 | 6.0 | — | — | — |
| 1982/83 | 3.1 | −0.7 | 3.1 | — | — | — |
| 1983/84 | 7.7 | 9.6 | 7.7 | 45.3 | 35.7 | 43 |
| 1984/85 | 4.3 | 1.5 | 4.3 | — | — | — |
| 1985/86 | 4.5 | 0.7 | 4.5 | — | — | — |
| 1986/87 | 4.3 | −0.6 | 4.3 | 38.8 | 34.3 | 37.7 |
| 1987/88 | 3.8 | −1.3 | 3.8 | 39.2 | 36.2 | 38.5 |
| 1988/89 | 10.5 | 15.5 | 10.5 | 39.1 | 36.6 | 38.4 |
| 1989/90 | 6.7 | 1.5 | 6.7 | 34.3 | 33.4 | 34.1 |
| 1990/91 | 5.6 | 4.1 | 5.6 | 36.4 | 32.8 | 35.5 |
| 1991/92 | 1.3 | −1.5 | 1.3 | 37.4 | 33.2 | 36.3 |
| 1992/93 | 5.1 | 5.8 | 5.1 | 43.4 | 33.7 | 40.9 |
| 1993/94 | 5.9 | 4.1 | 5.9 | 36.7 | 30.5 | 35 |
| 1994/95 | 7.3 | 5.0 | 7.3 | 39.8 | 33.5 | 38.4 |
| 1995/96 | 7.3 | −0.9 | 7.3 | 37.5 | 28 | 35 |
| 1996/97 | 7.8 | 9.6 | 7.8 | — | — | — |
| 1997/98 | 4.8 | −2.4 | 4.8 | 35.7 | 30 | 34.4 |
| 1998/99 | 6.5 | 6.2 | 6.5 | — | — | — |
| 1999/2000 | 6.1 | 0.3 | 6.1 | 27.1 | 23.6 | 26.1 |
| 2000/01 | 4.4 | −0.1 | 4.4 | 24.9 | 24.3 | 24.7 |
| 2001/02 | 5.8 | 6.5 | 5.8 | 29.0 | 25.1 | 27.9 |
| 2002/03 | 4.0 | −5.2 | 4.0 | 23.7 | 23.8 | 30.4 |
| 2003/04 | 8.2 | 9.1 | 8.2 | 24.0 | 22.6 | 23.6 |
| 2004/05 | 7.2 | −0.5 | 7.2 | 28.3 | 25.7 | 27.5 |
| 1981/82 to 1990/91 | 5.6 | 3.5 | 5.6 | — | — | — |
| 1992/93 to 2004/05 | 6.1 | 3.4 | 6.1 | — | — | — |

Sources: National Accounts Statistics (various issues) for GDP; World Bank (2000) and Radhakrishna and Panda (2006) for poverty.
Notes: GDP, gross domestic product. —, missing data.
[a]Head count ratio indicates the proportion of the population below the poverty line.

The incidence of poverty (the head count ratio), measured using data from the National Sample Survey Organization, declined by about 9 percentage points during the 1980s. It increased immediately following the reforms, to reach a peak in 1992/93 at around 41 percent. It has since fallen, though with some fluctuations. On the whole, however, the 1990s did not witness a reduction in the poverty level comparable to that achieved in the 1980s. The absence of a decline in the incidence of poverty may reflect the faster rise in agricultural prices relative to the price index since the mid-1990s. This would conform with the predictions of the ex ante analysis (Figure 3.6).

Rising food prices can have an adverse effect on food security not only for the poor, but even for those who are marginally above the poverty line. To what extent can India pursue a policy of food price stabilization under a liberalized trade regime?

**Figure 3.6   Movements in wholesale price indexes**

Wholesale price index

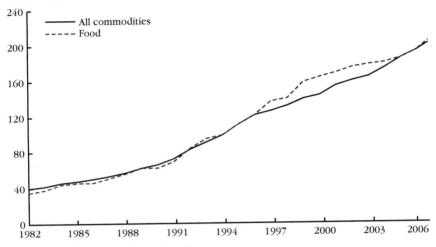

Source: Reserve Bank of India (various issues).

Ganesh-Kumar and Parikh (1998) analyze this issue. Using Monte Carlo simulations that compare the cost of domestic stock operations (at market price) with the cost of international trade, they show that it is feasible to combine buffer stocks with a liberal trade regime to pursue price stability, targeting a level at which domestic supply equals demand for rice and wheat. Such a stock-trade policy can be pursued at a low cost to the government and would require only modest levels of stocks of these two crops: 4.0 and 0.5 MMT of rice and wheat, respectively.

Their analysis also shows that with just these levels of stocks, India's dependence on imports for smoothing domestic availability during domestic production shortfalls would be very modest, amounting to 3.5 MMT for rice and 1.2 MMT for wheat (average + 1 standard deviation). The simulations also show that significantly large imports—in excess of 6.7 MMT of rice and 2.4 MMT of wheat (average + 3 standard deviations)—occur with very low frequency: 0.27 percent and 0.85 percent of years for rice and wheat, respectively. Importantly their analysis also accounts for rainfall-induced production variability and variability in world prices, as well as large-country effects of India's trade. Thus a liberal trade regime combined with buffer stocks can be expected to stabilize food prices and is compatible with the WTO Agreement on Agriculture. A critical requirement, however, is that government's stocking operations (procurement and sales) take place at market price and not at an administratively fixed price.

In reality, however, the government procures grains at the preannounced MSP and releases them at the CIP—both administratively fixed. The period since the late

1990s has highlighted the incompatibility of the current system with a liberal trade regime. During the late 1990s and early 2000s, in response to political lobbying, the government kept raising its MSP even while, in the international markets, cereal prices exhibited a dramatic downward trend. Consequently selling to the government was more profitable than exporting; given the open-ended public procurement policy, this led to a significant increase in public procurement.

Faced with mounting costs of procurement, the government increased its ration prices, resulting in a fall in sales by the PDS. This combination of increasing procurement and declining public distribution resulted in an unprecedented accumulation of public foodgrains stocks, reaching 63 MMT by July 2002 (Figure 3.7). To bring down these stocks, in subsequent years the government subsidized exports, by an amount that was about 50 percent lower than its procurement costs. Moreover 2002/03 and 2004/05 turned out to be drought years that saw a significant drop in grain production. As a result stocks plummeted to just 16 MMT by April 2006. In the case of wheat the fall was particularly sharp, from about 41 MMT in July 2002 to just 4 MMT in April 2006.

All these studies on trade liberalization implicitly assume a single integrated market for food in the country as a whole. In reality the numerous central and state government restrictions on domestic trade have prevented spatial integration of markets across the country. When markets are not spatially integrated, local shortages can translate into rising local food prices, even though the country as a whole may not experience any serious food shortage and the national average food price may be fairly stable.

What is the impact of interstate barriers on movement of foodgrains across different states? This question is addressed in the following sections, using a spatial model of rice and wheat markets that allows for interstate and international trade in these grains. This model is then used to analyze the impact of liberalizing the interstate trade in grains, as well as the impact of a reduction in interstate transport costs.

## Domestic Liberalization in India:
## A Multicommodity Spatial Equilibrium Model

Welfare impacts of market deregulation and freeing of interstate trade from controls can best be analyzed using a spatial equilibrium model.[7] Jha and Srinivasan (2004) build a multiregional, multicommodity partial equilibrium model to analyze the impact of domestic liberalization for rice and wheat. In the model the country is divided into 18 major states (regions) that account for 99 percent of the total production of these grains. Demand and supply functions are specified for each state, based on elasticity

**Figure 3.7    Buffer stocks of cereals with central pool in India**

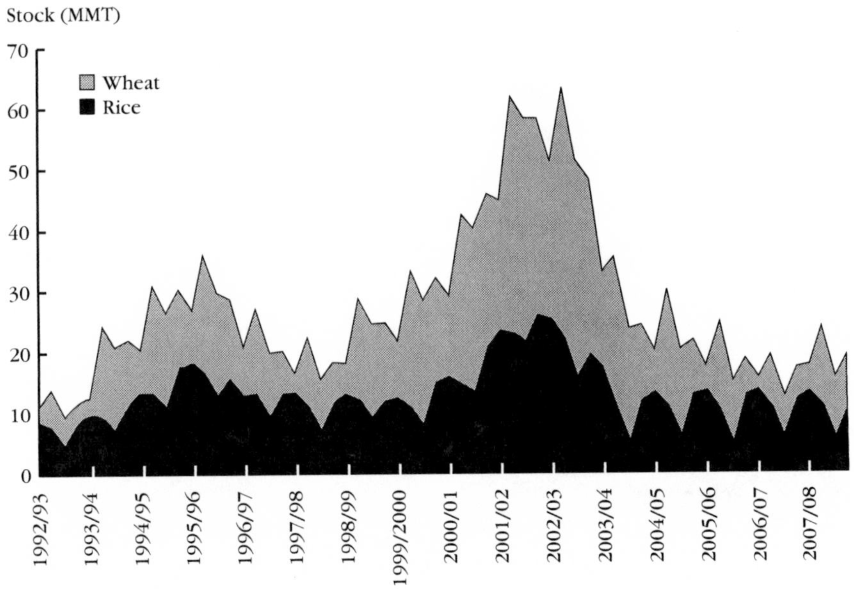

Stock (MMT)

Source: Ministry of Agriculture, Government of India.
Notes: For each financial year, stocks as on the first day of April, July, October, and January.
MMT, million metric tons.

estimates from the literature.[8] These functions are calibrated for the base year 2000/01 using data on all exogenous and endogenous variables. In the model regional demand and supply of rice and wheat interact through the substitution possibilities in both consumption and production. Equilibrium prices and other variables are obtained as solutions to the commodity balance equations, subject to the constraints imposed by government interventions. The set of equations that clear the markets and the set of inequalities that represent price interventions by the government are solved as a mixed complementarity problem using PATH Solver in GAMS.

**Demand and Supply Functions**

Jha and Srinivasan consider linear demand functions, which incorporate the effects of own price, cross prices, and income. For region $i$ the open-market demand function is specified as follows:

$$D(i) = \alpha(i) + \beta(i)\mathrm{pr}(i) + \gamma(i)\mathrm{qr}(i) + \lambda(i)y(i), \qquad (1)$$

where $pr(i)$ is own retail price, $qr(i)$ is the retail price of the other crop, and $y(i)$ is per capita income.

The supply function is also assumed to be linear. It depends on the weighted average of market and procurement prices received by the farmers[9]:

$$S(i) = a(i) + b(i)\text{wap}(i) + c(i)\text{qf}(i), \tag{2}$$

where $S(i)$ is production, $\text{wap}(i)$ is the weighted average of procurement and market prices, and $\text{qf}(i)$ is the weighted average farm harvest price of the other crop. Note that

$$\text{wap}(i) = [\lambda \text{pf}(i) + (1 - \lambda)\text{lvp}(i)],$$

where $\text{pf}(i)$ is own-farm harvest price and lvp is procurement price (MSP in the case of wheat and levy procurement price for rice).

### Interstate Trade

Jha and Srinivasan assume that restrictions due to policy or infrastructure bottlenecks manifest themselves in the form of an implicit tariff on interstate trade. In the base case the implicit tariff is obtained endogenously from the model, by imposing a constraint that total interstate trade in equilibrium not exceed the trade observed in the base year. Given the base interstate trade, the implicit tariff variable (ita) adjusts to keep the sum of all regional imports (tm, also equal to the sum of all exports) from exceeding that level. This is specified as the following complementarity condition:

$$\text{tm} \geq \Sigma_j \Sigma_i T(i,j) \perp \text{ita} \geq 0, \tag{3a}$$

where tm is the total observed interstate trade in the base year and $T(i,j)$ denotes the amount exported by region $i$ to region $j$ (or equivalently the amount imported by region $j$ from region $i$). This complementarity condition implies that if ita > 0 then $\Sigma_j \Sigma_i T(i,j)$ = tm. If total trade, $\Sigma_j \Sigma_i T(i,j)$, is less than tm, then ita = 0.

Trade from region $i$ to region $j$ is determined by the following complementarity condition:

$$T(i,j) \geq 0 \perp [p(i) + \text{tc}(i,j) + \text{traders' margins}](1 + \text{ita}) \geq p(j), \tag{3b}$$

where $\text{tc}(i,j)$ is the transportation cost from state $i$ to state $j$, and $p(i)$ is wholesale price.

Equation (3b) implies zero trade, $T(i,j) = 0$, if the sum of the purchase cost in state $i$ plus the cost of transporting grains to state $j$, inflated by the implicit tariff, exceeds the returns—that is, the open-market price in state $j$, $[p(i) + \mathrm{tc}(i,j)](1 + \mathrm{ita})$ $> p(j)$. Based on the assumption of perfect competition, $T(i,j) > 0$ implies that $[p(i) + \mathrm{tc}(i,j)](1 + \mathrm{ita}) = p(j)$.

### Foreign Trade

The rest of the world is treated as another region, where trade involves additional costs of transport from the nearest or cheapest port. Given the potentially large size of India in world trade, Jha and Srinivasan assume that higher imports into India cost more, while higher exports fetch lower prices. Export (import) price as a function of exports (imports) is expressed as

$$\text{Export price} = \text{Border price} - \mathrm{ec} \times \text{total exports} - \text{port clearance charges}$$

and

$$\text{Import price} = \text{Border price} + \mathrm{ic} \times \text{total imports} + \text{port clearance charges},$$

where "border price" is expressed in domestic currency, ic is the import coefficient, and ec is the export coefficient. These are obtained from their respective price elasticities, evaluated at the base-year values. Exports take place as long as the export price is higher than the purchase cost of grain, including transport costs to the port. Imports take place if it is cheaper to import than to buy in the domestic local market. Trade with the rest of the world (ROW) follows the complementarity conditions

$$\mathrm{EX}(i, \text{"ROW"}) \geq 0 \perp [p(i) + \mathrm{tc}(i, \text{"ROW"}) + \text{traders' margins}] \geq \mathrm{XP} \quad (4a)$$

and

$$\mathrm{IM}(i, \text{"ROW"}) \geq 0 \perp [\mathrm{MP} + \mathrm{tc}(i, \text{"ROW}) + \text{traders' margins}] \geq p(i), \quad (4b)$$

where EX and IM denote exports and imports, and XP and MP denote their respective prices.

### Price Relationships

Equilibrium prices in the model refer to wholesale prices. Retail price (which enters the demand equation) is given as

$$\mathrm{pr}(i) = p(i) \times (1 + \text{retail margin}). \quad (5)$$

In the absence of data on retail profit margins, it is assumed to be the same percentage as the wholesale margin.[10] Farm harvest price (which enters the supply equation) is given as

$$pf(i) = p(i)/(1 + \text{wholesale margin} + \text{marketing cost}). \qquad (6)$$

Procurement price (exogenous and the same for all states) is the fixed levy price for rice, while for wheat it is the fixed MSP. The PDS price in state $i$ for both rice and wheat is expressed as a fixed percentage, lower than the market price:

$$PDSP(i) = v_i p(i).$$

### Procurement

Due to the levy, rice procurement is fixed exogenously as a percentage of production:

$$\text{proc\_R}(i) = \mu_i S(i),$$

where $\mu_i$ is the levy fraction of output in state $i$. Wheat procurement, however, is determined endogenously based on MSP and is determined by the complementarity condition:

$$\text{proc\_W}(i) \geq 0 \perp p(i) \geq MSP, \qquad (7)$$

where $\text{proc\_W}(i)$ is government procurement of wheat. The complementarity condition implies zero wheat procurement if the open-market price is higher than the MSP. Positive procurement implies that the open-market price is equal to the MSP. Out of the grains procured, exogenously fixed quantities are distributed through the PDS for each state.

### Welfare Gains

The welfare gains equal the sum of producers' and consumers' surpluses. There is also a change in welfare of the traders. Trade reforms also have implications for the government's fiscal position.

Change in producer surplus is obtained from

$$PS = S(i)(\text{wap}_1 - \text{wap}_0) + \tfrac{1}{2}(\text{spe})S(i)(\text{wap}_1 - \text{wap}_0)^2/\text{wap}_0,$$

where $\text{wap}_0$ is the base-year weighted average of farm and market prices, $\text{wap}_1$ is the current-year weighted average of farm and market prices, and spe is the price elasticity of supply.

Change in consumer surplus is written as

$$CS = -D(i)(pr_1 - pr_0) - \tfrac{1}{2}(dpe)D(i)(pr_1 - pr_0)^2/pr_0,$$

where $pr_0$ is the own retail base-year price, $pr_1$ is the own retail current-year price, and dpe is the price elasticity of demand.

Traders earn profits at three levels of intermediation: within state, from farm to wholesale market (*wholesale traders*); from wholesale to retail market (*retail traders*); and from *interstate trading*. The margins by themselves do not constitute the income of traders, as they also incur costs to provide services (for example, finding a buyer). Using data on profit margins, the gains to traders in each state have been calculated by comparing the surpluses in different scenarios to the base scenario.

Wholesale traders' surplus is obtained by multiplying the margin by the wholesale price and local production (net of procurement, net exports abroad, and net exports to other states):

$$WTS(i) = Margin \times p(i) \times$$
$$\{S(i) - proc(i) - [E(i) - M(i)] - [\Sigma_j T(i,j) - \Sigma_j T(j,i)]\}.$$

Retail traders' surplus is obtained by applying the margin to the free market demand times the retail price:

$$RTS(i) = Margin \times pr(i) \times D(i).$$

Savings in government costs arise from changes in procurement, storage, and distribution costs and are obtained as follows:

Total government cost = Purchase cost + procurement
incidental cost + storage cost + distribution cost,

where

Purchase cost = Government procurement × MSP,

Procurement incidental cost = Government procurement × incidental cost,

Storage cost = (Procurement – PDS) × per-unit storage cost,

and

$$\text{Distribution} = \text{PDS} \times \text{distribution cost.}$$

Thus

$$\text{Sales realization} = \text{PDS} \times \text{central issue price}$$

and

$$\text{Net government cost} = \text{Total government expenditure} - \text{sales realization.}$$

### Market Equilibrium

The market clearing condition equates net availability to demand in each state. Since PDS quantities are exogenously specified, it implies equating open-market demand with net supply. Net availability equals production minus the outflows from the state, which consist of net regional imports, government procurement, and net foreign exports. The equilibrium condition for state $i$ is

$$S(i) + [\Sigma_j T(i,j) - \Sigma_j T(j,i)] - \text{proc}(i) - [E(i) - M(i)] = D(i), \qquad (8)$$

and the markets are cleared by $p(i)$.

The MSP is fixed so that the quantity procured covers the PDS requirements. The difference between procurement and PDS equals stocks held by the government.

## Scenarios and Simulations

### Reference Scenario

The base scenario (S0) is one in which movement restrictions exist. Consequently total interstate trade cannot exceed a certain level, equal to the equilibrium level observed in the base period. Trade and transport costs for interstate trade, as well as the tariff rate for external imports, are set at actual levels in the base period 2000/01. The model equilibrium gives the implicit tariff in the base case as 8.4 percent for rice and 4.9 percent for wheat, as mark-ups on the cost of purchase plus interstate transport.[11]

### Changed Scenarios

The relaxation of interstate trade restrictions is captured by eliminating the implicit interstate tariff. The analysis also takes into account reduction in transport costs for improving interregional trade. Two scenarios are considered. Scenario 1 (S1) considers complete elimination of implicit tariffs. In scenario 2 (S2), in addition to the removal of tariffs, transport costs are reduced by 25 percent. S1 should be feasible in the short to medium run, and S2 in the medium to long run.[12] In both S1 and S2 the tariff rate for external imports is kept fixed at the base scenario levels. Thus we model only domestic trade liberalization here.

## Results: Regional Redistribution and Efficiency Gains

Compared to the base scenario in S1, the aggregate production and market demand for rice change little with relaxation of movement restrictions (Tables 3.6 and 3.7). Since PDS quantities are assumed fixed, total consumption changes are also small. There is, however, a distinct change in the spatial pattern of consumption and production between surplus and deficit states, creating a ripple effect through the country (Tables 3.8 and 3.9).[13] In the major surplus states (Andhra Pradesh, Haryana, Punjab, and Uttar Pradesh), domestic consumption of rice falls while production rises. In the case of wheat, production impacts are negligible, but aggregate national consumption rises by more than 1.6 MMT in scenario 2 over the base case. Consumption picks up in particular in major consuming states, including Bihar, Gujarat, and Madhya Pradesh. The effect on wholesale prices in different states is along expected lines, with deficit states witnessing a fall in wholesale prices and surplus states, a rise.

In the case of rice procurement, the simulation results reveal that with fixed levy percentages, the level of procurement rises marginally (in S2) due to higher production, by 0.06 MMT (Tables 3.6 and 3.7). In S2, without a levy, there is a reduction in wheat procurement by 1.8 MMT, reflecting better price offers from other states. While Punjab and Uttar Pradesh decrease sales to FCI at MSP by 0.86 and 1.1 MMT, respectively, Haryana gives away an extra 0.2 MMT in procurement. Since there is little change in production and consumption in Haryana, the higher procurement comes out of reduced trade with Gujarat and Himachal Pradesh, where prices are lower due to interstate trade liberalization. Since a major part of rice output is under levy, most changes occur through wheat. Wheat's domestic consumption (including private storage) rises by more than 2 MMT, mainly on account of lower stock holding by the FCI.

As the decrease in wheat procurement is of greater magnitude than the increase in rice procurement, the net effect is lower total procurement, reducing buffer stock holdings of FCI. When interstate transaction cost is reduced, surplus states increase their trade with other states and depend less on price support. With the elimination of movement restrictions, total government stocks go down by 2.45 MMT. This trend is driven largely by lower procurement of wheat, as PDS demand is assumed fixed.

**Table 3.6   Aggregate effects on quantities and prices**

| Scenario | Open market demand (MMT) | Net production (MMT) | Wholesale price (Rs/quintal) | Procurement (MMT) | PDS (MMT) | Total regional trade (MMT) | External imports (MMT) | External exports (MMT) | Closing FCI stocks (MMT) |
|---|---|---|---|---|---|---|---|---|---|
| Rice | | | | | | | | | |
| S0 | 48.175 | 79.454 | 1,312 | 31.56 | 7.29 | 7.71 | 0.281 | 0 | 24.27 |
| S1 | 48.176 | 79.532 | 1,333 | 31.61 | 7.29 | 8.75 | 0.251 | 0 | 24.32 |
| S2 | 48.181 | 79.552 | 1,337 | 31.62 | 7.29 | 8.98 | 0.247 | 0 | 24.33 |
| Wheat | | | | | | | | | |
| S0 | 43.490 | 67.205 | 775 | 23.82 | 3.87 | 5.33 | 0.102 | 0 | 19.95 |
| S1 | 44.481 | 67.142 | 766 | 22.75 | 3.87 | 6.27 | 0.089 | 0 | 18.89 |
| S2 | 45.150 | 67.100 | 759 | 22.02 | 3.87 | 6.93 | 0.075 | 0 | 18.16 |
| Total | | | | | | | | | |
| S0 | 91.67 | 146.66 | 2,087 | 55.38 | 11 | 13.04 | 0.383 | 0 | 44.22 |
| S1 | 92.66 | 146.67 | 2,098 | 54.36 | 11 | 15.02 | 0.340 | 0 | 43.20 |
| S2 | 93.33 | 146.65 | 2,096 | 53.64 | 11 | 15.90 | 0.322 | 0 | 42.49 |

Source: Authors' calculations from model simulations.

Notes: FCI, Food Corporation of India; MMT, million metric tons; PDS, public distribution system; Rs, rupees.

Table 3.7   Efficiency gains relative to base scenario

| Scenario | Total regional trade (MMT) | Regional price variation (coefficient of variation of prices) | PDS cost (Rs 10 million) | Procurement cost (Rs 10 million) | Storage cost (Rs 10 million) | Sales realization (Rs 10 million) | Net government cost (Rs 10 million) | Total consumer surplus (Rs 10 million) | Total producer surplus (Rs 10 million) | Total consumer and producer surplus (Rs 10 million) |
|---|---|---|---|---|---|---|---|---|---|---|
| Scenario 1 | | | | | | | | | | |
| Rice | 1.04 | −0.048 | 0 | 48 | 10 | 0 | 58 | 1,437 | 1,369 | 2,806 |
| Wheat | 0.94 | −0.019 | 0 | −1,011 | −265 | 0 | −1,276 | 1,069 | −544 | 525 |
| Total | 1.98 | | 0 | −963 | −255 | 0 | −1,218 | 2,506 | 825 | 3,331 |
| Scenario 2 | | | | | | | | | | |
| Rice | 1.27 | −0.068 | 0 | 60 | 12 | 0 | 72 | 2,838 | 1,637 | 4,475 |
| Wheat | 1.60 | −0.040 | 0 | −1,698 | −445 | 0 | −2,143 | 1,802 | −898 | 904 |
| Total | 2.86 | | 0 | −1,639 | −433 | 0 | −2,072 | 4,640 | 739 | 5,379 |

Source: Authors' calculations from model simulations.
Notes: MMT, million metric tons; PDS, public distribution system; Rs, rupees.

**Table 3.8  Simulation results: Rice**

| State | Open-market demand S0 (MMT) | S1 (% change over S0) | S2 (% change over S0) | Wholesale price S0 (Rs/quintal) | S1 (% change over S0) | S2 (% change over S0) | Procurement S0 (MMT) | S1 (% change over S0) | S2 (% change over S0) | Net regional imports S0 (MMT) | S1 (% change over S0) | S2 (% change over S0) |
|---|---|---|---|---|---|---|---|---|---|---|---|---|
| Andhra Pradesh | 5.94 | −2.53 | −1.85 | 1,365 | 2.42 | 1.54 | 5.31 | 0.19 | 0.00 | −0.24 | 66.67 | 45.83 |
| Assam | 2.37 | 3.80 | 6.33 | 1,582 | −3.54 | −6.32 | 1.82 | −0.55 | −0.55 | 0.25 | 40.00 | 68.00 |
| Bihar | 7.23 | 3.04 | 3.46 | 1,425 | −3.09 | −3.65 | 0 | 0.00 | 0.00 | 1.73 | 13.29 | 15.61 |
| Goa | 0.08 | 0.00 | 0.00 | 1,312 | 2.52 | 2.59 | 0.07 | 0.00 | 0.00 | −0.07 | 0.00 | 0.00 |
| Gujarat | 0.81 | −3.70 | −6.17 | 1,223 | 2.70 | 4.66 | 1.87 | 0.53 | 0.53 | −0.14 | 28.57 | 42.86 |
| Haryana | 0.17 | −5.88 | −11.76 | 1,153 | 5.72 | 8.59 | 0 | 0.00 | 0.00 | −0.66 | 1.52 | 3.03 |
| Himachal Pradesh | 0.23 | −13.04 | −17.39 | 913 | 17.09 | 24.75 | 0 | 0.00 | 0.00 | −0.88 | 4.55 | 6.82 |
| Jammu and Kashmir | 0.45 | −4.44 | −8.89 | 1,081 | 6.66 | 9.62 | 1.14 | 0.88 | 0.88 | 0.04 | −75.00 | −100.00 |
| Karnataka | 1.86 | −3.76 | −3.23 | 1,329 | 2.48 | 2.26 | 0 | 0.00 | 0.00 | −0.74 | 10.81 | 10.81 |
| Kerala | 2.04 | 5.39 | 7.35 | 1,561 | −5.64 | −7.62 | 0.45 | 0.00 | 0.00 | 1.27 | 9.45 | 12.60 |
| Madhya Pradesh | 3.59 | 1.95 | 1.95 | 1,388 | −2.95 | −2.88 | 0 | 0.00 | 0.00 | 3.07 | 2.28 | 1.95 |
| Maharashtra | 2 | 7.50 | 7.50 | 1,444 | −5.33 | −5.61 | 0 | | | 0.02 | 800.00 | 800.00 |
| Orissa | 3.74 | 3.74 | 4.28 | 1,425 | −3.09 | −3.65 | 2.18 | −0.46 | −0.46 | 1.2 | 12.50 | 14.17 |
| Punjab | 0.17 | −5.88 | −11.76 | 1,153 | 5.72 | 8.59 | 6.39 | 0.31 | 0.63 | −2.66 | 1.13 | 1.50 |
| Rajasthan | 0.13 | −15.38 | −15.38 | 1,231 | 4.47 | 5.77 | 0.07 | 0.00 | 0.00 | 0.05 | −40.00 | −60.00 |
| Tamil Nadu | 4.32 | 4.63 | 6.25 | 1,548 | −4.84 | −6.85 | 3.39 | −0.59 | −0.59 | 0.09 | 277.78 | 366.67 |
| Uttar Pradesh | 5.12 | −6.05 | −8.01 | 1,204 | 5.48 | 7.14 | 5.39 | 0.37 | 0.37 | −1.15 | 29.57 | 38.26 |
| West Bengal | 7.91 | −3.92 | −5.18 | 1,204 | 5.48 | 7.14 | 3.48 | 0.29 | 0.57 | −1.17 | 29.06 | 38.46 |

Source: Authors' calculations from model simulations.

Note: MMT, million metric tons; Rs, rupees.

Table 3.9   Simulation results: Wheat

| State | Open-market demand | | | Wholesale price | | | Procurement | | | Net regional imports | | |
|---|---|---|---|---|---|---|---|---|---|---|---|---|
| | S0 (MMT) | S1 (% change over S0) | S2 (% change over S0) | S0 (Rs/quintal) | S1 (% change over S0) | S2 (% change over S0) | S0 (MMT) | S1 (% change over S0) | S2 (% change over S0) | S0 (MMT) | S1 (% change over S0) | S2 (% change over S0) |
| Andhra Pradesh | 0.19 | 5.26 | 15.79 | 928 | -2.59 | -7.00 | 0 | 0.00 | 0.00 | 0.19 | 5.26 | 10.53 |
| Assam | 0.17 | 0.00 | 5.88 | 1,062 | -2.82 | -9.70 | 0 | 0.00 | 0.00 | 0.08 | 0.00 | 12.50 |
| Bihar | 5.66 | 2.47 | 4.24 | 892 | -4.60 | -7.74 | 0 | 0.00 | 0.00 | 1.19 | 13.45 | 22.69 |
| Goa | 0.03 | 0.00 | 0.00 | 977 | -6.86 | -11.16 | 0 | 0.00 | 0.00 | 0.03 | 0.00 | 0.00 |
| Gujarat | 1.75 | 6.86 | 11.43 | 904 | -4.65 | -7.96 | 0 | 0.00 | 0.00 | 1.1 | 10.91 | 19.09 |
| Haryana | 2.03 | 0.99 | 0.99 | 740 | 0.00 | 0.00 | 7.4 | 0.95 | 2.57 | -0.22 | -40.91 | -95.45 |
| Himachal Pradesh | 0.29 | 3.45 | 6.90 | 933 | -4.61 | -8.57 | 0 | 0.00 | 0.00 | -0.31 | -3.23 | -9.68 |
| Jammu and Kashmir | 0.63 | 4.76 | 7.94 | 1,067 | -8.72 | -14.15 | 0 | 0.00 | 0.00 | 0.48 | 8.33 | 12.50 |
| Karnataka | 0.22 | 0.00 | 4.55 | 890 | -2.47 | -6.07 | 0 | 0.00 | 0.00 | -0.03 | -33.33 | -66.67 |
| Kerala | 0.11 | 9.09 | 18.18 | 1,050 | -6.76 | -12.48 | 0 | 0.00 | 0.00 | 0.08 | 50.00 | 62.50 |
| Madhya Pradesh | 4.43 | 5.19 | 9.03 | 892 | -4.60 | -7.74 | 0 | 0.00 | 0.00 | 0.53 | 47.17 | 83.02 |
| Maharashtra | 2.19 | 2.74 | 5.02 | 910 | -4.62 | -8.13 | 0 | 0.00 | 0.00 | 1.21 | 4.96 | 9.92 |
| Orissa | 0.17 | 11.76 | 17.65 | 910 | -4.62 | -8.13 | 0 | 0.00 | 0.00 | 0.16 | 6.25 | 18.75 |
| Punjab | 2.19 | 0.91 | 1.37 | 740 | 0.00 | 0.00 | 12.01 | -4.25 | -7.08 | -1.35 | 36.30 | 61.48 |
| Rajasthan | 5.77 | 3.81 | 5.37 | 846 | -4.61 | -6.62 | 0 | 0.00 | 0.00 | 0.3 | 80.00 | 113.33 |
| Tamil Nadu | 0.07 | 28.57 | 71.43 | 1,008 | -3.17 | -8.83 | 0 | 0.00 | 0.00 | 0 | 0.00 | 0.00 |
| Uttar Pradesh | 16.9 | 0.53 | 0.71 | 740 | 0.00 | 0.00 | 4.4 | -14.32 | -25.45 | -3.08 | 17.53 | 32.47 |
| West Bengal | 0.71 | -2.82 | -1.41 | 757 | 2.51 | 1.32 | 0 | 0.00 | 0.00 | -0.35 | 5.71 | 0.00 |

Source: Authors' calculations from model simulations.

Note: MMT, million metric tons; Rs, rupees.

The direction of trade follows arbitrage opportunities from regional price differences resulting from the removal of restrictions. Gujarat, Himachal Pradesh, and Rajasthan find it cheaper to import wheat from Punjab than from Haryana (Table 3.10). The combination of lower consumption and higher production for rice results in higher net exports by surplus states to other states, as expected with freer domestic trade (Tables 3.6 and 3.7). As with rice, there is an increase in the quantity of wheat traded domestically. Regional wheat exports grow substantially from Punjab, while the major importing states of Bihar, Gujarat, and Maharashtra buy more wheat from other states.

When the implicit tariff on domestic trade is reduced, the quantity traded domestically increases for both commodities, while quantities traded externally decrease. World prices being lower than domestic prices, the simulations show no rice or wheat exports. However, some states find it cheaper to import from abroad than from neighboring states. Tamil Nadu imports both rice and wheat, whereas Kerala opts for wheat imports from abroad as well as from Karnataka and Madhya Pradesh, replacing its base-period imports (mainly from Uttar Pradesh).

In the deficit states, due to increased supply from interstate trade, wholesale and weighted average prices fall and so does production (weighted average prices are not shown in the figures). The opposite holds true in the surplus states, except for wheat-growing regions, where the equilibrium price continues to be the MSP. The net effect is that with lower trading costs, prices stabilize across states, even though the average national price for rice rises and the price for wheat falls. A reduction in transport costs, in addition to lowering implicit tariffs, has a much larger impact on regional price stability. Thus infrastructure is perhaps more important to improved domestic trade than policy reforms.

Comparing scenario 2 with scenario 0, the 100 percent implicit tariff reduction and 25 percent reduction in transport cost result in a rise in consumer surplus for both rice and wheat, though some states gain and some lose (Figure 3.8). As seen earlier, the producer surplus rises for rice and falls for wheat (Table 3.7). In the case of wheat, there is a fall in producer surplus and a rise in consumer surplus in almost all states. Since the local market prices remain unchanged in wheat surplus states like Haryana, Punjab, and Uttar Pradesh, they show no change in producer or consumer surplus (Table 3.11). Consumer surplus is positive everywhere but in the states with the largest deficits (Bihar, Kerala, and Rajasthan). While traders incur a net welfare loss in rice, they gain in wheat. This is due to the policy of MSP-based free procurement for wheat but a levy for rice. The magnitude of traders' surplus is much smaller than that of consumers and producers. At the national level, total surpluses for producers, consumers, and wholesale traders are positive. There is a small loss in retail traders' surplus, but overall there is a net positive gain in the economy (Table 3.11). Since

Table 3.10   Changing trading partnerships with freer domestic trade

**Rice**

| Trading state | Scenario 0 | Scenario 2 |
|---|---|---|
| Andhra Pradesh | Kerala | Kerala, Tamil Nadu |
| Goa | Kerala | Kerala |
| Gujarat | Kerala | Kerala, Maharashtra, Tamil Nadu |
| Haryana | Kerala, Madhya Pradhesh, Orissa, Tamil Nadu | Madhya Pradhesh, Orissa, Rajasthan |
| Himachal Pradesh | Haryana, Jammu & Kashmir, Punjab, Rajasthan | Haryana, Punjab |
| Karnataka | Kerala | Kerala, Tamil Nadu |
| Punjab | Kerala, Madhya Pradhesh, Orissa, Tamil Nadu | Madhya Pradhesh, Orissa, Rajasthan |
| Uttar Pradesh | Bihar, Maharashtra | Bihar |
| West Bengal | Assam, Bihar, Orissa | Andhra Pradesh, Assam, Bihar, Orissa |

**Wheat**

| Trading state | Scenario 0 | Scenario 2 |
|---|---|---|
| Andhra Pradesh | Gujarat | Kerala, Tamil Nadu |
| Haryana | Jammu & Kashmir, Himachal Pradesh, Rajasthan | Gujarat, Himachal Pradesh, Rajasthan |
| Himachal Pradesh | | Jammu & Kashmir |
| Karnataka | Goa, Kerala | Goa, Kerala |
| Madhya Pradesh | | Kerala, Tamil Nadu |
| Maharashtra | | Goa |
| Punjab | Gujarat, Himachal Pradesh, Rajasthan | Gujarat, Himachal Pradesh, Rajasthan |
| Uttar Pradesh | Bihar, Kerala, Madhya Pradesh, Maharashtra | Bihar, Madhya Pradesh, Maharashtra, Orissa |
| West Bengal | Andhra Pradesh, Assam, Orissa | Andhra Pradesh, Assam, Orissa |

Source: Authors' calculations from model simulations.

**Figure 3.8    Changes in total surplus in scenario 2 over base**

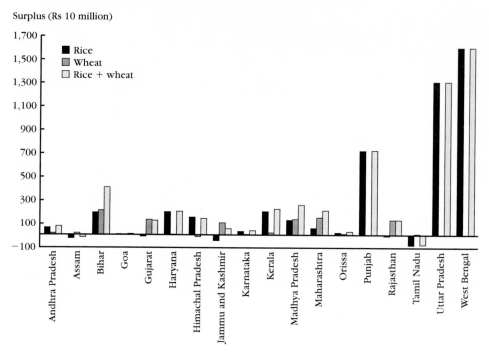

Surplus (Rs 10 million)

Note: Rs, rupees.

PDS quantities and prices are kept unchanged in the model, the costs of PDS remain unchanged due to reforms. However, the costs of procurement and storage both fall. These savings equal Rs 12 billion with simple policy reform (scenario 1) and Rs 20 billion with both short- and long-term policy changes (scenario 2) (Table 3.7).

## Conclusions

This chapter evaluates international and domestic trade and marketing policies in India, examining the effects of deregulating domestic markets and liberalizing external trade in the foodgrains sector. To alleviate household food insecurity, the government of India supports several food-based programs that are among the largest in the world. But pervasive inefficiencies in implementation in several of these programs seriously undermine their ability to achieve the intended goals.

Traditionally the government fixed prices for both producers and consumers: it decided how much to distribute where, how much of its stocks to release or accumulate to achieve price stabilization, and so on. Public policy toward foodgrains markets

Table 3.11  Welfare gains from base case trade restrictions eliminated and transport cost reduced 25 percent (Rs 10 million)

| | Rice | | | | | Wheat | | | | | Aggregate total surplus |
|---|---|---|---|---|---|---|---|---|---|---|---|
| | Change in surpluses of type | | | | | Change in surpluses of type | | | | | |
| States | CS | PS | Wholesale traders | Retail traders | Total surplus | CS | PS | Wholesale traders | Retail traders | Total surplus | |
| Andhra Pradesh | −146 | 199 | −0.77 | −0.88 | 51.35 | 15.57 | −0.32 | 0.00 | 0.00 | 15.25 | 67.36 |
| Assam | 284 | −317 | −0.10 | −0.11 | −33.21 | 20.69 | −7.33 | 0.00 | 0.00 | 13.36 | −19.21 |
| Bihar | 419 | −229 | −0.97 | −1.07 | 187.96 | 465.61 | −254.96 | 0.00 | 0.55 | 211.2 | 399.51 |
| Goa | −3 | 4 | −0.05 | −0.05 | 0.9 | 3.67 | 0.00 | 0.00 | 0.00 | 3.67 | 4.9 |
| Gujarat | −55 | 47 | −0.63 | −0.77 | −9.4 | 163.91 | −38.94 | 0.00 | 0.29 | 125.26 | 115.89 |
| Haryana | −19 | 216 | −0.22 | −0.26 | 196.52 | 0.00 | 0.00 | 7.59 | 0.05 | 7.64 | 204.16 |
| Himachal Pradesh | −54 | 204 | 0.17 | 0.20 | 150.37 | 28.37 | −40.10 | 0.00 | 0.03 | −11.7 | 138.4 |
| Jammu and Kashmir | −83 | 35 | 0.08 | 0.14 | −47.78 | 116.22 | −18.29 | 0.00 | 0.03 | 97.96 | 49.25 |
| Karnataka | −60 | 92 | −1.01 | −1.09 | 29.9 | 12.93 | −10.77 | 0.00 | 0.20 | 2.36 | 33.1 |
| Kerala | 275 | −73 | −0.90 | −0.99 | 200.11 | 16.93 | 0.00 | 0.00 | 0.03 | 16.96 | 217.14 |
| Madhya Pradesh | 159 | −32 | −1.73 | −1.88 | 123.39 | 354.17 | −222.29 | 0.00 | 0.29 | 132.17 | 255.68 |
| Maharashtra | 186 | −128 | 1.24 | 1.39 | 60.63 | 208.06 | −60.11 | 0.00 | 0.63 | 148.58 | 208.26 |
| Orissa | 213 | −196 | 0.67 | 0.72 | 18.39 | 14.92 | −0.80 | 0.00 | 0.00 | 14.12 | 32.39 |
| Punjab | −19 | 738 | −0.18 | −0.22 | 718.6 | 0.00 | 0.00 | 11.16 | 0.01 | 11.17 | 729.76 |
| Rajasthan | −10 | 9 | −0.51 | −0.58 | −2.09 | 380.48 | −252.94 | 0.00 | 0.33 | 127.87 | 125.24 |
| Tamil Nadu | 541 | −621 | −1.86 | −2.16 | −84.02 | 7.77 | 0.00 | 0.00 | 0.00 | 7.77 | −76.02 |
| Uttar Pradesh | 492 | 813 | −2.41 | −2.76 | 1,299.83 | 0.00 | 0.00 | 3.28 | 0.89 | 4.17 | 1,304.0 |
| West Bengal | 718 | 876 | 4.64 | 4.97 | 1,603.61 | −7.38 | 8.73 | 0.00 | 0.53 | 1.88 | 1,605.14 |
| All India | 2,838 | 1,637 | −4.54 | −5.4 | 4,465.06 | 1,801.92 | −898.12 | 22.03 | 3.86 | 929.69 | 5,394.95 |

Source: Authors' calculations from model simulations.

Note: CS, consumer surplus; PS, producer surplus.

has tended to be interventionist, with the central and state governments actively involved in storing grain and placing restrictions on the movement of foodgrains across states. These restrictions are often based on the assumption that markets cannot be expected to perform well in alleviating local scarcities. While some limited reforms have been implemented with regard to the international trade in foodgrains, and to a lesser extent in domestic trade, overall the government continues to dominate all aspects of foodgrains marketing.

An assessment of the costs and functioning of the FCI—the main parastatal agency entrusted with the tasks of procurement, storage, transport, and distribution of foodgrains on behalf of the government—reveals enormous inefficiencies and substantial scope for improvement. Private traders are shown to operate at costs much lower than public costs, for both storage and trade, despite several controls and restrictions and notwithstanding the freight and credit subsidies provided to the FCI.

Liberalization of the international trade in foodgrains has primarily taken the form of removal of export controls on grains and other agricultural products, and the replacement of quantitative restrictions on imports with tariffs (which are among the highest in the world). Studies of the impact of trade liberalization predicted that it would lead to higher agricultural prices and lower industrial prices; in the short run this would adversely affect both growth and equity, while in the medium and long run it would result in acceleration of growth through more efficient allocation of resources across sectors, in turn helping to reduce poverty. The actual experience of the 1990s and 2000s has more or less confirmed these expectations.

Past studies have also shown that it is possible to effectively stabilize food prices and protect household access to food through a combination of a liberal trade regime and publicly operated buffer stocks, with government procurement and sales taking place at market prices rather than at administratively fixed prices. Such a policy would also be compatible with India's commitments under the WTO Agreement on Agriculture. But in reality, with government interventions in foodgrains markets continuing to take place at administratively set prices, the incompatibility of such intervention with a liberal trade regime is manifest in the wild swings in the public stock of foodgrains since the late 1990s.

An underresearched aspect of the foodgrains policy in India is the impact of domestic market regulations relating to intracountry movement and storage of grains. A multimarket spatial model of rice and wheat markets in India has been used here to study the impacts of domestic market deregulation—specifically the impacts of removal of all interstate movement restrictions, along with improvement in transport efficiency. Simulation results show that grain storage and interstate movement restrictions are welfare-reducing. When the constraints imposed on private trade through such restrictions are binding, zoning policies systematically increase (rather than reduce) interstate food price dispersion. This worsens the situation of food-deficit households in deficit states. In that sense the movement restrictions have a direct bearing on household-level food security.

The simulation results also show that private trade occurs between neighboring states (not directly over long distances, as practiced by government agencies) and thus does not compete directly with FCI. The direction of trade between any two states is therefore determined by the arbitrage possibilities over shorter distances rather than by the deficit or surplus status of the states. In these simulations exports to the rest of the world do not occur for either rice or wheat, due to unattractive international prices and the absence of export subsidies. However, some states do find it more attractive to buy from abroad than from other states. The consumers in the deficit states with ports benefit more from external trade than do those in the interior surplus states. In particular Kerala (in the case of wheat) and Tamil Nadu (both rice and wheat) find it cheaper to import from abroad than to buy domestically.

The model results also show that aggregate procurement of rice and wheat falls, as traders prefer to trade with other states rather than sell to FCI at MSP. This holds especially for wheat, which has no levy. In the case of rice, levy procurement curtails the possibility of trade with other regions, particularly since the levy is as high as 50–75 percent in some states. The immediate effect of lower procurement is that FCI's buffer stocks fall, leading to a cost savings in procurement and storage. Policy changes aimed at bringing down restrictions on interstate trade and transport costs can have a potentially large impact on aggregate welfare (more than Rs 50 billion) and its distribution across states.

The simulations also show that domestic trade liberalization can be facilitated by long-term policy changes that reduce the transaction costs of traders. These include encouraging investment and modernization through improved infrastructure, enabling a larger scale of operation (for example, through bulk handling and transport), and innovations (for example, fuel-efficient trucks); and development of improved institutions for market information, grading and labeling, and so forth.

These reform measures need to be complemented by other major reform measures that will gradually but significantly reduce government intervention in all aspects of foodgrains markets—procurement, storage, transportation, and distribution—so that the private sector can play an effective role in foodgrains marketing. Given the close interdependence of foodgrains markets with public distribution and the operations of the FCI, it is critical that reforms follow an integrated approach, covering not just the operations of the FCI but also the government's pricing policies, and more critically its safety-net programs.[14] Piecemeal reforms that do not address the conflicting needs of farmers (who want higher returns for their crops) and consumers (who want cheap food) will not elicit popular consensus in a vibrant democracy, and would only lead to pressures for rolling back the reform measures.

## Notes

1. In fact international trade in grains was a state monopoly until the early 1990s.

2. See, for example, Krishna and Raychaudhuri (1980); Gulati (1989); Gulati, Hanson, and Pursell (1990); Pursell and Gulati (1993); Radhakrishna et al. (1997).

3. The Department of Consumer Affairs in the Ministry of Consumer Affairs, Food, and Public Distribution regulates domestic and interstate trade; its mission is to implement the ECA and prevent black marketing, while ensuring uniform standards of grades and measures across the country.

4. The railways, owned by the government, sometimes deny wagons to private grain traders in order to restrict interstate grain movement.

5. FCI is unable to do so, as it is apparently required to pay mandi charges on *all* its purchases, adding to its costs.

6. During the 1990s the stock of rice held by the government of India varied between 10 and 15 MMT as compared to the volume of the world rice market of about 15–20 MMT.

7. Shikha Jha and P. V. Srinivasan are the authors of the multicommodity spatial model presented here. The simulations presented later in this chapter were also carried out by them. For complete details on the model and the simulations see Jha and Srinivasan (2004).

8. See Jha and Srinivasan (2004) for detailed information on the sources of elasticities.

9. Based on production patterns, rice and wheat can be substituted only in some states. The literature provides insignificant cross-elasticity estimates; they are thus dropped from the supply equations for all states.

10. Measurements of retail and wholesale margins in the base scenario, along with the interstate transport cost, come from Chand (2002). In some states (like Jammu and Kashmir) the estimates of transport cost from Chand (2002) have been doubled to take into account difficult geography. For details see Jha and Srinivasan (2004).

11. Note that these implicit tariff rates are uniform for all states.

12. Jha and Srinivasan (2004) report results for experiments with a 50 percent reduction in implicit tariffs, a 50 percent reduction in transport costs, and a combination thereof.

13. The changes in net production are negligible across all states and are not reported here. Detailed results are available in Jha and Srinivasan (2004).

14. Several studies have elaborated on the set of comprehensive reforms that the Indian foodgrains sector requires. See, for example, World Bank (1999, 2005) and Ganesh-Kumar, Gulati, and Cummings (2007).

## References

Acharya, S. S. 2001. Domestic agricultural marketing policies, incentives and integration. In *Indian agricultural policy at the crossroads: Priorities and agenda,* ed. S. S. Acharya and D. P. Chaudhri. New Delhi: Rawat.

Administrative Staff College of India (ASCI). 2001. *A study of the costs of acquisition and distribution of food grains by the Food Corporation of India.* Hyderabad.

Chand, R. 2002. *Government intervention in food grain markets in the new context.* New Delhi: National Center for Agricultural Economics and Policy Research.

———. 2003. Domestic reforms for trade liberalization: Analysis and approaches. Paper presented at the South Asia Initiative Workshop on Analysis of Trade Liberalization for Poverty Alleviation, held at Colombo, Ceylon, April 21–25.

Debroy, B., and P. D. Kaushik. 2002. *Barriers to inter-state trade and commerce: The case of road transport.* New Delhi: Commission for Contemporary Studies, Rajiv Gandhi Institute.

Drèze, J., and A. Sen. 1993. *Hunger and public action.* New Delhi: Oxford University Press.

Ellis, F., P. Senanayake, and M. Smith. 1997. Food price policy in Sri Lanka. *Food Policy* 22 (1): 81–96.

Expenditure Reforms Commission. 2001. *Report on food security.* New Delhi: Government of India.

Food Corporation of India (FCI). 2009. Transport management. http://fciweb.nic.in/transport_management/transport_management.htm. Accessed December 21, 2009.

Ganesh-Kumar, A., A. Gulati, and R. Cummings, Jr. 2007. *Foodgrains policy and management in India: Responding to today's challenges and opportunities.* PP-056. New Delhi and Mumbai: International Food Policy Research Institute and Indira Gandhi Institute of Development Research.

Ganesh-Kumar, A., and K. S. Parikh. 1998. A stock-trade policy for national level food security for India. Mimeo. Mumbai: Indira Gandhi Institute of Development Research.

Government of India (GOI). 1965. *Report of the Jha Committee on Food Grain Prices for 1964–65.* New Delhi: Department of Agriculture.

———. 1991. *Report on the operations of the Food Corporation of India, Bureau of Industrial Costs and Prices.* New Delhi: Ministry of Industry.

———. 2001. *Report of the Tenth Plan Working Group on Public Distribution System and Food Security.* New Delhi: Development Policy Division, Planning Commission.

———. 2002. *Report of High Level Committee on Long-Term Grain Policy.* New Delhi: Department of Food and Public Distribution, Ministry of Consumer Affairs, Food and Public Distribution.

———. 2006. *Economic Survey 2005–06.* New Delhi: Ministry of Finance.

Gulati, A. 1989. Food subsidies: In search of cost-effectiveness. *Economic and Political Weekly* 24 (28): 1584–1590.

Gulati, A., J. Hanson, and G. Purcell. 1990. *Effective incentives in India's agriculture.* Policy Planning and Research Working Paper 332 (Trade Policy). Washington, D.C.: World Bank.

Gulati, A., S. Kahkonen, and P. Sharma. 2000. The Food Corporation of India: Successes and failures in Indian foodgrain marketing. In *Institutions, incentives and economic reforms in India,* ed. S. Kahkonen and A. Lanyi. New Delhi: Sage.

Jha, S. 2002. Domestic trade restrictions and food security. In *India development report,* ed. K. Parikh and R. Radhakrishna. New Delhi: Oxford University Press.

Jha, S., and P. V. Srinivasan. 1997. Food grain price stabilization: Implications of private storage and subsidized food distribution. *Journal of Policy Modelling* 19 (6): 587–604.

———. 2001. Taking the PDS to the poor: Directions for further reform. *Economic and Political Weekly,* September 29, 3779–3786.

———. 2004. *Achieving food security in a cost effective way: Implications of domestic deregulation and reform under liberalized trade.* MTID Discussion Paper 67. Washington, D.C.: International Food Policy Research Institute.

Kherallah, M., H. Löfgren, P. Gruhn, and M. M. Reeder. 2000. *Wheat policy reform in Egypt: Adjustment of local markets and options for future reforms.* Research Report 115. Washington, D.C.: International Food Policy Research Institute.

Krishna, R., and G. S. Raychaudhuri. 1980. *Some aspects of wheat and rice price policy in India.* Staff Working Paper 381. Washington, D.C.: World Bank.

Minot, N., and F. Goletti. 2000. *Rice market liberalization and poverty in Vietnam.* Research Report 114. Washington, D.C.: International Food Policy Research Institute.

Panda, M., and J. Quizon. 2001. Growth and distribution under trade liberalization in India. In *Trade and industry: Essays by NIPFP–Ford Foundation Fellows,* ed. A. Guha, K. L. Krishna, and A. K. Lahiri. New Delhi: National Institute of Public Finance and Policy.

Parikh, K., A. Ganesh-Kumar, and G. Darbha. 2003. Growth and welfare consequences of rise in MSP. *Economic and Political Weekly,* March 1, 891–895.

Parikh, K. S., N. S. S. Narayana, M. Panda, and A. Ganesh-Kumar. 1995. *Strategies for agricultural liberalization: Consequences for growth, welfare and distribution.* PP-016. Mumbai: Indira Gandhi Institute of Development Research.

———. 1997. Agricultural trade liberalization: Growth, welfare and large country effects. *Agricultural Economics* 17 (1): 1–20.

Pursell, G., and A. Gulati. 1993. *Liberalizing Indian agriculture: An agenda for reform.* Working Paper 1172. Washington, D.C.: World Bank.

Radhakrishna, R., and M. Panda. 2006. *Macroeconomics of poverty reduction: India case study.* PP-057. Mumbai: Indira Gandhi Institute of Development Research.

Radhakrishna, R., K. Subbarao, S. Indrakant, and C. Ravi. 1997. *India's public distribution system: A national and international perspective.* Discussion Paper 380. Washington, D.C.: World Bank.

Rao, V. M. 2001. The making of agricultural price policy: A review of CACP reports. *Journal of Indian School of Political Economy* 13 (1): 1–28.

Rashid, S., A. Gulati, and S. M. Dev. 2008. Parastatals and food policies: The Indian case. In *From para-*

*statals to private trade: Lessons from Asian agriculture,* ed. S. Rashid, A. Gulati, and R. Cummings, Jr. Baltimore, Md., U.S.A.: Johns Hopkins University Press.

Reserve Bank of India. Various years. *Handbook of statistics on the Indian economy.* CD-ROM. Mumbai.

Tyagi, D. S. 1990. *Managing India's food economy: Problems and alternatives.* New Delhi: Sage.

World Bank. 1999. *India—Food grain marketing policies: Reforming to meet security needs.* Rural Development Unit, South Asia Region, Working Paper 18329. Washington, D.C.

———. 2000. *India: Policies to reduce poverty and accelerate sustainable development.* Report 19471-IN. Washington, D.C.

———. 2005. *India: Re-energizing the agricultural sector to sustain growth and reduce poverty.* New York: Oxford University Press.

# Chapter 4

# Liberalization and Food Security in Nepal

## Bishwambher Pyakuryal, Y. B. Thapa, and Devesh Roy

With agricultural trade liberalization becoming part of a multilateral agenda, there is widespread concern that trade liberalization may have an adverse impact on poverty and food security in developing countries—even when liberalization is unilateral. Nepal is a least-developed country, with a gross national product of US$235.00 per capita in 2001 and the second lowest per capita wealth in the world. Within South Asia Nepal has the lowest per capita income, the highest dependence of population on agriculture, and the second highest poverty rate.

Among South Asian countries Nepal liberalized the most extensively during the 1980s and 1990s, on both the domestic and external fronts. The country now has the lowest average tariffs in South Asia and has taken several steps to downsize its public distribution system and to remove a host of agricultural subsidies. This contrasting scenario, in which the country with the lowest per capita income is also the most liberalized, presents an interesting case for policy analysis.

What has been the impact of domestic and external liberalization in Nepal on food security? Since liberalization several aggregate-level indicators of food sufficiency and security (per capita food availability and extent of malnourishment) have indeed shown improvement. However, many other indicators of food security, such as agricultural productivity, have shown little or no improvement. Taking other South Asian countries as a benchmark, Nepal presents a mixed picture (Appendix Tables A4.1 and A4.2; Appendix Figures A4.1–A4.3). For some indicators (for example, extent of undernourished population) it has better outcomes than other countries, while for other indicators (such as stunting of children), Nepal has the worst outcomes in the region.[1]

A unique feature of Nepal's linkage between liberalization and food security is the wide disparity in outcomes across regions. Nepal is a landlocked country with a high population density (158 persons per square kilometer in 2001) and immense physical diversity. Some 86 percent of the population lives in rural areas. The country has a uniquely hierarchical geography, divided into three ecological regions: the mountains, the hills, and the terai (foothills).

These regions have always been extremely diverse in such basic respects as population share, arable land, foodgrains production, and the extent of malnourishment and undernourishment (Appendix Figure A4.4). They also exhibit different degrees of amenability to markets and access to food. More importantly, the effect of liberalization on these segregated regions seems to have reinforced their hierarchical ranking, with the terai reaping the fruits of liberalization and remote regions suffering its adverse impacts—a pattern that reflects the country's lack of spatial integration and in turn the lack of government investment in the infrastructure of spatial integration.

This strong interregional disparity in food security and poverty continues to provide the government with a strong rationale to manage food trade flows between the food-surplus and food-deficient regions and to create safety nets and support programs for the remote regions. The most important component of the safety net is the public distribution system, the Nepal Food Corporation (NFC). As part of the domestic reforms, the NFC has undergone several changes. However, despite those reforms, the public sector continues to be mistargeted and relatively inefficient, with marketing and transportation costs resulting in substantial accumulated losses.

The next section presents background information on the food security situation in Nepal. In the third section we document the main elements of external liberalization. The fourth section presents evidence from computable general equilibrium models that support the regional variation in impacts of trade liberalization. The following section outlines the role of the public procurement and distribution system, and the sixth section looks at reforms in the public system and their impacts. The seventh section assesses the trend of NFC cost effectiveness postreform, and the eighth section concludes by summarizing the main findings and suggesting the way forward.

## Evolution of the Agricultural Sector, Policies, and Food Security Outcomes

### Evolution of Indicators of Food Security

Agriculture contributed to 38 percent of the gross domestic product (GDP) and 66 percent of employment in 2001 (75 percent, if agriculture-related trade and manufacturing are included). During 1991–2001, the agricultural growth rate (2.66

percent per year) was marginally higher than the population growth rate, and it was volatile due to its dependence on the monsoon. Over the two decades from 1976 to 1996, the growth rate was only 2.8 percent in agriculture, while non-agriculture grew at 6.6 percent (Bajracharya 2001). The average GDP growth rate over the same period was 4.7 percent (but only 1.6 percent per capita). GDP grew by only 0.8 percent in 2001, partly because of political unrest. In the 1990s GDP growth was negative in three out of eight years—lower than the population growth rate and more volatile.[2] Absolute poverty in Nepal increased from 36 percent to 42 percent during the period 1977–96.

The incidence of poverty does not vary significantly between the hills and the terai, but it is extremely high in the mountains (Appendix Figure A4.4 and Table 4.1). Consequently the most food-insecure area is the far western region in the mountains. The Nepal Living Standards Survey for 1995/96 estimated that 40 percent of the population was under the absolute poverty line, based on a daily intake of 2,124 calories and the expenditure required to procure a minimum level of nonfood goods and services (CBS 1996a, 1996b).

In an agrarian economy landownership is the most important source of food security. Larger landholdings also provide a greater marketable surplus. Landownership in Nepal is extremely skewed and varies significantly across regions. According to the National Sample Census of Agriculture for 1992, the average farm size was only 0.9 hectare per holding (Table 4.2). Marginal farmers make up 43 percent of households but operate only 11 percent of the farmed area (Table 4.3). Landholding sizes decrease moving from the terai into the mountains, as does percentage of land area cultivated. With such small sizes, especially in the hills and mountains, there is little prospect for raising farm productivity and, accordingly, negligible investment in land improvement.

**Table 4.1    Poverty incidence across regions in Nepal**

| Region and years | Rural | Urban | Overall |
|---|---|---|---|
| 1984/85 | | | |
| Terai | 35.4 | 24.1 | 34.5 |
| Hills | 52.7 | 14.5 | 50.0 |
| Mountains | 44.1 | — | 44.1 |
| Nepal total | 43.1 | 19.2 | 41.4 |
| 1995/96 | | | |
| Terai | 37.3 | 28.1 | 36.7 |
| Hills | 52.7 | 14.5 | 50.0 |
| Mountains | 62.4 | — | 62.4 |
| Nepal total | 46.6 | 17.8 | 44.6 |

Sources: National Planning Commission (1985, 1998).

Note: —, Measure not available.

Table 4.2    Farm statistics by region, 1992

| Statistic | Terai | Hills | Mountains | Nepal |
|---|---|---|---|---|
| Area under cultivation (%) | 38 | 14 | 3 | 16 |
| Farm size (ha/holding) | 1.23 | 0.77 | 0.68 | 0.95 |
| Owner-tiller tenure (%) | 87.1 | 95.4 | 94.2 | 90.9 |
| Gini index with households | 0.55 | 0.47 | 0.43 | 0.52 |
| Gini index with population | 0.46 | 0.40 | 0.39 | 0.44 |

Source: CBS (1994).

Table 4.3    Distribution of farmholdings and operational land by farm sizes, 1992

| Statistic | Marginal (<0.5 ha) | Small (0.5–2.0 ha) | Large (>2.0 ha) |
|---|---|---|---|
| Farm households (%) | 43.1 | 45.9 | 11.0 |
| Operational land area (%) | 11.3 | 46.8 | 41.9 |

Source: Compiled from Table 2.6 of CBS (1994).

In terms of food security outcomes at a national level, Nepal was food secure until the early 1970s (except in periods of unfavorable weather, as in 1972). The food balance for 1970/71 showed a surplus of 294,000 metric tons (MT); an even greater surplus, 539,000 MT, occurred in 1974/75 (FAMSD 1982). Food was exported from the terai, although the hills remained food deficient. In 1977 the government estimated the national food deficit at 1.5 percent. Alternative estimates from Gurung (1989) are much higher: 15–19 percent in 1976 and 18–22 percent in 1977. During the drought of 1980 Nepal received food aid to meet the shortages.

Though Nepal has experienced sporadic food insufficiency at the national level, food security concerns are most pronounced at the household level, owing to poverty, and most severe in the hills and mountains. Estimates of the average per capita food deficit as of 2001 were 47 kilograms in the mountains and 32 kilograms in the hills—even though the national level shows a per capita *surplus* of 45 kilograms. The ratio of food deficits to requirements has fluctuated heavily depending on the weather. From a deficit of 12.5 percent during 1990–94, the net food balance moved to a 1.9 percent surplus in 2001. The food deficits are most pronounced in the mountains and hills, while the terai exhibits a surplus (Table 4.4). The share of the terai in grain production increased from 51 to 58 percent, while that of the hills and mountains decreased (Table 4.4). Food production per capita in the terai is nearly 50 percent higher than in the hills and two times higher than in the mountains.

The per capita gross foodgrains production at the national level decreased from 376 to 277 kilograms during 1974–92 (APROSC and JMA 1995), a decline of 1.85 percent per annum. The average gross per capita production of 277 kilograms dur-

Table 4.4   Food availability and requirement of cereals by region, 2000/01

| Ecological region | Population (thousands) | Food available (thousands of MT) | Food requirement (thousands of MT) | Food Balance (thousands of MT) |
|---|---|---|---|---|
| Mountains | 1,715 | 248 | 328 | −80 |
| Hills | 10,335 | 1,742 | 2,077 | −336 |
| Terai | 11,189 | 2,524 | 2,025 | 499 |
| Nepal total | 23,239 | 4,513 | 4,430 | 83 |

Source: CBS (2002).

ing this period translates to 190 kilograms of foodstuffs (edible form)—just slightly more than the official minimum requirements of 180 kilograms (Wallace 1987; Uma 1993).

Yields for most crops (except wheat) were stagnant or increased only marginally during 1985–99 (NPC 2001). The productivity increase was 1.5 percent for paddy, 0.2 percent for maize, and 1.9 percent for wheat. Sharma (2002) compares the yields in Nepal to those in the rest of South Asia: the average yield in Nepal shows a dramatic decline since the 1960s, from 157 to a poor 61 percent of the South Asian average.

The export of agricultural products was a major source of foreign exchange until 1979. During 1974–79, foodgrains accounted for 25 percent of merchandise exports (Ministry of Finance 1997). The deficit in food trade has increased from about NRs 1 billion to 4 billion on a three-year average basis during the interval 1991–2001. Nepal's spending on food imports increased sharply between 1993 and 1999, from NRs 0.622 to NRs 1.641 billion. The trade balance appears positive for a few years only if pulses are included.

Declining yields and consequently rising imports imply an adverse outcome for national-level food self-sufficiency. But even with increased self-sufficiency at the national level, household-level outcomes might worsen. Furthermore average nutrition outcomes in Nepal show mixed results over time, with improvement in some indicators and a worsening in others.

### Structural Adjustment: A Break in Nepal's Trade Policy

According to Sharma (2000), the evolution of Nepal's trade policies has passed through three distinct phases, moving from a free trade regime (1923–56) to an increasingly closed, protectionist regime (1956–85) and then toward an open, liberal regime (1985–86).

The thrust for reforms in the 1980s came from structural adjustment programs mandated by the International Monetary Fund (IMF). Nepal faced severe balance of payments problems and budget deficits in the mid-1980s, due to rising government expenditures aimed at offsetting the sluggish economic growth rates. Monetization of the deficit fueled inflation, leading to an import surge and consequently large current account deficits. The decline in export earnings and foreign aid inflows led to a crisis situation in the early 1980s, culminating in IMF loans that carried with them structural adjustment requirements as part of the package. Nepal implemented the IMF-supported stabilization program beginning December 1985, and the second-phase structural adjustment program in 1988.

The liberalization policies pursued since 1985/86 began gradually, consisting mainly of dismantling quantitative restrictions and simplifying the industrial licensing regime. Tariffs (including sales tax, excise duties, and additional duties) were subsequently reduced, and disparities in tariff rates were narrowed, especially beginning in the late 1980s (Sharma 2000). The tariffs were reduced gradually, with the most significant reduction happening in 1992.

Since the liberalization process was gradual, we can identify cutoff points that demarcate the pre- and postliberalization periods: 1986 was the starting point for liberalization, and 1992 marked the phase of significant tariff reduction. We treat 1986 as the cutoff point in analyzing food security outcomes, since the most comprehensive changes occurred in 1986 following the advent of the structural adjustment programs.

For the computable general equilibrium (CGE) model, focusing only on tariff reduction, 1992 would be the most appropriate cutoff. The social accounting matrix (SAM), however, is based on 1995/96 data, so the tariff reductions in 1995/96 are already included in the baseline for the CGE analysis. As a result, the model-based analysis of counterfactual scenarios for food security outcomes begins from a vantage point of lowered tariffs. In the case of domestic markets, we consider the restructuring of the NFC, a process that started only in 2000, as a measure of reform. The liberalization policies following the structural adjustment programs included significant changes in food policy as well, as did some autonomous reforms (such as those involving the NFC). Box 4.1 lists the milestones in Nepal's food policy.

Thus, beginning in 1985/86, structural policy changes represented a gradual movement toward Nepal's becoming the most liberalized and trade-dependent economy in South Asia, a movement that culminated in 1995. (Significant tariff reductions first appeared in 1992.) Since the 1980s Nepal has implemented substantial trade liberalization, eliminating quantitative restrictions and reducing and rationalizing tariffs, including those in agriculture. In 2002 Nepal's agricultural tariffs were the lowest in South Asia (Box 4.2 and Table 4.5).

Tariffs on live animals and animal products and on vegetable products were 5 and 15 percent, respectively, and those on animal or vegetable fats and oils and on prepared foodstuffs were 10 and 25 percent, respectively. There is no tariff on staples and no quantitative restriction on agricultural products. Nepal's applied tariff on agricultural imports is 14.5 percent. The country's bound tariffs are about 50 percent

---

**Box 4.1    Tariffs and taxes on food trade**

1. Import tariff: Nepal has the lowest tariffs within the South Asian Association for Regional Cooperation for almost all products. The average tariff on agricultural products is 14.5 percent. For processed or frozen products it ranges between 25 and 40 percent.

2. A local development tax (LDT) and a security tax are levied on imports. The LDT replaced an earlier octroi (local-level entry tax). The security tax is levied temporarily for the purpose of maintaining law and order.

3. An export tax of 5 percent is levied on few commodities like soybean oil, ghee, and vegetable oil. Most other countries in the region provide some export incentives.

4. Nepal does not have significant nontariff barriers, except a quarantine standard and product composition standards on inputs such as fertilizers. Nepal has been harmonizing as per the Codex Alimentarius standards.

5. Within the WTO Nepal has committed to an average tariff of 51 percent, to be lowered to an average of 42 percent after three years.

---

lower than those for India. The main element of the domestic market reforms was the restructuring of the NFC, a process that began only in 2000. Other domestic policies, such as removal of subsidies, had been initiated much earlier, during the structural adjustment program.

The last major policy change (or, more correctly, change in the policy environment) was membership in the WTO in 2004. Given Nepal's already liberalized economy, the actual changes in policies resulting from WTO membership were minimal. In agriculture subsidies were not an issue, as Nepal had eliminated most of them. In the government's view certain irrigation and agricultural subsidies might need to be reviewed, but under WTO rules they could be accommodated under aggregate measures of support to agriculture. Similarly the treaty with India and regional agreements like the South Asian Preferential Trade Agreement were not inconsistent with WTO rules.

What has been the impact of trade liberalization in Nepal? At an aggregate level, as we have seen, there have been improvements in some social and food security

**Box 4.2    Chronology of government initiatives in food policy**

Early 1960s—The government instituted and funded the Valley Food Arrangement Committee.

1964—The government replaced the committee with the Food Arrangement Corporation (FAC) to distribute food obtained locally.

1965—The Food Management Corporation (FMC) was established under the Corporation Act to replace the FAC (which nevertheless continued until 1972).

1971/72—Droughts and excess rains in hilly and remote regions underscored the need for a national agency. The government created the Agricultural Marketing Corporation by merging the FMC and the Agricultural Supply Corporation. The objectives of the corporation were to

1. Provide a regular and organized supply of agricultural inputs,

2. Make foodgrains available at a reasonable price to the poor in food-deficit districts,

3. Achieve better coordination by bringing both the input and output distribution functions under a single management,

4. Promote exports of foodgrains to countries other than India,

5. Stabilize prices of foodgrains, and

6. Increase agricultural production by providing incentives to producers.

1973—The government merged the Agricultural Supply Corporation and the FAC to form the Agriculture Purchase and Sales Corporation. The FAC had been responsible for food supply throughout the country.

1974—The Agriculture Purchase and Sales Corporation was split into the Agriculture Inputs Corporation (AIC) and the NFC under the Corporation Act. The NFC was responsible for handling foodgrains distribution, while the AIC was responsible for providing inputs to farmers. The NFC was entrusted with the procurement, storage, and distribution of foodgrains, as follows:

1. Procure, store, transport, and distribute foodgrains at a fair price, in order to meet food requirements in remote and food-deficit areas and to maintain farm incomes.

2. Ensure adequate supply of foodgrains and other essential commodities.

3. Implement the rice exports program of the government.

4. Maintain a reserve stock in relation to domestic requirements.

5. Construct and maintain warehouses for storage and distribution.

Although the NFC was established to distribute food in deficit areas (mainly in the hills and mountains), in fact a major part of the food has been sold in the Kathmandu valley.

1986—The National Planning Commission began to monitor price movements across the border with India. India's minimum support price (MSP), along with other prices fixed by the government of India, was factored into Nepal's MSP and the selling price of fertilizers.

1995—The government implemented the Agriculture Perspective Plan (APP). The APP aims to increase food security through greater efficiency in agriculture production, and to increase demand for agriculture output through creation of employment in the agriculture sector.

1998/99 to present—Policies have focused on downsizing the NFC and increasing the role of the private sector in food marketing. Since the mid-1990s the NFC has reduced the scope of its operations.

2004—The government announced the Food Procurement at the Local Level program. The program aimed to increased food production in hilly and remote areas by purchasing locally produced foodgrains, at a price equal to the total of the purchase price in the terai region plus the NFC's transportation cost to the destination.

2005—The government announced the Food for Students program in 21 districts.

2008—The government banned the export of foodstuffs (including rice) to prevent shortages; it increased the subsidy to NFC through its annual budget for effective supply of foodgrains.

**Table 4.5    Bound and applied tariffs on major agricultural products, August 2002 (percent)**

| Product | Bangladesh | Bhutan | India | Nepal | Pakistan | Sri Lanka |
|---|---|---|---|---|---|---|
| Bound tariff | 50–200 (90% of products have 200; 10% of products have 59) | Has not entered into WTO | Mostly 100 (300 on edible oils) | 42–51 | 100–120 | 50 for all agriculture products |
| Cereals | 36 | 30 | 36 | 10 | 25 | 30 |
| Vegetables | 26–36 | 20 | 35 (onions: 5) | 10 | 10–20 | 30–60 (garlic: 12) |
| Fruits | 26–75.8 (betel nuts: 102.3) | 20 | 35.2–45.2 (dried grapes and betel nuts: 108–113.2) | 10–15 | 20–25 | 30 (dates: 6) |
| Preparations of fruits and vegetables | 36–86.4 | 30 | 35.2–40.4 | 25–40 | 25 | 30 |
| Coffee and tea | 36 | 20 | 108 | 10–25 | 20–25 | 30 (QR for tea) |
| Spices | 26–102.3 | 20 | 35.2–76.8 (QR for cardamom) | 5–10 | 20 | 6–60 |
| Animals | 11 | 20 | 35.2 | 10 | 10–20.25 | 30 |
| Poultry | 26 + QR | 20 | 35.2 | 10 | 20 – octroi[a] | 30 |
| Egg | 36 + QR | 10 | 35.2 + QR | 10 | 20 | 30 |
| Meats and skin | 0–36 | 10–30 | 0–35 | 5–10 | 0–25 + octroi | 12–30 |
| Fish and crustaceans | 36–62.5 | 20 | 35.2 | 10 | 10 | 12 |
| Dairy products | 36–86.5 | 30 | 15–60 | 10–15 | 20–25 | 10–30 |
| Rice | 26 | 20 | 87.2 | 10 | 10 | 60 |
| Wheat and wheat flour | 11–18.5 | 20 | 35.2–50 | 10 | 20–25 | 0–10 |
| Coarse grains and flours | 3.5–18.5 | 20 | 19.6–50 | 10 | 10–25 | 0–30 |
| Processed cereals | 36–75.8 | 20 | 36–56 + QR | 10 | 20–25 | 5–30 |
| Spices | 36–75.8 | 20 | 35.2 + QR | 5–10 | 20 | 30 |
| Edible oils | 18.5–36 | 30 | 75–85 | 5–15 | — | 26–30 |
| Fibers | 3.5–26 | 0 | 9.2–19.6 | 5–10 | 5–10 | 0 |
| Sugar | 86.4 | 20 | 60 + QR | 40 | 25 | 3.5 |
| Rubber | 18.5 | 20 | 30–76.8 | 5 | 5 | 12 |
| Raw tobacco | 18.5 | 100 | 36 | 10 | 25 | 90 |
| Wood and wood products | 3.5–36 | 10–30 | 5–36 | 5–15 | 10–25 | 0–30 |

Source: NRB (2002).

Notes: QR, quantitative restrictions; —, data not available.

[a]Local-level entry tax.

indicators, both absolutely and in relation to South Asia. However, the impacts may not have been uniform across regions within Nepal. In the next section we review the evidence from CGE models. Estimates of the gains and losses across regions provide some evidence for the conjecture that, as in the baseline conditions, the results of trade liberalization could differ significantly across regions.

## Results from the CGE Models

The impacts of trade liberalization on poverty in Nepal have been studied using CGE models by Cockburn (2001) and Sapkota (2002). Both studies use the same model but differ in their base data. Cockburn's study is based on the SAM for 1986, while Sapkota's study uses that for 1996/97. Their findings are quite similar qualitatively, except for some small differences in the magnitude of the impacts. Here we present mainly the results from Sapkota (2002).

The model distinguishes seven household categories, based on location and occupational status: urban; small farm, large farm, and nonfarm terai; and small farm, large farm, and nonfarm hills and mountains. Firms, the government, and the rest of the world are defined as other agents. The model distinguishes five primary factors: unskilled labor, skilled labor, land, and agricultural and non-agricultural capital; these are further distinguished by category of household.

The model considers sixteen commodity-producing sectors, disaggregated by location (urban, rural, terai, and hills and mountains). Production is modeled as a nested constant elasticity of substitution structure. The model allows for intersectoral but not interregional factor mobility. Households receive income from factor payments as well as transfers from firms, the government, and the rest of the world. Transfers from the government and the rest of the world are assumed fixed. Consumption is modeled using a linear expenditure system. The model allows for imperfect substitutability of domestically produced goods and their imported counterparts, and between exports and local sales for domestically produced goods. The values for volume of investment, foreign savings, government consumption, and world prices for exports and imports all remain fixed in the model.

Tables 4.6 and 4.7, drawn from Sapkota (2002), summarize the results from model simulations that eliminate all import tariffs, assuming a compensatory uniform consumption tax designed to maintain government revenue. The output changes are determined by both the initial level of trade taxes (which are driven to zero in the simulations) and the import penetration of the product. Consider, for example, paddy that has high tariffs but low import penetration (just 0.2 percent): the net impact on outputs of reducing tariffs on paddy to zero will be negligible.

**Table 4.6 CGE model results: Effect on output variables**

| Sector | $\delta M_j$ | $\delta D_j$ | $\delta EX_j$ | $\delta XS_j = \delta VA_j$ Urban | Terai | Hills | Nepal |
|---|---|---|---|---|---|---|---|
| Paddy | 5.9 | 0 | 2.1 | 0.2 | –0.1 | –0.1 | 0 |
| Other food crops | 6.2 | 0 | 2 | 0.1 | –0.1 | –0.1 | 0 |
| Cash crops | 1.7 | 0 | 2.2 | 0.2 | –0.2 | –0.2 | 0.1 |
| Livestock and fisheries | 1.3 | –0.1 | 2 | 0.1 | –0.2 | –0.2 | 0 |
| Forestry | 0.0 | 0.2 | 2.3 | 0.4 | –0.1 | 0 | 0.2 |
| **Total agriculture** | **2.3** | **0.0** | **2.1** | **0.2** | **–0.1** | **–0.2** | **0.0** |
| Mining | 5.8 | –0.7 | — | –0.8 | –0.6 | –0.5 | –0.7 |
| Manufacturing | 2.9 | –0.3 | 1.7 | –0.3 | 0 | 0.1 | 0 |
| Construction | 0.0 | –1 | — | –1.8 | –0.8 | –0.6 | –1 |
| Utilities | 7.0 | 0.3 | — | –0.1 | 0.3 | 0.4 | 0.3 |
| **Total industry** | **3.0** | **–0.2** | **1.7** | **–1.1** | **–0.5** | **–0.4** | **–0.6** |
| Hotels and restaurants | 0.0 | 0.7 | 3.3 | 1.8 | 2.2 | 2.3 | 2.2 |
| Transport | 1.5 | 0.3 | 2.8 | 0.7 | 1.1 | 1.3 | 1.1 |
| Trade | –0.1 | 0.7 | 3.6 | 0.4 | 1.3 | 1.6 | 1.3 |
| Banking and real estate | — | 0.6 | — | –0.1 | 0.8 | 1 | 0.6 |
| Public services | — | 0 | — | 0.7 | –0.2 | –0.2 | 0 |
| Other services | — | 0.3 | 1.8 | 0.3 | 0.3 | 0.3 | 0.3 |
| **Total services** | **1.1** | **0.4** | **3.1** | **0.5** | **0.7** | **0.8** | **0.7** |
| Total | 2.67 | –0.01 | 2.62 | 0.0 | 0.02 | –0.02 | 0.14 |

Source: Simulation results.

Note: $\delta D_j$, change in local demand for domestic production; $\delta EX_j$, change in export volume; $\delta M_j$, change in import volume; $\delta VA_j$, change in local value added; $\delta XS_j$, change in local production volume; —, not applicable.

**Table 4.7 Nominal income, prices, and real income change as a percentage of base income**

| | U | T1 | T2 | T3 | H1 | H2 | H3 | All |
|---|---|---|---|---|---|---|---|---|
| Change in nominal income | –2.91 | –3.02 | –3.42 | –2.95 | –2.81 | –2.62 | –2.71 | –2.92 |
| Change in consumer price index | –3.29 | –2.43 | –2.46 | –2.50 | –2.53 | –2.37 | –2.25 | –2.39 |
| Percentage change in real income | 0.38 | –0.59 | –0.96 | –0.45 | –0.28 | –0.25 | –0.46 | –0.53 |

Source: Sapkota (2002).

Note: H1, hills and mountain small farm household; H2, hills and mountain large farm household; H3, hills and mountain off-farm household; T1, terai small farm household; T2, terai large farm household; T3, terai off-farm household; U, urban household.

The findings suggest that trade liberalization brings about reallocation of resources away from some agriculture and industry (in particular mining and manufacturing) and toward services (hotels and restaurants, and trade, transport, and communication); this is reflected in a fall or rise in the output of these sectors. Prices decline most dramatically in agriculture, in the range of 4.0–4.3 percent. This is in line with agriculture's high initial level of protection.

Most importantly, the changes in agricultural output are not uniform across regions. While paddy output declines in all regions, the decline is sharpest in the hills and mountains. Output of other food crops increases in the terai but declines in the hills and mountains. This pattern is reversed only in the case of cash crops, livestock and fisheries, and forestry. In contrast, the changes (increase or decline) in industrial and services output are more or less constant across regions.

Wages (both skilled and unskilled) decline the least in urban areas; the decline in returns to agricultural capital and land is least in the hills and mountains. While all household categories experience a decline in their incomes, the loss is least (−1.8 percent) for urban households, while it is high (−3.3 percent) for households in the hills and mountains (where households derive most of their income from land and unskilled labor) that experience a large fall in their factor prices.

The impact of trade liberalization on poverty (head count ratio) shows a negligible decline (−0.01 percent) for the country as a whole. At a regional level the urban and terai regions show a decline in poverty (−0.07 and −0.19 percent, respectively), but there is a rise in poverty in the hills and mountains (0.15 percent). The poverty gap measure (Foster, Greer, Thorbecke index), evaluated for various poverty lines, reveals a slight reduction in the depth of poverty in rural areas among the very poorest and a clear rise in poverty among the moderately poor, while very wealthy households experience increased income from trade liberalization.

Given these effects of liberalization, with winners and losers, there is a clear basis for public safety nets. Nepal has a long history of government intervention in food markets, the most important being the NFC. The domestic food market reforms in Nepal considered here are related to significant changes in the NFC.

## Food Security Policies and the Place of the NFC

The NFC was established to serve as a safety net for the vulnerable sections of the population. Food distribution in the remote hill and mountain districts is managed through the NFC and District Disaster Management Committees. The NFC is intended to act as a conduit between the food-surplus and food-deficit regions, thereby improving the availability of food in remote regions. How well has the NFC met its objectives?

During 1996–2001 NFC sales declined by almost 50 percent, while the share of sales to remote areas increased (Table 4.8). This allocation trend seems to be in the right direction, yet it may still be suboptimal given the relative needs of the areas. One relevant outcome indicator is the level of food prices: in the absence of intervention, these should be much higher in remote areas, so a relatively more even price distribution would reflect an effective market intervention. Wallace (1987) demonstrated that food prices were lower in the Kathmandu valley (with its richer population) than elsewhere.

Table 4.8    Food distribution quota and sales by district (MT)

| Year/indicator | Inaccessible districts | | Accessible districts | |
|---|---|---|---|---|
| | Quota | Sales | Quota | Sales |
| 1998/99 | 15,435 | 17,790 | 26,000 | 30,097 |
| 1999/2000 | 13,500 | 14,648 | 22,500 | 10,519 |
| 2000/01 | 11,170 | 9,607 | 20,000 | 9,307 |
| 2001/02 | 10,219 | 7,119 | 20,000 | 15,073 |
| Average | 12,581 | 12,291 | 22,125 | 16,249 |
| Quota as percentage of total | 36.3 | — | 63.7 | — |
| Sales as percentage of total | — | 43.1 | — | 56.9 |
| Sales as percentage of quota | — | 97.7 | — | 73.4 |

Source: NFC (2002).

In the Kathmandu valley the NFC met 15.5 percent of the demand in 1997 (Adhikari and Bohle 1999), a figure that declined to 9 percent in 2002 (Pandey 2003).

Though the share of remote areas has risen over time, the NFC's distribution to those areas has not been targeted effectively at needy households. Data for 1998–2002 indicate that the NFC apportioned only 36 percent of its target quota for the inaccessible regions as against 64 percent for the accessible regions (Table 4.8 and Figure 4.1). The government expenditure is nevertheless quite high: the NFC system has been beset with leakages and inefficiency.

Since the 1975 famine the government has delivered food by air to the Karnali region, which receives about 40–50 percent of the subsidized food. (But note that in 1998 60 percent of the Karnali allocation was for government employees and teachers.) A big part of the subsidy thus accrues to the airlines, with air transport costs in the range of NRs 40–60/kilogram of rice. In contrast, road transport via Tibet would cost only NRs 20/kilogram—and, being more labor intensive, would also generate employment. In 1988, Jumla received 800 MT of rice, 615 MT of it airlifted and the rest transported by mules and porters. Transportation of 185 MT to Jumla requires about 27,550 man-days, or 6 man-days for every 40 kilograms. If the 615 MT had been transported by porters instead of aircraft, it would have generated over 92,000 man-days (353 man-years) of employment. Indeed, in the mountainous regions of Nepal, the World Food Program (WFP) runs a food-for-portering program, selecting porters from among the poor and landless. This option, however, has not been applied by government on any significant scale.

As a result of all the factors discussed, NFC's distribution in most food-deficit and moderately food-deficit areas (38 districts) mitigated less than 4 percent of the food deficit in 1994 (ANZDEC 2002). Much of the distribution of the NFC is directed toward the richer Kathmandu valley, as Figures 4.2 and 4.3 show.

Figure 4.1    Sales by Nepal Food Corporation, 1990–2001

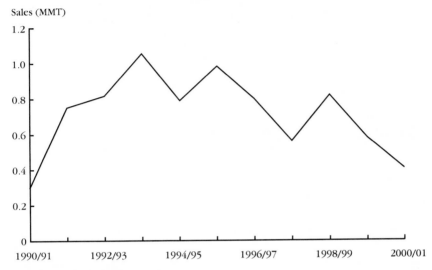

Source: Nepal Food Corporation (2002).

Figure 4.2    Total grain distributed by Nepal Food Corporation, 1974–2002

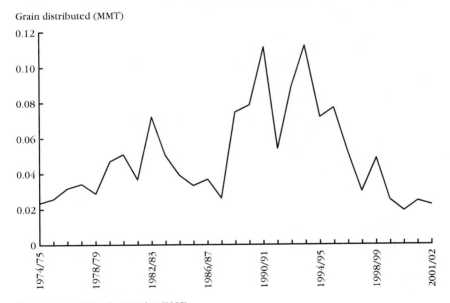

Source: Nepal Food Corporation (2002).

**Figure 4.3    Share of Kathmandu valley in Nepal Food Corporation distribution, 1974–2002**

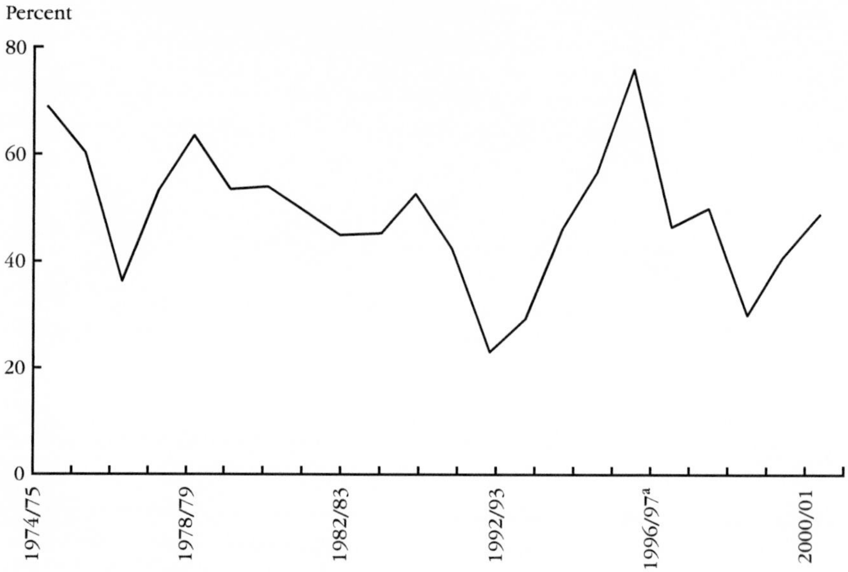

Percent

Source: Nepal Food Corporation (2002).
[a]Years with distribution of only rice.

The accumulated losses of the NFC were a whopping NRs 884 million (Nepal rupees) until 1990 and grew to NRs 905 million by 1996 (APROSC 1998). Perry (2000) estimated that the NFC requires US$7–1,176/MT in internal transport and handling costs (ITHC), depending upon the remoteness of the district. Based on NFC accounts, we estimate the average ITHC at NRs 27/kilogram. The cost of transporting rice is estimated at NRs 49/kilogram (for 2004)—higher than the average price of rice per kilogram even at the height of the food price crisis. NFC has not been successful in meeting its food security objectives in a cost-effective manner. Various reforms have been attempted to improve its functioning.

## Reforms of the NFC

Reforms of the NFC have included closure of depots, downsizing, and a greater reliance on open-market operations for procurement. The NFC withdrew sales depots from 29 districts and reduced the number of depots from 135 to 67 (effective January 1, 2000). Branch offices were also reduced, from 26 to 19. Has this reform improved efficiency?

Most of the 68 abandoned depots are located in accessible areas rather than remote areas. The reform proposal specified a preference for maintaining NFC service in the areas affected by Maoist political activity. Nevertheless, two depots in the Maoist-affected Jajarkot district were also closed. Depots in areas lacking accessible roads—like Humla, Jumla, and Mugu—were also withdrawn. As part of its downsizing, the NFC terminated 305 temporary employees and accepted the resignation of 125 staff members based on voluntary retirement. Further downsizing seems unlikely due to pressure from the employees' union.

Historically the NFC procured food from local markets or directly from farmers in food-surplus areas, at a price equal to or above the MSP. Following liberalization, the government discontinued the MSP, so the NFC procured rice on the open market. The amount of its direct purchases from farmers varied over time (Figure 4.4). Appendix Figure A4.5 shows the trends in procurement price. The greater reliance on open-market operations has led to a decline in food procurements by the NFC and consequent declines in government stocks and godown capacity utilization (Figure 4.5).

One of the most pertinent indicators of the effect of reforms is improvement in the cost effectiveness of food procurement and distribution. As we will see, inefficiencies continue to keep cost effectiveness low, even after reforms.

**Figure 4.4    Purchases by Nepal Food Corporation, 1990–2001**

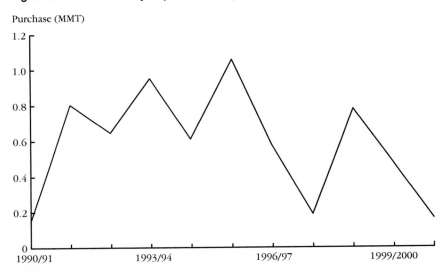

Purchase (MMT)

Source: Nepal Food Corporation (2002).

**Figure 4.5   Trends in godown capacity utilization ratio, 1974–2001**

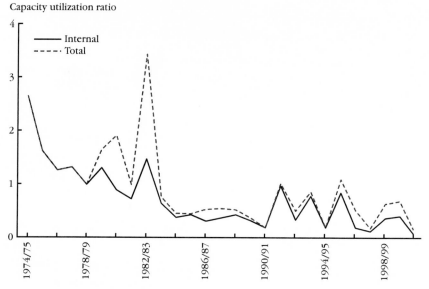

Source: Nepal Food Corporation (2002).

## Effectiveness of the Public Distribution System Pre- and Postreform

In order to assess the efficiency of the NFC, we estimate the average market handling ratio (that is, the quantity of food handled per unit of staff) for total volume as well as internal purchases. The total market handling ratio peaked at 132 MT per staff member in 1982/83. But by 1997/98, the ratio had decreased to 20 MT, reflecting an increase in the number of permanent staff and the lower quantity of goods distributed (Figure 4.5). The performance for domestic procurement was even worse: the efficiency ratio declined from 74 MT to 10 MT during 1991–2001. As discussed previously, air transport of grains has been very expensive—and it continues even after reforms. Moreover, the transport subsidy increased every year until 1998–2001.

In comparing the cost effectiveness of the private sector, it is important to note that, though it has expanded over the past decade, the private sector in Nepal is still comparatively small. Furthermore there are several operational differences, particularly in terms of grades and standards. Compared to that for the private sector, the NFC price is in fact lower. In Jumla, for example, the average market price of coarse rice in 2003 was NRs 50/kg, while the NFC price was NRs 24/kilogram—though the cost of air transportation has not been factored in. In addition the government has to make provision for godowns in the food-deficit districts (these have also been left out of the price estimate). This raises the NFC's overhead costs relative to those of the private sector.

The handling charges for the NFC are also much higher, but these are not necessarily related to inefficiency (Table 4.9). The NFC adheres to minimum quality standards as per the Food Grain Quality Act 1966 (in terms of moisture content, foreign materials, and so forth). The quality of the food in the private sector, in contrast, is poorer and unmonitored. Transportation costs are also higher for the public sector, due to a 10 percent value added tax, and the standard truckload for the public sector is smaller, owing to regulations. The private sector usually hires vehicles without any bid bond requirement.

Little information is available regarding marketing costs in the private sector. When we estimate marketing cost as a fraction of the prevailing sales price for the NFC, the results show that the NFC incurs a loss of 52 percent of the consumer price in the Kathmandu valley; losses are expected to be even higher in remote areas. On items for which marketing costs are somewhat comparable, the public sector has much higher costs. Particularly in packaging, processing, and physical loss—where economies of scale have little effect on the unit price—costs are much higher for the public sector.

The losses of NFC are indeed largely attributable to high marketing costs, mainly handling costs (accounting for 36 percent of total marketing cost, or 16 percent of the consumer price). On the revenue side, conversely, NFC prices are lower

Table 4.9  Marketing cost of coarse rice in Kathmandu, by agency, 1982 (NRs/MT)

| Operation | NFC | Private sector |
|---|---|---|
| Sales price | 3,651 | 5,017 |
| Farmer's share | 3,706 | 3,464 |
| Marketing cost | 1,614 | 951 |
| Transport cost | 293 | 522 |
| Physical losses | 115 | 71 |
| Milling cost | 72 | 67 |
| Packaging | 101 | 24 |
| Handling | 580 | 71 |
| Storage | 433 | 188 |
| Taxes | 20 | 8 |
| Wholesaler | 161 | 251 |
| Miller | 13 | 201 |
| Retailer | 55 | 150 |
| Institution (NFC) | (–1,898) | — |

Source: Estimates are based on Munakarmi (1985).

Note: —, missing data.

than open-market prices. Higher administrative costs, interest charges on accumulated losses, and a lower sales price have resulted in heavy losses for the NFC.

Thus, in spite of the several reforms of the NFC, efficiency indicators do not show improvements vis-à-vis the private sector. Given the higher efficiency of the private sector and its still limited role, there is a basis for exploring public-private partnership to ensure greater food security overall and to mitigate the disparity across sectors. For example, collaboration with the private sector in packaging, processing, or storage could minimize physical loss of foodgrains.

## Conclusions

Following border trade liberalization, several indicators of food security did improve in Nepal, reflected particularly in a rise in per capita food availability and a decline in malnourishment. However, the impact has been markedly asymmetric across regions. The remote areas in the hills and the mountains have not benefited from liberalization, while the terai have reaped most of the benefits.

The domestic reforms in Nepal have mostly taken the form of restructuring the NFC. There has been an active downsizing of the NFC, with a closure of depots and a reduction in personnel. However, the NFC continues to be mistargeted and comparatively inefficient relative to the private sector.

Two categories of policy suggestions can be made for Nepal. The short- to medium-run policy should aim for greater involvement of the private sector in handling, transport, storage, and marketing, by providing incentives in these areas, where the private sector seems to be more efficient. Partnership might entail, for example, sharing transportation and storage facilities. The government could explore other options for reducing costs, for instance by shifting to ground transportation of grains, which would not only reduce costs but also create employment. This by itself would contribute to food security, along the lines of the food-for-portering program undertaken by the WFP.

In the long run the government must ultimately take steps toward greater spatial integration of markets by creating needed marketing and physical infrastructure, especially to link remote regions with food-surplus regions and with the entry points for international trade. In South Asia the experience of Nepal contrasts starkly with that of Bangladesh. Bangladesh invested in the integration of markets through building roadways and to a lesser extent waterways, and as a result the benefits of liberalization in that country have been much more widespread than in Nepal.

**Appendix Table A4.1    Profile of South Asia, 2002**

| Indicator | Unit | Bangladesh | India | Nepal | Pakistan | Sri Lanka |
|---|---|---|---|---|---|---|
| GDP | Constant 1995 US$ (millions) | 53,758.7 | 517,263.2 | 5,806.3 | 75,118.6 | 17,048.8 |
| Growth rate (%) | | 5.1 | 5.4 | 3.6 | 3.2 | 3.5 |
| GDP per capita | Constant 1995 US$ | 396.2 | 493.3 | 240.7 | 518.4 | 898.8 |
| Growth rate (%) | | 3.3 | 3.6 | 1.2 | 0.7 | 2.1 |
| Agricultural GDP | Percent of total GDP | 22.7 | 22.7 | 40.8 | 23.2 | 20.1 |
| Growth rate (%) | | 3.7 | 1.5 | 3.3 | 2.0 | 1.6 |
| Employment in agriculture | Percent of total employment | 62.1 | 66.7 | 78.5 | 48.4 | 41.6 |
| Trade | Percent of GDP | 33.3 | 30.8 | 44.9 | 37.7 | 79.0 |
| Trade in goods | Percent of GDP | 29.4 | 20.8 | 35.8 | 35.8 | 65.2 |
| Poverty gap | At US$1.00 a day (%) | 8.1 | 8.2 | 9.7 | 2.4 | 1.0 |
| | At US$2.00 a day (%) | 36.3 | 35.3 | 37.5 | 22.0 | 13.5 |
| Poverty headcount, national | Percent of total population | 49.8 | 28.6 | 42.0 | 32.6 | 25.0 |
| | Percent of rural population | 53.0 | 30.2 | 44.0 | 35.9 | 27.0 |
| | Percent of urban population | 36.6 | 24.7 | 23.0 | 24.2 | 15.0 |
| GINI index | Percent | 31.8 | 32.5 | 36.7 | 33.0 | 34.4 |
| Undernourished population | Percent in 1999–2001 | 32.0 | 21.0 | 17.0 | 19.0 | 25.0 |
| Underweight children under age 5 | Percent in 1996–2002 | 48.0 | 47.0 | 48.0 | 38.0 | 33.0 |
| Stunted children under age 5 | Percent in 1996–2002 | 45.0 | 45.0 | 51.0 | 36.0 | 20.0 |
| Low birth weight | Percent of births in 1998–2000 | 30.0 | 30.0 | 21.0 | 19.0 | 22.0 |
| Infant mortality rate | Per 1,000 live births | 48.0 | 65.0 | 62.0 | 76.0 | 16.0 |
| Under-5 mortality rate | Per 1,000 live births | 73.0 | 90.0 | 83.0 | 101.0 | 19.0 |

**Source: World Bank (2004).**

**Appendix Table A4.2    Production, availability, and consumption of cereals in South Asia (thousands of MT)**

| Year | Production | Imports | Stock change[a] | Exports | Availability[b] | Consumption | Net imports as percentage of availability | Availability (kg per capita per annum) | Consumption (kg per capita per annum) |
|---|---|---|---|---|---|---|---|---|---|
| Bangladesh | | | | | | | | | |
| 1971–75 | 11,380 | 2,036 | −924 | 0 | 12,492 | 11,512 | 16.3 | 174.6 | 160.9 |
| 1981–85 | 15,668 | 1,854 | −688 | 4 | 16,829 | 15,597 | 11.0 | 183.1 | 169.7 |
| 1991–95 | 18,948 | 1,472 | 1,354 | 0 | 21,774 | 20,025 | 6.8 | 185.1 | 170.2 |
| 2002 | 26,924 | 2,826 | −460 | 1 | 29,289 | 26,912 | 9.6 | 203.7 | 187.1 |
| India | | | | | | | | | |
| 1971–75 | 93,739 | 3,960 | −1,116 | 160 | 96,423 | 85,293 | 3.9 | 162.4 | 143.6 |
| 1981–85 | 127,882 | 1,560 | −3,285 | 529 | 125,628 | 111,248 | 0.8 | 171.3 | 151.7 |
| 1991–95 | 166,434 | 431 | 388 | 2,067 | 165,186 | 144,765 | −1.0 | 184.1 | 161.4 |
| 2002 | 174,655 | 54 | 23,826 | 9,485 | 189,051 | 165,662 | −5.0 | 180.1 | 157.8 |
| Nepal | | | | | | | | | |
| 1971–75 | 2,809 | 4 | −156 | 166 | 2,491 | 2,029 | **−6.5** | 193.7 | 157.8 |
| 1981–85 | 3,186 | 50 | −20 | 45 | 3,171 | 2,701 | **0.1** | 199.4 | 169.9 |
| 1991–95 | 4,478 | 45 | −5 | 2 | 4,516 | 3,805 | **0.9** | 226.1 | 190.6 |
| 2002 | 5,839 | 38 | 57 | 10 | 5,924 | 4,773 | **0.5** | 240.7 | 193.9 |
| Sri Lanka | | | | | | | | | |
| 1971–75 | 945 | 938 | 112 | 2 | 1,992 | 1,898 | **47.0** | 152.9 | 145.7 |
| 1981–85 | 1,635 | 731 | −7 | 1 | 2,360 | 2,205 | **31.0** | 155.4 | 145.3 |
| 1991–95 | 1,745 | 1,025 | −37 | 16 | 2,718 | 2,509 | **37.1** | 155.9 | 143.9 |
| 2002 | 1,938 | 1,306 | −252 | 10 | 2,982 | 2,745 | **43.5** | 157.7 | 145.2 |

Source: FAO (2005).

Note: Average values are reported for the five-year periods, except for 2001 and 2002, which are annual data.

[a]Positive (negative) values indicate stock depletion (addition to stocks).

[b]Availability = Production + imports + stock change − exports.

**Appendix Figure A4.1   Daily per capita calorie consumption, South Asia,
1971–2002**

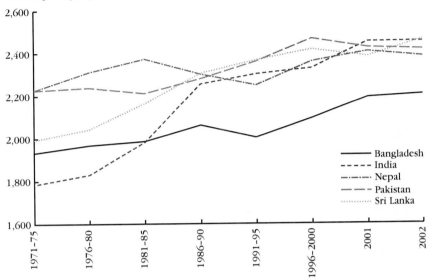

Source: FAO (2005).

**Appendix Figure A4.2   Daily per capita protein consmption, South Asia,
1971–2002**

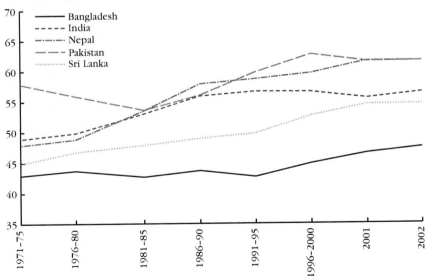

Source: FAO (2005).

## Appendix Figure A4.3  Daily per capita fat consumption, South Asia, 1971–2002

Fat per capita per day (grams)

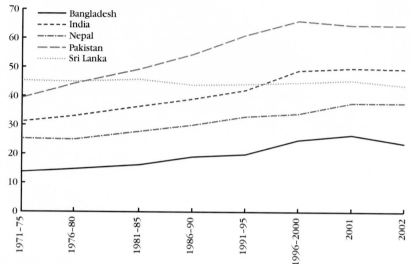

— Bangladesh
--- India
-·-·- Nepal
---- Pakistan
········ Sri Lanka

Source: FAO (2005).

## Appendix Figure A4.4  Hierarchical geography in Nepal, selected years

Outcomes

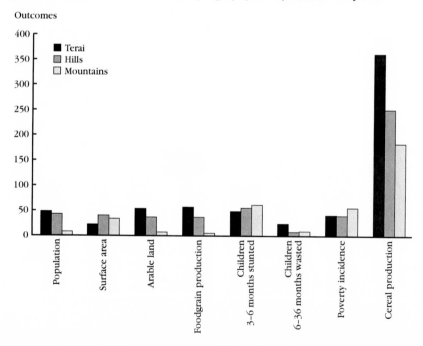

■ Terai
▨ Hills
☐ Mountains

Notes: Population (year 2001), surface area (year 2001), arable land (year 1992), and foodgrain production (during the 1990s) represent percentage shares. Children 3–6 months stunted, children 6–36 months wasted, and poverty incidence (all year 2001) are expressed as percentages. Cereal production is expressed as kilograms per capita per year during the 1990s.
Sources: Sharma (2002), World Bank (2004), and FAO (2005).

**Appendix Figure A4.5    Trends in public procurement prices, 1990–2001**

Procurement price (thousands NRs/MT)

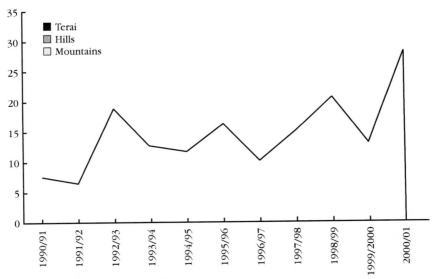

Source: Nepal Food Corporation (2002).

## Notes

1. Indicators like stunting and wasting depend also on a country's health care delivery systems; the systems in Nepal are generally inferior to those in the rest of south Asia.

2. Poverty and food insecurity in Nepal have been checked to some extent only by remittances from abroad; these totaled NRs 100 billion in 2002.

## References

Adhikari, J., and H.-G. Bohle. 1999. *Food crisis in Nepal.* New Delhi: Adriot.

Agricultural Projects Services Center (APROSC). 1998. *A comprehensive study on future role of the Nepal Food Corporation.* Kathmandu.

Agricultural Projects Services Center (APROSC) and John Mellor Associates (JMA). 1995. *Nepal: Agricultural perspective plan.* Kathmandu and Washington, D.C.

ANZDEC. 2002. *Nepal agriculture sector performance review,* Volume 1: *Main text.* Draft final report. Auckland, New Zealand: ANZDEC.

Bajracharya, B. B. 2001. *Poverty reduction: National strategies for sustainable development.* Paper presented at the National Consultative Workshop, held in Kathmandu, Nepal, January 30.

Central Bureau of Statistics (CBS). 1994. *National Sample Census of Agriculture Nepal, 1991/92, Analysis of Results.* Kathmandu.

———. 1996a. *Nepal living standards survey report,* Volume 1. Kathmandu.

———. 1996b. *Nepal living standards survey report,* Volume 2. Kathmandu.

———. 2002. *Nepal Multi-Indicator Surveys.* Kathmandu.

Cockburn, J. 2001. A computable general equilibrium (CGE) micro-simulation model: An application to Nepal. Paper presented at the meeting on Micro Impacts of Macroeconomic and Adjustment Policies Modelers, held in Singapore, April 30–May 5.

Food and Agricultural Marketing Services Department (FAMSD). 1982. *Food statistics of Nepal 1981.* Kathmandu.

Food and Agriculture Organization of the United Nations (FAO). 2005. FAOstat. http://faostat .fao.org/. Accessed November 2007.

Gurung, H. 1989. *Nepal: Dimensions of development.* Kathmandu: Saroj Gurung.

Ministry of Finance. 1997. *Economic survey of Nepal 1996/97.* Kathmandu.

Munakarmi, R. B. 1985. *A case study: Marketing cost and margins of major commodities in Nepal.* Kathmandu: Department of Food and Agriculture Marketing Services.

National Planning Commission (NPC). 1985. *The seventh five-year plan (1985–90).* Kathmandu.

———. 1998. *The ninth plan (1997–2002).* Kathmandu.

———. 2001. *Approach paper to tenth plan (2002–07).* Kathmandu.

National Sample Census of Agriculture (NSCA). 1992. *National sample census of agriculture.* Kathmandu.

Nepal Food Corporation (NFC). 2002. *Progress reports* (various issues). Kathmandu.

Nepal Rastra Bank (NRB). 2002. *WTO and Nepal.* Research Department. Kathmandu.

Pandey, P. R. 2003. Agreement on agriculture: Issues of market access for South Asian countries. *South Asia Economic Journal* 4 (1): 19–40.

Perry, S. 2000. *Enabling development: Food assistance in Nepal (final draft).* Kathmandu: World Food Program, Nepal.

Sapkota, P. R. 2002. *Trade liberalization and poverty in Nepal: An applied general equilibrium analysis.* Ottawa: International Development Research Centre.

Sharma, K. 2000. *Liberalization and structural change: Evidence from Nepalese manufacturing.* Center Discussion Paper 812. New Haven, Conn., U.S.A.: Economics Growth Center, Yale University.

Sharma, S. K. 2002. Food security in Nepal. In *Economic reforms and food security: The impact of trade and technology in South Asia,* ed. S. C. Babu and A. Gulati. Washington, D.C.: International Food Policy Research Institute.

Uma, G. 1993. Sustainable livelihood security of villages surrounding the Pichavaram Mangrove Forest, India. *Indian Geographical Journal.* 68 (1): 33–47.

Wallace, M. B. 1987. *Food price policy in Nepal.* Research Report 3. Winrock Project. Kathmandu: His Majesty's Government of Nepal, U.S. Agency for International Development (USAID), German Agency for Technical Cooperation (GTZ), International Development Research Centre (IDRC), and Ford Foundation.

World Bank. 2004. *World development indicators.* CD-ROM. Washington, D.C.

# Chapter 5

# Impact of Domestic Agricultural Trade Liberalization and Market Reform Policies on Food Security in Pakistan

Munir Ahmad, Caesar Cororaton, Abdul Qayyum,
Muhammad Iqbal, and Paul Dorosh

Agriculture is an important sector of Pakistan's economy, contributing 23 percent to gross domestic product (GDP) and 42 percent to employment. The performance of the agricultural sector over the four decades from 1960 to 2008 was satisfactory, with an average growth rate of 3.5 percent per annum, although there were wide year-to-year fluctuations. The livestock subsector grew relatively faster than other agricultural subsectors, with an annual growth rate of 3.6 percent. The growth in cereal production was nearly 3.3 percent. Cereals constitute roughly 96 percent of the total foodgrains output, including all pulses. Within cereals, wheat is the major foodgrain, contributing about 73 percent to the total production of cereals.

Among foodgrains, wheat and rice production grew the most rapidly, at 3.7 percent per annum over the same period, while the growth rates of maize, other cereals, gram, and other pulses were 3.4, 0.13, 0.05, and 0.3 percent, respectively (Table 5.1). The major factor contributing to the growth in production of wheat, rice, and maize has been higher productivity per unit of land; for other foodgrains land productivity growth is only marginal. This difference reflects, first, the disparity in technological breakthroughs in seed and production technologies (with public-sector research and development focusing on major crops, including wheat, cotton, and rice), and second, a shift in consumption patterns toward superior cereals.

Table 5.1    Growth rates of area, yield, and production for various foodgrains, 1959/60 to 2007/08 (percent)

| Parameter | Wheat | Rice | Maize | Other cereals | All cereals | Gram | Other pulses |
|---|---|---|---|---|---|---|---|
| Area | 1.17 | 1.60 | 1.52 | −0.78 | 1.01 | −0.34 | −0.35 |
| Yield | 2.50 | 1.99 | 1.80 | 0.93 | 2.44 | 0.39 | 0.66 |
| Production | 3.72 | 3.66 | 3.38 | 0.13 | 3.50 | 0.05 | 0.30 |

Source: Government of Pakistan (2008, various years).

The government of Pakistan has a history of intervening in agricultural markets, resulting in underpricing of commodities relative to world levels (Dorosh and Valdes 1990; Hamid, Nabi, and Nasim 1990; Chaudhry 2001). Most government interventions have now been removed, and the markets operate freely—except that for wheat. The wheat market is characterized by significant government interventions in pricing, procurement, stocking, distribution, and transportation. These interventions involve high levels of subsidy every year, ranging from Rs 2.8 billion in 1990/91 to Rs 12.4 billion in 2002/03 (Faruqee 2005).

Various empirical studies on government interventions in wheat marketing in Pakistan have relied on partial equilibrium analysis, which does not capture the policy effects in all sectors of the economy (Dorosh and Valdes 1990; Hamid, Nabi, and Nasim 1990; Barkley 1992; Abedullah and Ali 2001; Ashfaq, Griffith, and Parton 2001). This chapter adds to that literature by providing a detailed review of government policies in agriculture (and for wheat in particular), using the computable general equilibrium (CGE) framework to analyze the economywide effects of trade liberalization in wheat. The impacts of "liberalization" of wheat quantified in this chapter are, it must be emphasized, the results of counterfactual simulations using the CGE model; they indicate the potential gains or losses that actual reforms could bring about.

The chapter is divided into six sections. The second section reviews the interventions of the government in agriculture, particularly in output and trade. This section also discusses how the government intervenes in the procurement and distribution of two major crops: wheat and rice. The third section examines major food security issues in the country in terms of stability in supply of foodgrains, food accessibility, and nutritional status of the population. In the fourth section, the chapter evaluates the effectiveness of these interventions. In the fifth section, it assesses the welfare implications of removing consumption subsidies and producer taxes using a general equilibrium model. The last section gives a summary of findings and conclusions.

## Government Interventions in Agriculture: An Overview

The history of government interventions in both agricultural output and inputs markets in Pakistan goes back to the inception of the country in 1947. As in most other developing countries, these interventions have sought to supply food to urban consumers at low prices—to the detriment of farmers. These policies present a contrast to the situation in developed countries, where farming communities are supported at the expense of taxpayers. Table 5.2 summarizes the evolution of important policies affecting agriculture in Pakistan.

## Output Markets and Trade

After independence the country was confronted with major problems relating to settlement, shortage of food in deficit areas, revenue constraints, and the balance of payment (Hamid, Nabi, and Nasim 1990). In response the government resorted to interventionist policies in trade and domestic markets. It pursued import substitution in manufacturing by imposing duties and controls on imports of manufactures, and it levied export taxes on raw cotton and jute in order to supply cheap raw materials to the local textile industry.

This policy resulted in an overvalued exchange rate that acted as an indirect tax on agriculture (Hamid, Nabi, and Nasim 1990). The prices for most agricultural commodities were kept considerably lower than world prices, and moreover these commodities were subject to compulsory procurement by government agencies. To ensure procurement, the movement of agricultural goods from one district to another was banned in most cases, with the exception of cotton (Turvey and Cook

**Table 5.2    Evolution of policies affecting agriculture**

| Date | Milestone |
|---|---|
| 1960s | Price support system for wheat. Later extended to rice, cotton, sugarcane, maize, potato, onion, gram, and oilseeds. |
| | Compulsory procurement replaced by voluntary procurement. |
| 1972 | Devaluation of currency by 131%. |
| 1970s | Establishment of REC and PASSCO. |
| 1979–80 | Structural adjustment program initiated; change from fixed to flexible exchange rate. |
| 1981 | APCOM established to recommend prices based on cost of production. |
| | System of sugar rationing, zoning of sugar mills, and compulsory rice procurement discontinued. |
| 1985–86 | Private sector allowed limited role in rice trading. |
| 1990s | REC and CEC merged with TCP. |
| | Private sector allowed entry to export rice, raw cotton, fruits, and vegetables. |

Note: APCOM, Agricultural Prices Commission; CEC, Cotton Export Corporation; PASSCO, Pakistan Agricultural Storage and Supplies Corporations; REC, Rice Export Corporation; TCP, Trading Corporation of Pakistan.

1976; Chaudhry 2001). As a result the agriculture sector performed poorly, resulting in countrywide food crises during the 1950s.

To overcome these crises, a formal support price system was initiated in the 1960s by fixing the price of wheat. Later rice, cotton, sugarcane, maize, potato, onion, gram, and oilseed crops were also included. The objective was to shield farmers against a fall in prices during the postharvest period. The policy of compulsory procurement was replaced by a voluntary one, and agricultural prices were set higher than the world level. Exports and movement of commodities, however, were still banned (Chaudhry 1995).

This farmer-friendly trend in commodity price policy was reversed in the 1970s. Pakistan devalued the rupee against the U.S. dollar by about 131 percent in 1972. Since most agricultural inputs were imported, the prices of inputs increased significantly. Various institutional and structural changes were also introduced, establishing state-owned enterprises and nationalizing existing ones to enhance government control over marketing and distribution. Among the several state-owned enterprises established during the 1970s, two played a direct role in foodgrains marketing. These were the Rice Export Corporation (REC), responsible for procurement and monopoly in rice exports, and the Pakistan Agricultural Storage and Supplies Corporations (PASSCO), which (along with the provincial food departments) attended to price stabilization, mainly for wheat.

The new policy of nationalization and excessive government control adversely affected the country's macroeconomic situation. To stabilize the economy the government undertook a structural adjustment program in 1979/80, supported by the International Monetary Fund (IMF) and the World Bank. The objective of the program was to eliminate price and trade distortions by gradually moving away from interventionist policies. As part of the reforms, there was a shift from a fixed exchange rate to flexible rates; this resulted in a devaluation of more than 30 percent in the early 1980s, reaching 100 percent in 1991.

Interventions in commodity markets continued during the 1980s, with a new system under which prices were fixed according to the recommendations of the Agricultural Prices Commission (APCOM), set up in 1981; these price recommendations were based on the cost of production. In contrast, the system of sugar rationing, the zoning of sugar mills, and compulsory rice procurement were discontinued. The private sector was permitted to play a limited role in rice trading beginning in 1985/86, and the government reduced the intervention of the REC. PASSCO was assigned the implementation of the support price for paddy, though its role overall remained negligible.

The process of trade liberalization continued during the 1990s. The role of the REC gradually declined, and it, along with the Cotton Export Corporation (CEC), was merged into the Trading Corporation of Pakistan (TCP). The private sector was allowed to participate in the export of agricultural commodities like rice, raw cotton, fruits, and vegetables. Some incentives were also provided to the private sector: a duty drawback; a 25 percent freight subsidy on fruits, vegetables, and fresh fish; and export financing. The government encouraged the export of wheat and its milling products by both the private and public sectors, with an announced subsidy of Rs 3,250 per metric ton (amounting to about US$1 million in 2001). The subsidy was reduced to Rs 2,500 per metric ton in 2002/03.

Despite efforts to liberalize agriculture, the government continues to fix support prices and procure certain commodities, and it continues to promote parastatal organizations such as the provincial food departments (PFDs), PASSCO, and the TCP.

As part of the structural adjustment program, a reduction in border protections was also initiated during the mid-1980s. The maximum applied tariff rates were reduced from 225 percent in 1987/88 to 70 percent in 1995, and in recent years to 25 percent (Table 5.3). Though there are no domestic market distortions, high rates of border protection continue in edible oils. All nontariff barriers have been dismantled completely. Import surcharges and license fees were removed during 1993–95 (FAO 2000). All items, including textile products, are freely importable, except for 30 that are restricted (mostly on religious, environmental, security, and health grounds).

Table 5.3   Bound and applied tariff rates, selected years, 1995–2005 (percent)

| Products | Bound rate | 1995 | 1998 | 2000 | 2002 | 2005 |
|---|---|---|---|---|---|---|
| Cereals | 100–150 | 0–65 | 0–25 | 0–15 | 0–25 | 0–25 |
| Wheat | 150 | 0 | 0 | 0 | 25 | 0 |
| Wheat flour | 150 | 10 | 10 | 10 | 10 | 10 |
| Rice | 100 | 25 | 25 | 15 | 5–10 | 5–10 |
| Oilseeds | 100 | 10–70 | 0–45 | 0–15 | 0–10 | 0–10 |
| Vegetable oils[a] | 100 | 25–70 | 15–45 | 15–35 | 10–25 | 5–25 |
| Live animals | 100 | 15–65 | 10–45 | 10–35 | 5–25 | 5–25 |
| Meat | 100 | 35–70 | 15–45 | 10–35 | 10–25 | 5–25 |
| Dairy | 100 | 25–70 | 25–45 | 25–35 | 25 | 5–25 |
| Sugar | 100 | 35–70 | 25–45 | 15–35 | 10–25 | 5–25 |
| Coffee and tea[b] | 100–150 | 15–70 | 15–45 | 25–35 | 20–25 | 5–25 |
| Fruits and vegetables | 100 | 35–65 | 35–65 | — | 10–25 | 5–25 |

Sources: CBR (various years) and FAO (2000).

Note: —, missing data.

[a]There are also specific rates for some oils, for example, soybean oil (crude and refined) at Rs 9,050 per metric ton and palm oil at Rs 10,200–16,850 per metric ton.

[b]The bound rate for coffee is 100 percent and that for tea is 150 percent; the applied rates for tea are also high.

## Procurement and Distribution of Foodgrains for Food Security

The marketing and distribution of foodgrains involves both the private and public sectors. The intermediaries in the marketing chain include village shopkeepers, arthies (commission agents), wholesalers, and beoparies (traders). Foodgrains reach consumers either unprocessed or processed through processors or millers, wholesalers, and retailers. While the private sector deals in all grains, wheat marketing has remained primarily within the purview of the public sector.

### Wheat Marketing

The price of wheat has been a politically sensitive issue in Pakistan. Therefore the federal and provincial governments intervene heavily in wheat marketing, using various instruments to serve their policy objectives, which are to

1. protect producers from price fluctuations through guaranteed minimum support prices;

2. achieve desired output targets;

3. encourage adoption of new technologies;

4. shield consumers against rises in price (particularly urban consumers); and

5. ensure food security.

The government decides the support price according to the recommendations of the APCOM, which are based on the cost of production (Faruqee 2005). The support price is normally announced before the sowing of a crop, in order to enable farmers to respond to the price incentives. The support price represents a minimum floor price, which the government protects through public procurement, and that in fact becomes the de facto procurement price for wheat (Dorosh 2004). Wheat is then procured by PASSCO and the PFDs.

During the interval 1990–2008, the amount of wheat procured has ranged between 15 and 41 percent of total production in the country (Table 5.4). The PFDs procure the major portion (63 percent in 1990, 83 percent in 1999), and the remainder is procured by PASSCO. Punjab is the only surplus province in wheat: up to 95 percent of total procurement comes from this province, and the rest mainly from Sindh. To achieve the procurement targets set by the government, interprovincial

Table 5.4    Government procurement of wheat as a percentage of wheat production,
1990–2008

| Year | Procurement as percent of production | Year | Procurement as percent of production |
|------|-----|------|-----|
| 1990–91 | 21.69 | 1999–2000 | 40.71 |
| 1991–92 | 20.72 | 2000–01 | 21.45 |
| 1992–93 | 25.50 | 2001–02 | 22.19 |
| 1993–94 | 23.95 | 2002–03 | 18.32 |
| 1994–95 | 22.00 | 2003–04 | 17.72 |
| 1995–96 | 20.39 | 2004–05 | 18.23 |
| 1996–97 | 16.37 | 2005–06 | 21.22 |
| 1997–98 | 21.31 | 2006–07 | 18.98 |
| 1998–99 | 22.79 | 2007–08[a] | 14.74 |

Source: Ministry of Finance (2008).
[a]Provisional data.

movement of wheat (and often interdistrict movement as well) is usually banned from May to August.

PASSCO and the PFDs procure wheat either directly from producers or through marketing agents. Suppliers are required to offer fair average quality for procurement or the product is rejected. The supplier bears the cost of transportation to the procurement centers, while the cost of shifting to government storage is borne by the PFD. The procurement centers accept wheat in bulk lots of 10 bags or more (the standard weight of a bag is 100 kilograms). The bags themselves are given to suppliers by the procurement centers, on loan or for purchase.

In addition to their own storage facilities (with a capacity of about 4.5 million tons for all foodgrains), both the PFDs and PASSCO rent space from the private sector. PASSCO normally distributes wheat grain to the armed forces, the Northern Areas, and Pakistan-administered Kashmir. Some of the stock is also sold to the deficit provinces through the PFDs. These are responsible for the public distribution system, releasing wheat at a predetermined uniform issue price to registered millers, based on a quota decided by the provincial and federal governments.[1] Imported wheat is also routed through the PFDs for distribution at the same issue price.

The system of uniform issue prices (which continued until 2001) did not cover all the costs from procurement to distribution. In May 2001 the government introduced cascading release prices, adjusting the issue price for wheat released from its stock according to the month of delivery; this resulted in higher issue prices in the later months of the crop year. The main reason for this change is to reduce government losses and to encourage the participation of the private sector in providing foodgrain storage.

Restrictions on the movements of wheat within the provinces were removed in May 2001 in order to ensure a smooth supply and widespread availability of food, and also to help wheat producers benefit from the price differentials—though in practice that never happened. Furthermore the State Bank of Pakistan allowed banks to finance the private sector's wheat purchases; other incentives included tax exemptions and reduced import duties on materials and facilities used for grain handling and storage (FAO 2003). In principle the government has also allowed the private sector to participate in the export and import of wheat.

The present public procurement and distribution system involves a heavy subsidy, ranging from Rs 2.75 billion in 1990/91 to Rs 12.35 billion in 2002/03; this import subsidy represents the difference between the procurement price and the issue price plus incidental costs (Table 5.5). The major beneficiaries in this process are the flour mills, particularly some of the selected and registered ones. The subsidized rates are applied only to wheat purchased from the government, which accounts for only a part of total capacity; the remaining amount is purchased on the open market. Flour prices are thus determined mainly by market forces.

The wheat pricing and procurement system does not help farmers—particularly the marginal and small farmers, who have only a small marketable surplus or none at all. Though marginal and small farmers may have to buy back wheat during later months of the year, they generally sell wheat grain in the market immediately after the harvest in order to repay loans. As the PFDs and PASSCO accept wheat grain only in bulk (at least 10 bags of 100 kilograms each), they are not an option for these

**Table 5.5    Total federal and provincial budgeted subsidies, 1990–2003 (millions of rupees)**

| Year | Provincial subsidy | Federal subsidy | Total subsidy | Real subsidy[a] |
|---|---|---|---|---|
| 1990–91 | 1,988 | 762 | 2,750 | 6,322 |
| 1991–92 | 1,831 | 2,175 | 4,006 | 8,451 |
| 1992–93 | 1,325 | 2,148 | 3,473 | 6,666 |
| 1993–94 | 2,760 | 354 | 3,114 | 5,378 |
| 1994–95 | 1,890 | 1,449 | 3,339 | 5,098 |
| 1995–96 | 3,169 | 6,648 | 9,817 | 13,522 |
| 1996–97 | 5,173 | 5,761 | 10,934 | 13,482 |
| 1997–98 | 2,443 | 4,119 | 6,562 | 7,499 |
| 1998–99 | 9,375 | — | 9,375 | 10,135 |
| 1999–00 | 6,045 | 923 | 6,968 | 7,273 |
| 2000–01 | 5,502 | 1,356 | 6,858 | 6,858 |
| 2001–02 | 5,940 | 2,668 | 8,608 | 8,317 |
| 2002–03 | 6,671 | 5,681 | 12,352 | 11,566 |

Source: Faruqee (2005).

Note: —, missing data.

[a]Real subsidy computed using the Consumer Price Index, assuming 2000/01 = 100.

farmers. Moreover the PFDs themselves—the main procurers of wheat—operate in the grain markets through commission agents and do not have their own procurement centers.

### Rice Marketing

Rice procurement and trading were long a monopoly of the government, which purchased rice mainly through dealers at procurement centers in the controlled areas. Rice growers were allowed to pool their output to assemble the required 240-bag lots. The dealers would have the paddy processed into rice only at authorized mills; the government banned rural rice-husking mills in controlled areas during procurement season. No dealer was allowed to remove rice from the mills without obtaining a disposal order from the PFD. Rice marketing is now within the purview of the private sector. It remains subject to the support price managed by PASSCO, although no paddy procurement has been reported since 1995/96.

## Trends in Food Security in Pakistan

Trends in food security are assessed along four dimensions: availability, stability, access, and nutritional status.

### Availability of Foodgrains

Pakistan has made significant progress in production of major cereals. Per capita availability of cereals increased from 118 kg in 1961 to 154 kg in 2002; more than 80 percent of the 2002 amount is accounted for by wheat alone (Table 5.6). As the staple food, wheat accounts for over 37 percent of cultivated area. Its performance affects not only economic growth and the import bill but also the nutritional status of the people of Pakistan. It occupies a pivotal position in national food security goals.

The government has tried to maintain availability at the level of 2,400 calories per person per day since the early 1990s, increased from 1,754 calories per person per day in 1961 (Table 5.7). However, daily average availability of calories per person in Pakistan is substantially lower than the averages of other developing and developed countries, by 10 percent and 26 percent, respectively.[2] Changes over time in the composition of food intake show a shrinking share of wheat in total calories available and a rising share from animals and other sources (Table 5.7): the share of wheat declined from 48 percent in 1990 to 41 percent in 2002, while the share of other cereals declined from 20 percent in 1970 to 11 percent in 1990 (remaining at that level since). The share of livestock products in calorie intake increased from 12 percent in 1970 to 18 percent in 2002. The share of other items (vegetable oils, vegetables, fruits, and sweeteners) has been nearly constant since 1980.

Table 5.6     Production and per capita availability of cereals in Pakistan, selected years, 1961–2002 (thousands of tons)

| Year | Production | Change in stock | Imports – Exports | Total availability | Consumption | Per capita availability (kg/year) |
|---|---|---|---|---|---|---|
| | | | Cereals | | | |
| 1961 | 6,167 | −308 | 912 | 6,771 | 6,044 | 117.8 |
| 1970 | 10,999 | 336 | −108 | 11,227 | 10,087 | 153.4 |
| 1980 | 15,513 | −1,216 | −544 | 13,753 | 11,753 | 137.8 |
| 1990 | 19,328 | 248 | 1,305 | 20,881 | 18,504 | 155.2 |
| 1995 | 22,834 | −2,328 | 847 | 21,353 | 18,729 | 137.5 |
| 2000 | 28,062 | −2,204 | −1,023 | 24,835 | 21,570 | 151.2 |
| 2001 | 25,109 | 3,277 | −3,090 | 25,296 | 22,287 | 152.4 |
| 2002 | 24,936 | 3,818 | −2,678 | 26,076 | 23,099 | 154.1 |
| | | | Wheat | | | |
| 1961 | 3,814 | −308 | 1,080 | 4,586 | 4,204 | 81.9 |
| 1970 | 7,294 | 336 | 121 | 7,751 | 7,137 | 108.6 |
| 1980 | 10,856 | −1,217 | 601 | 10,240 | 9,104 | 106.7 |
| 1990 | 14,316 | 248 | 2,045 | 16,609 | 15,162 | 127.3 |
| 1995 | 17,002 | −2,328 | 2,692 | 17,366 | 15,748 | 115.6 |
| 2000 | 21,079 | −1,995 | 987 | 20,071 | 17,959 | 125.9 |
| 2001 | 19,024 | 1,982 | −686 | 20,320 | 18,415 | 125.9 |
| 2002 | 18,227 | 3,469 | −1,013 | 20,683 | 18,859 | 125.8 |

Source: FAO (2004) (August).

Table 5.7     Per capita availability of calories and shares of various sources, selected years, 1961–2002

| | Total | | Wheat | | Other grains | | Pulses | | Animal | | Others | |
|---|---|---|---|---|---|---|---|---|---|---|---|---|
| Year | Calories | Share (%) | Calories | Share (%) | Calories | Share (%) | Calories | Share (%) | Calories | Share (%) | Calories | Share (%) |
| 1961 | 1,754 | 100 | 742 | 42 | 342 | 19 | 114 | 6 | 260 | 15 | 296 | 17 |
| 1970 | 2,203 | 100 | 984 | 45 | 438 | 20 | 77 | 3 | 257 | 12 | 447 | 20 |
| 1980 | 2,124 | 100 | 967 | 46 | 304 | 14 | 49 | 2 | 261 | 12 | 543 | 26 |
| 1990 | 2,410 | 100 | 1,153 | 48 | 274 | 11 | 58 | 2 | 309 | 13 | 616 | 26 |
| 1995 | 2,345 | 100 | 1,048 | 45 | 212 | 9 | 59 | 3 | 353 | 15 | 673 | 29 |
| 2000 | 2,447 | 100 | 1,000 | 41 | 244 | 10 | 68 | 3 | 436 | 18 | 699 | 29 |
| 2001 | 2,426 | 100 | 1,000 | 41 | 256 | 11 | 58 | 2 | 436 | 18 | 676 | 28 |
| 2002 | 2,419 | 100 | 999 | 41 | 275 | 11 | 59 | 2 | 437 | 18 | 649 | 27 |

Source: FAO (2004) (August).

Domestic production, commercial imports, and food aid are the main constituents of food availability at the national level. The production of cereals and pulses has increased more than 3.5-fold since the early 1960s. Nevertheless Pakistan has been importing significant quantities of wheat and pulses to meet the needs of its fast-growing population. The share of imports in wheat consumption during the interval

1961–2003 has varied, declining from 26 percent in 1961 to less than 1 percent in 2003 (Table 5.8). The large wheat deficit during the early 1960s was largely reduced during the 1970s as a consequence of the Green Revolution. Later, however, an increased dependence on wheat imports re-emerged. In the case of rice, in contrast, Pakistan has been quite successful in producing enough for domestic consumption and even generating an exportable surplus (Table 5.9).

### Stability in Supply of Foodgrains

Stability is defined as a steady supply of food at the national level and is thus directly affected by the performance of the agriculture sector. Apart from production, it also entails better management of domestic production, integration of local markets, and rational use of buffer stocks and trade (FAO 2002). Pakistan faced severe floods during 1973 and 1992 and droughts in 1998, 2000, and 2001. Fluctuations and shortages have therefore been common. At times the government has had to import up to one-fifth of the wheat requirement. In order to meet the shortages in deficit and urban areas and to avoid high food prices for consumers, the government has been

Table 5.8   Food balance sheet for wheat, selected years, 1961–2004 (thousands of tons)

| Year | Production | Imports | Change in stock | Exports | Total | Feed, seed, and others | Availability | Import share (%) |
|------|-----------|---------|-----------------|---------|-------|------------------------|--------------|------------------|
| 1961 | 3,814  | 1,080 | −308   | —     | 4,586  | 385   | 4,201  | 26 |
| 1970 | 7,294  | 229   | 336    | 108   | 7,751  | 614   | 7,137  | 3  |
| 1975 | 7,673  | 1,345 | −482   | 4     | 8,532  | 629   | 7,903  | 17 |
| 1980 | 10,856 | 604   | −1,217 | 3     | 10,240 | 1,136 | 9,104  | 7  |
| 1985 | 11,703 | 982   | −589   | 51    | 12,045 | 1,174 | 10,871 | 9  |
| 1990 | 14,316 | 2,047 | −691   | 2     | 15,670 | 1,447 | 14,223 | 14 |
| 1991 | 14,565 | 972   | −983   | 2     | 14,552 | 1,456 | 13,096 | 7  |
| 1992 | 15,684 | 2,018 | −1,443 | 3     | 16,256 | 1,552 | 14,704 | 14 |
| 1993 | 16,156 | 2,890 | −1,965 | 4     | 17,077 | 1,616 | 15,461 | 19 |
| 1994 | 15,213 | 1,902 | 826    | 8     | 17,933 | 1,524 | 16,409 | 12 |
| 1995 | 17,002 | 2,706 | −2,243 | 4     | 17,461 | 1,702 | 15,759 | 17 |
| 1996 | 16,907 | 1,968 | −411   | 8     | 18,456 | 1,763 | 16,693 | 12 |
| 1997 | 16,650 | 2,500 | 215    | 5     | 19,360 | 1,667 | 17,693 | 14 |
| 1998 | 18,694 | 2,534 | −1,841 | 9     | 19,378 | 1,883 | 17,495 | 14 |
| 1999 | 17,856 | 3,240 | −1,507 | 9     | 19,580 | 1,788 | 17,792 | 18 |
| 2000 | 21,079 | 1,048 | −1,995 | 61    | 20,071 | 2,112 | 17,959 | 6  |
| 2001 | 19,024 | 149   | 1,982  | 835   | 20,320 | 1,905 | 18,415 | 1  |
| 2002 | 18,227 | 267   | 3,469  | 1,280 | 20,683 | 1,824 | 18,859 | 1  |
| 2003 | 19,183 | 94    | 590    | 43    | 19,824 | 1,918 | 17,906 | 1  |
| 2004 | 19,335 | 108   | −213   | 553   | 18,677 | 1,934 | 16,743 | 1  |

Source: FAO (2004) (August) and Government of Pakistan (2004).

Note: —, missing data.

Table 5.9    Food balance sheet for rice, selected years, 1961–2000 (thousands of tons)

| Year | Production | Imports | Stock change | Exports | Total | Feed, seed, and others | Availability | Exports share |
|------|-----------|---------|--------------|---------|-------|------------------------|--------------|---------------|
| 1961 | 1,127 | 2 | 0 | 173 | 955 | 109 | 846 | 0.15 |
| 1970 | 2,200 | 0 | 0 | 229 | 1,971 | 159 | 1,812 | 0.10 |
| 1975 | 2,619 | 0 | 0 | 476 | 2,143 | 190 | 1,953 | 0.18 |
| 1980 | 3,125 | 0 | 0 | 1,082 | 2,043 | 220 | 1,823 | 0.35 |
| 1985 | 2,920 | 0 | 0 | 715 | 2,205 | 220 | 1,985 | 0.24 |
| 1990 | 3,262 | 0 | 0 | 741 | 2,522 | 232 | 2,290 | 0.23 |
| 1995 | 3,968 | 0 | 0 | 1,844 | 2,125 | 263 | 1,862 | 0.46 |
| 2000 | 4,805 | 1 | −209 | 2,010 | 2,588 | 807 | 1,781 | 0.42 |

Sources: FAO (2004) (August) and Government of Pakistan (2004).

actively pursuing a policy of support and procurement prices combined with central-ized storage and distribution operations, though at a very high cost.

One of the important indicators of economic access to food is the proportion of people below the poverty line (FAO 1998). Poverty increased in Pakistan during the 1960s despite rapid economic growth, while it declined between 1970 and 1987/88 in spite of relatively slower growth (Table 5.10). The Pakistan economy has continued to grow at a slower pace, with the exception of a few years during the 1990s, and the declining trend in poverty reversed. Nevertheless the daily average *availability* of calo-ries per person has progressively increased over the past four and a half decades—even though this availability has not been consistently reflected in declining poverty. This finding suggests that enhanced food availability at the national level has not translated into actual increased consumption of calorie-rich food at the regional or household level. This could reflect either reduced access to food or a shift in preferences.

The level of poverty is not determined solely by overall income level. Increasing poverty could be due to worsening income inequality, as seen in the Gini coefficients reported in Table 5.10 and in the increasing numbers (and area) of small landhold-ings seen in Table 5.11. Another possible factor is a shift in preferences (away from calorie intake) with rising incomes.

### Nutritional Status

Effective biological absorption of food is as important for food security as availability. Biological food absorption is affected by such factors as sanitation, clean drinking water, quality of food, and consumer awareness of proper food storage and processing practices as well as basic nutrition.[3]

According to the Planning Commission of Pakistan, per capita food intake in the country is higher than the recommended average *at the national level* (Khan 2003).

Table 5.10  Poverty, GDP growth, and inequality, selected years, 1963–2001

| | Head count | | | Food poverty | | | Planning Commission | | | GDP growth (%) | Calories | Gini coefficient |
|---|---|---|---|---|---|---|---|---|---|---|---|---|
| | Overall | Rural | Urban | Overall | Rural | Urban | Overall | Rural | Urban | | | |
| 1963–64 | 40.25 | 38.94 | 44.53 | — | — | — | — | — | — | 6.5 | 1,987 | 0.386 |
| 1966–67 | 44.50 | 45.62 | 40.96 | — | — | — | — | — | — | 3.1 | 2,010 | 0.355 |
| 1968–69 | — | — | — | — | — | — | — | — | — | 6.5 | 2,270 | 0.336 |
| 1969–70 | 46.53 | 49.11 | 38.76 | — | — | — | — | — | — | 9.8 | 2,203 | 0.336 |
| 1970–71 | — | — | — | — | — | — | — | — | — | 1.2 | 2,199 | 0.330 |
| 1971–72 | — | — | — | — | — | — | — | — | — | 2.3 | 2,262 | 0.345 |
| 1978–79 | 30.68 | 32.51 | 25.94 | — | — | — | — | — | — | 5.5 | 2,262 | 0.373 |
| 1984–85 | 24.47 | 25.87 | 21.17 | — | — | — | — | — | — | 8.7 | 2,178 | 0.369 |
| 1985–86 | — | — | — | — | — | — | — | — | — | 6.4 | 2,170 | 0.355 |
| 1986–87 | — | — | — | 26.9 | 29.4 | 24.5 | — | — | — | 0 | 2,315 | 0.346 |
| 1987–88 | 17.32 | 18.32 | 14.99 | 26.4 | 29.9 | 22.7 | — | — | — | 6.4 | 2,175 | 0.348 |
| 1990–91 | 22.11 | 23.59 | 18.64 | 23.3 | 26.2 | 18.2 | — | — | — | 5.6 | 2,231 | 0.407 |
| 1992–93 | 22.32 | 26.24 | 21.70 | 20.3 | 22.5 | 16.8 | — | — | — | 2.3 | 2,356 | 0.410 |
| 1993–94 | 23.60 | 26.30 | 19.40 | 20.8 | 24.4 | 15.2 | — | — | — | 4.5 | 2,409 | 0.400 |
| 1996–97 | 31.00 | 32.00 | 27.00 | 23.6 | 26.3 | 19.4 | — | — | — | 1.9 | 2,466 | 0.373 |
| 1998–99 | 32.60 | 34.80 | 25.90 | 32.6 | 34.8 | 25.9 | 30.6 | 34.7 | 20.9 | 4.2 | 2,456 | 0.410 |
| 2000–01 | — | — | — | — | — | — | 32.1 | 39.0 | 22.7 | 1.8 | 2,426 | 0.454 |

Sources: Amjad and Kemal (1997), Jafri (1999), Qureshi and Arif (1999), Government of Pakistan (2004), and Kemal (2005).

Note: —, missing data.

Table 5.11    Farm classification by farm size, selected years, 1960–2000

| Farm size (ha) | Number of farms (%) | | | | | Farm area (%) | | | | |
|---|---|---|---|---|---|---|---|---|---|---|
| | 1960 | 1972 | 1980 | 1990 | 2000 | 1960 | 1972 | 1980 | 1990 | 2000 |
| <5 | 19.0 | 28.2 | 34.1 | 47.5 | 57.6 | 3.0 | 5.2 | 7.1 | 11.3 | 15.5 |
| 5 to <12.5 | 44.3 | 39.9 | 39.4 | 33.4 | 28.1 | 23.6 | 25.2 | 27.3 | 27.5 | 27.9 |
| 12.5 to <25 | 23.8 | 21.1 | 17.3 | 12.2 | 8.8 | 27.0 | 26.6 | 24.7 | 21.5 | 19.1 |
| 25 to <50 | 9.0 | 7.7 | 6.5 | 4.7 | 3.9 | 19.0 | 18.8 | 17.8 | 15.8 | 16.3 |
| 50 to <150 | 3.3 | 2.7 | 2.4 | 1.8 | 1.2 | 16.0 | 15.1 | 14.7 | 13.9 | 9.6 |
| >150 | 0.5 | 0.4 | 0.3 | 0.3 | 0.2 | 11.5 | 9.1 | 8.5 | 10.1 | 11.6 |
| Total | 100.0 | 100.0 | 100.0 | 100.0 | 100.0 | 100.0 | 100.0 | 100.0 | 100.0 | 100.0 |

Source: Malik (2003).

Nonetheless, one-third of all pregnant women were malnourished and over 25 percent of babies had low birth weight in 2001/02. Malnutrition was a major problem, responsible for more than 30 percent of all infant and child deaths in the country in 2001/02. The incidence of moderate to severe underweight, stunting, and wasting among children less than 5 years of age was about 38, 37, and 13 percent, respectively, in 2001/02 (Planning Commission and UNICEF 2004). Malnourishment among mothers (as reflected in body mass index) was 21 percent in 2001/02 (Khan 2003).

## Consequences and Cost Effectiveness of the Existing System

We review the effects of price policy in three areas: terms of trade in agriculture, relative to consumer prices, international commodity prices, and domestic input prices; resource transfers from the agriculture sector to the non-agriculture sector; and the monthly wholesale price of wheat and the support price.

### Aggregate Terms of Trade

The level of agricultural prices relative to consumer prices, international prices of agricultural commodities, and domestic prices for inputs (including fertilizer, diesel oil, water, and pesticides) constitutes the sector's terms of trade (TOT).[4] Tracking the changes in TOT can help us to evaluate the profitability of the farm sector and chart the changes in the standard of living of the farming community. Analyzing the terms of trade for 20 agricultural commodities, including wheat and rice, from 1973 to 1983, Zahid and Hyder (1986) concluded that the increase in producer prices relative to the consumer price index remained lower than the base year. Similarly, during the past two decades, the increase in the producer price index was relatively less than the increase in the consumer price index for the period 1983–2003, except during 1997–2000, indicating that the farming community remained relatively worse off than the country as a whole (Figure 5.1).

The evolution of the producer price index relative to international commodity prices shows that the terms of trade (the TOT international price index in Figure 5.1) were favorable for almost half the reference period. Interestingly, a regular three- to four-year cycle can be observed. However, the variations in the cycle have decreased over time. Two factors may contribute to these cyclical trends: (1) The government's announced support and procurement prices for various crops are maintained at the same level for a couple of years, and (2) government interventions have declined significantly over time, in compliance with IMF and World Bank conditionalities as well as commitments to the World Trade Organization.

Zahid and Hyder (1986) show that the ratio of the producer price index to input prices remained in favor of the farming community from 1973 to 1983, mainly due to input subsidies. Figure 5.1 shows that domestic producer prices of crops relative to the major agricultural input prices remained below the base year (1983), except for the period from 1997 to 2000, when international prices were very low and domestic prices of most of the agricultural commodities were fixed at a significantly higher level.

**Figure 5.1    Aggregate terms of trade in agriculture, 1983–2002**

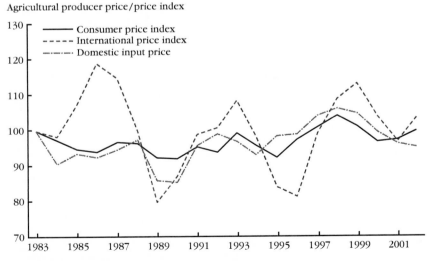

Source: Zahid and Hyder (1986) and authors' calculations.

### Nominal and Effective Protection Coefficients

Policy effects on agricultural incentives can also be evaluated by comparing domestic prices with parity prices, obtained by adjusting the world prices for transportation and other local costs. The nominal protection coefficient (NPC) measures the actual divergence between domestic and international prices, and it captures only the distortions in the output market. The effective protection coefficient (EPC) measures the net effect of government interventions on value added in any production process, incorporating distortions in the inputs markets as well. The NPC and EPC measures for the period from 1960 to 2002 for major agricultural commodities (for available years) are given in Table 5.12. Values at unity indicate no price distortion. Values greater (less) than one imply protection (disprotection), indicating incentive (disincentive) for production.

Table 5.12 shows that all major crops except basmati rice were highly protected against international prices during the 1960s. However, the domestic price relative to international prices started falling during the late 1960s. Afterward NPCs and EPCs for IRRI rice, cotton, and sugarcane remained either higher than or close to one except for a few years. On the other hand, those measures for wheat and basmati rice remained significantly lower than one for most of the 1980s and 1990s; basmati rice growers were the most adversely affected by the policy disincentives, followed by wheat growers.[5] These low and less-than-one measures also indicate a transfer of

**Table 5.12   Nominal and effective protection coefficients for selected commodities, selected years, 1960–2005**

| Year | Wheat NPC | Wheat EPC | Basmati NPC | Basmati EPC | IRRI NPC | IRRI EPC | Cotton NPC | Cotton EPC | Sugarcane NPC | Sugarcane EPC |
|------|-----------|-----------|-------------|-------------|----------|----------|------------|------------|---------------|---------------|
| 1960–61 | 1.20 | 1.24 | 0.84 | 0.85 | — | — | 1.05 | 1.07 | 2.71 | 2.75 |
| 1965–66 | 1.54 | 1.56 | 0.90 | 0.92 | — | — | 1.03 | 1.04 | 3.83 | 3.85 |
| 1970–71 | 1.59 | 1.56 | 0.84 | 0.83 | 0.87 | 0.87 | 1.20 | 1.19 | 2.15 | 2.13 |
| 1975–76 | 0.84 | 0.82 | 0.50 | 0.49 | 0.75 | 0.75 | 0.68 | 0.68 | 0.68 | 0.68 |
| 1982–83 | 0.73 | 0.70 | 0.46 | 0.38 | 0.95 | 1.01 | 0.92 | 0.95 | 0.75 | 0.73 |
| 1983–84 | 0.55 | 0.47 | 0.46 | 0.37 | 0.96 | 0.96 | 0.77 | 0.73 | 0.96 | 0.97 |
| 1999–2000 | 0.90 | 0.84* | 0.80 | 0.74 | 0.90 | 0.88 | 0.61 | 0.48 | 1.08 | 1.09 |
| 2000–01 | 0.79 | 0.69* | 0.79 | 0.75 | 1.30 | 1.54 | 0.99 | 0.94 | 0.83 | 0.81 |
| 2001–02 | 0.64 | 0.52* | 0.76 | 0.72 | 1.24 | 1.45 | 1.05 | 1.00 | 0.95 | 0.95 |
| 2002–03 | 0.63 | — | — | — | — | — | 1.12 | — | — | — |
| 2003–04 | 0.64 | — | — | — | — | — | 1.02 | — | — | — |
| 2004–05 | 0.76 | — | — | — | — | — | 1.00 | — | — | — |

Sources: EPCs for the years 1960–61 to 1975–76 are from Gotsch and Brown (1980), those from 1982–83 and 1983–84 are from Appleyard (1987), and the other measures are the authors' own calculations. NPCs for the years 2002–03 to 2004–05 are from Orden et al. (2006).

Note: *, EPC does not contain input subsidies; —, missing data.

resources from agriculture to non-agriculture, with adverse consequences for domestic production—especially of wheat, the main staple.

### Effects on Supply and Demand and Net Resource Transfers

Evaluating policy interventions, Hamid, Nabi, and Nasim (1990) show that production of major crops under interventions has been lower than in the counterfactual case of no interventions. The study estimates that wheat output would have been higher by 10–17 percent during the 1960s and 1970s and by 14 percent during the 1980s.[6] For basmati rice the comparable figures for the 1970s and 1980s are 25 percent and 40 percent, respectively.

Similarly Dorosh and Valdes (1990) concluded that production of wheat was lower by a full 24 percent and that of basmati rice by 52 percent during 1978–87, because of government interventions. The level of farm income without intervention could have been higher by 40 percent. The study further indicated that without intervention, Pakistan could have been a wheat exporter. Hamid, Nabi, and Nasim (1990) concluded that the consumption of all crops except sugar was higher than it would have been without government interventions. The overconsumption in wheat was in the range of 6–12 percent.

Ashfaq, Griffith, and Parton (2001), analyzing the welfare impact of wheat price policies, conclude that net welfare loss ranged from about Rs 11 billion during 1993–96 to about Rs 27 billion in 1974/75, and from about 4 percent to 15 percent of the GDP from agriculture. The flow of transfers has been from producers and government to consumers (Barkley 1992; Ashfaq, Griffith, and Parton 2001). Abedullah and Ali (2001) found that the support price benefits both the producers and the consumers and imposes a heavy cost on the government exchequer. The cost is higher than the ensuing benefits to producers and consumers, resulting in a net loss to society.

Thus government interventions in agriculture resulted in huge net resource transfers from the agriculture sector to the other sectors of the economy. These transfers amounted to about Rs 25 billion per annum during 1978–87 (Dorosh and Valdes 1990). A more recent study (Chaudhry 2001) shows that the annual resource transfer in nominal terms varied from Rs 40 billion in 1984/85 to Rs 214 billion in 1999/2000.

With rising incomes and urbanization, the demand for an efficient marketing structure increases (Kurosaki 1996). Market inefficiencies absorb significant amount of public and private resources, increase price risk, and discourage investment (Kurosaki 1996; Deomampo 1997). This section examines several aspects of market efficiency: marketing margins, market integration, and the cost of public and private distribution.

## Marketing Margins

Market efficiency can be assessed by quality, quantity, and price to consumers and by net returns to producers. Market inefficiencies result in a greater difference between producer and consumer prices (the marketing margin), reflecting higher marketing costs, higher profits for intermediaries, or both. Higher costs are usually caused by poor market infrastructure (roads, transport, storage, and utility services), high post-harvest losses, lack of grading, and improper handling of the products. Marketing profits are greater where there is greater risk of losses, greater marketing investment, or simply an exploitative system.

In Pakistan certain commodities involve very high marketing margins—45 percent for onions and 85 percent for bananas—that consist mainly of intermediaries' profits (Siddiqui 1979; Mohy-ud-Din 1992; Khushk and Smith 1996; Mustafa and Iqbal 1996; Lashari et al. 2002; Khushk et al. n.d.). In onions a 5 percent margin is attributable to costs, with the remaining 40 percent representing profit to intermediaries; in bananas, similarly, a 30 percent margin reflects actual marketing cost, and 49 percent represents profit. Pulses also involve huge marketing margins, ranging from 55 to 74 percent and similarly dominated by the profits shared by various intermediaries (Siddiqui 1979). Since the prices of wheat and wheat flour are controlled by the government, those marketing margins are generally not high. The marketing margin for wheat varies from 5 percent for grain to 58 percent for milled wheat.

## Market Integration

The competitiveness of markets can be evaluated based on how well price formation is interrelated over time and space. A high association between prices over time and space indicates good integration and the proper operation of price signals. With poor spatial integration, localized shortages or gluts translate into localized high or low prices. By providing marketing and transport infrastructure, the government improves spatial integration and enables private trade to arbitrage the price differentials, thus reducing regional price spreads. Where government intervenes directly in the market for some commodities (such as wheat in Pakistan), those commodity prices also become a measure of government effectiveness in smoothing prices spatially.

Qureshi (1974) estimated the correlation coefficients between price movements in village markets and wholesale markets for six commodities (wheat, cotton, gur, oilseeds, gram, and paddy) and concluded that the markets are well integrated. Mohammad (1977) supported these results, using average weekly wholesale price data for wheat in 12 districts.

Kurosaki (1996) concluded that in the case of wheat, the farmgate prices were almost perfectly explained by the government support price and the distance from the town. Even though most farmers sell their wheat to private traders and not to the procurement centers, the farmgate prices are integrated with the support price. This follows from active competition among private traders and substantial procurement by the government: government releases of stock significantly suppress market prices of wheat. The farmgate price of basmati paddy, in contrast, was not explained well by the support price, reflecting negligible procurement by the government.

Tahir and Riaz (1997) examined weekly prices of cotton, wheat, and rice in selected markets of southern Punjab and concluded that the agricultural markets are integrated only in the long run, with short-run integration only in special cases. The study found only long-run integration of wheat markets, since wheat is heavily regulated and the procurement centers actively participate in purchases at the time of harvest and a few months after. Moreover the movement of wheat is banned for a few months after the harvest. Therefore wheat markets are expected to be less integrated in the short run.

### Incidental Costs

During their procurement and distribution operations, the parastatals incur heavy incidental costs for packaging, handling, and so forth. The increasing incidental costs, coupled with the narrow margin between the procurement and release prices of wheat, continue to be a matter of great concern. High incidentals also make the export of wheat uncompetitive in the international market (Slam 2003). Table 5.13 shows that the PFDs' incidentals ranged from Rs 920 to Rs 2,350 per metric ton from 1996/97 to 2002/03, while for PASSCO the range was from Rs 1,218 to Rs 2,431 per metric ton during the same period. (The difference between the two parastatals' costs mainly reflects the use of gunny bags [Slam 2003].) A comparison of

Table 5.13   Incidental costs in wheat procurement and storage, 1996–2003 (Rs/MT)

| Year | PFDs | PASSCO | Private traders |
|------|------|--------|-----------------|
| 1996–97 | 919.6 | 1,217.59 | — |
| 1997–98 | 1,079.87 | 1,718.99 | — |
| 1998–99 | 1,439.95 | 1,778.85 | — |
| 1999–2000 | 1,482.22 | 1,906.44 | — |
| 2000–01 | 1,637.35 | 1,680.73 | 1,687–1,920 |
| 2001–02 | 2,130.6 | 2,125.83 | — |
| 2002–03 | 2,350 | 2,430.96 | 1,427–1,730 |

Source: Slam (2003).

Note: PASSCO, Pakistan Agricultural Storage and Supplies Corporations; PFDs, provincial food departments; —, missing data.

private traders' costs with those of the parastatals shows that incidentals were much lower recently for private traders than for the state-owned enterprises, ranging from Rs 1,427 to Rs 1,920 per metric ton (Table 5.13).

## Welfare Analysis of Wheat Policy

In order to analyze the welfare impacts of wheat policy in Pakistan, we construct a CGE model and calibrate it to the 2001/02 social accounting matrix (SAM) developed by Dorosh, Niazi, and Nazli (2004). We conduct policy experiments to analyze the household effects of possible reforms in wheat policy. Specifically we analyze the impact of removal of consumer subsidies and producer taxes on wheat. We first estimate the rates of consumer subsidies and producer taxes in the wheat sector, based on a simple analysis of the structure of the wheat economy and the linkage between wheat production and the overall economy.

Ahmad et al. (2006) estimate the consumer subsidies and producer taxes entailed in the extensive government intervention in wheat marketing in Pakistan. For the various seasonal phases of wheat marketing, over the period 1996/97 to 1999/2000, they analyze *quantities* (production, home consumption, feed seed, and wastage; government procurement and open-market sales; imports and marketed consumption); *prices* (government support price, issue price, wholesale price, import parity price, government's import price); and *costs* (government's storage cost, private storage cost).

This partial equilibrium analysis shows that total producer welfare loss was Rs 37.96 billion, and the policy costs to government amounted to about Rs 14.74 billion, while millers' *gain* from the wheat policy was Rs 11.05 billion. The overall financial loss was about Rs 3.37 billion, reflecting mainly the difference between the gain to the millers and the subsidy provided by the government—a gap apparently unaccounted for in the system. Their analysis also highlights the fact that consumers are subsidized at the expense of the farmers, and that the millers absorb almost all of the subsidy provided by the government to implement wheat policy. Ahmad et al. estimate the implicit production tax and consumption subsidy during this period at 23 percent and 22 percent, respectively. The effects of removing the consumption subsidy and producer tax are analyzed using a CGE model.[7]

### The CGE Model

The model is a static, one-period model. It has 34 production sectors; 10 labor types; values for capital, land, and water; and 19 household categories. The model specifies a constant elasticity of transformation (CET) function between export ($E$) and domestic sales ($D$). In the case that the export price ($Pe$) increases relative to the local price ($Pl$), export supply will increase while domestic sales will decline. The supply side of the model assumes profit maximization. The first-order conditions for profit maximization generate the necessary supply and input demand functions.

A slight variation on this structure is used in the case of agricultural production, wherein value added is a Cobb-Douglas combination of three factor inputs: aggregate capital, an aggregate labor input, and an aggregate land and water input. Capital is fixed, while labor is specified as a nested Cobb-Douglas function of 10 labor types. Following Robinson and Gehlhar (1995) and Cororaton (2005), the aggregate land and water input is specified as a nested linear combination of land and water. Following Lofgren and Robinson (1997), underutilization of land and water resources is allowed in the model, which is solved as a mixed complementarity problem.

On the demand side, substitution is allowed between imports and domestic goods using a constant elasticity of substitution (CES) function. This substitution indicates product differentiation, where imports and domestically produced goods are treated as imperfect substitutes. If the import price (in local currency) ($Pm$) declines relative to the domestic price ($Pd$), the demand for imports will rise while the demand for local goods will decline. The demand side assumes cost minimization; the first-order conditions generate the import and domestic demand functions. The trade elasticities in the CES and CET functions are reported in Ahmad et al. (2006).[8]

The pricing mechanism operates as follows. The output price ($Px$) is a composite of export ($Pe$) and local ($Pl$) prices. Indirect taxes are added to the local price to determine the domestic price ($Pd$), which together with import price ($Pm$) will determine the composite commodity price ($Pq$). The composite price ($Pc$) is the price paid by consumers and incorporates any consumption tax or subsidy. The import price ($Pm$) is denominated in domestic currency, and it is affected by the world price of imports, the exchange rate ($er$), the tariff rate ($tm$), and the indirect tax rate ($itx$). The direct effect of a tariff reduction is a reduction in $Pm$—if large enough, this will in turn reduce the composite price ($Pq$).

The consumption function of households uses a linear expenditure system. Intermediate demand is determined by a set of fixed Leontief coefficients. Sectoral capital is fixed, as is labor supply.

A traditional macroeconomic closure is used, where total savings is equal to total investment. Total savings is composed of four items: foreign, household, firm, and government savings. Foreign savings is assumed fixed. The nominal exchange rate is the numeraire. The foreign trade sector is effectively cleared by changes in the real exchange rate, which is the ratio of the nominal exchange rate multiplied by world prices and divided by the domestic price index. Government consumption expenditure is fixed. The rest of the savings items are endogenously determined.

**Policy Experiments**

In the original calibration of the model, there is no consumer subsidy or production tax on wheat. In the SAM imports of wheat amount to just 2.5 percent of total supply. Since the analysis will attempt to capture the second half of the 1990s, we recalibrated the model by increasing the import-supply ratio from 2.5 percent to 9 percent; by increasing the subsidy so that the import price of wheat is 22 percent higher than the consumer price; and by increasing the production tax so that the producer price is 23 percent lower than the import price. We run two policy experiments—with and without price distortions—and compare the static results.

Table 5.14 presents the effects of removing price distortions on a range of household categories, expressed in income, consumer prices, and net welfare. We trace these effects in their impact on the wheat market, on factor prices, and on other sectors of the economy.

Removing the distortion in wheat prices is welfare improving on the whole, across all household categories. Overall welfare improves by 0.29 percent of total disposable income of households. This effect is not very sensitive to large changes in trade elasticities for wheat (±20 percent and 40 percent). Across household groups, the net positive effects reflect income effects that dominate price effects. Price effects are calculated from changes in commodity prices weighted by the expenditure share of each group. Since expenditure shares vary across household types, price effects vary as well. Income effects come largely from changes in factor prices, as discussed later.

Household group h6 (medium farmers in other Pakistan) enjoy the highest improvement in welfare (1.26 percent of income), based on a relatively higher improvement in income and a lower increase in expenditure-weighted prices. This is followed by group h1 (large farmers in Sindh), with a 1.21 percent improvement in welfare. Nonfarm households, both poor and nonpoor, have the lowest improvement in welfare, as their increase in income is not far above the increase in their expenditure-weighted prices.

The effects of removing price distortions on the wheat grain sector are presented in Table 5.15. The large drop in imports (−58 percent) is expected as the distortions are removed.[9] Production improves by 8.1 percent as the tax is eliminated. The amount sold on the domestic market increases by 6 percent. The price received by farmers increases by 2.2 percent. There are two opposing effects on the demand price: upward pressure, due to the removal of subsidy, and downward pressure, due to the improvement in supply. The result shows the demand price of wheat decreasing (−5.1 percent), which means that the supply effect dominates the price increase of the removal of subsidy. As a result, demand for wheat improves by 1 percent.

The effects on wheat milling (flour) are presented in Table 5.16. The effects are similar to those for wheat grain but smaller. This is expected because only 66.2 per-

Table 5.14   Household-level effects

| | | Change (%) | | Welfare change | Sensitivity analysis: Welfare change (% of trade elasticities in wheat sector) | | | |
|---|---|---|---|---|---|---|---|---|
| Group | Household | Disposable income | Prices[a] | (% of disposable income) | +20% | -20% | +40% | -40% |
| h1 | Large farmers in Sindh | 1.81 | 0.62 | 1.21 | 1.42 | 1.01 | 1.66 | 0.82 |
| h2 | Large farmers in Punjab | 1.55 | 0.64 | 0.92 | 1.07 | 0.77 | 1.24 | 0.64 |
| h3 | Large farmers in other Pakistan | 1.21 | 0.56 | 0.67 | 0.75 | 0.59 | 0.83 | 0.52 |
| h4 | Medium farmers in Sindh | 1.23 | 0.62 | 0.63 | 0.71 | 0.55 | 0.80 | 0.47 |
| h5 | Medium farmers in Punjab | 1.11 | 0.65 | 0.48 | 0.54 | 0.43 | 0.60 | 0.38 |
| h6 | Medium farmers in other Pakistan | 1.80 | 0.56 | 1.26 | 1.47 | 1.06 | 1.70 | 0.88 |
| h7 | Small farmers in Sindh | 1.11 | 0.64 | 0.48 | 0.52 | 0.44 | 0.56 | 0.41 |
| h8 | Small farmers in Punjab | 1.16 | 0.67 | 0.50 | 0.55 | 0.46 | 0.60 | 0.41 |
| h9 | Small farmers in other Pakistan | 1.02 | 0.66 | 0.37 | 0.38 | 0.36 | 0.40 | 0.35 |
| h10 | Small farm renters, landless in Sindh | 1.27 | 0.65 | 0.64 | 0.70 | 0.58 | 0.76 | 0.52 |
| h11 | Small farm renters, landless in Punjab | 1.18 | 0.64 | 0.55 | 0.60 | 0.50 | 0.66 | 0.46 |
| h12 | Small farm renters, landless in other Pakistan | 1.06 | 0.62 | 0.45 | 0.48 | 0.43 | 0.51 | 0.40 |
| h13 | Rural agricultural workers, landless in Sindh | 1.26 | 0.62 | 0.65 | 0.68 | 0.63 | 0.71 | 0.61 |
| h14 | Rural agricultural workers, landless in Punjab | 1.23 | 0.65 | 0.59 | 0.62 | 0.57 | 0.64 | 0.55 |
| h15 | Rural agricultural workers, landless in other Pakistan | 1.03 | 0.58 | 0.46 | 0.45 | 0.47 | 0.43 | 0.48 |
| h16 | Rural nonfarm, nonpoor | 0.84 | 0.65 | 0.21 | 0.19 | 0.22 | 0.18 | 0.23 |
| h17 | Rural nonfarm, poor | 0.85 | 0.59 | 0.26 | 0.24 | 0.29 | 0.21 | 0.31 |
| h18 | Urban nonpoor | 0.80 | 0.69 | 0.13 | 0.12 | 0.13 | 0.12 | 0.14 |
| h19 | Urban poor | 0.84 | 0.62 | 0.22 | 0.22 | 0.23 | 0.21 | 0.24 |
| | Overall | | | 0.29 | 0.30 | 0.28 | 0.32 | 0.26 |

Source: Authors' calculations.

[a]Change in commodity prices, weighted by household expenditure shares.

Table 5.15   Effects on the wheat grain sector

| Item | Change (%) |
| --- | --- |
| Imports | −58.0 |
| Production | 8.1 |
| Sold to domestic market | 6.0 |
| Price received by farmers[a] | 2.2 |
| Demand price | −5.1 |
| Demand | 1.0 |

Source: Authors' calculations.

Note: Values are for irrigated wheat only.

[a]Value-added price of wheat.

Table 5.16   Effects on wheat milling (flour)

| Item | Change (%) |
| --- | --- |
| Imports | −4.42 |
| Production | 0.87 |
| Sold to domestic market | 0.78 |
| Demand price | −1.12 |
| Demand | 0.54 |

Source: Authors' calculations.

cent of wheat grain goes to wheat milling; the rest goes to other sectors such as live-stock. Imports of wheat flour drop by −4.4 percent as expected. Production improves by 0.87 percent, including a 0.78 percent increase in production sold to the domestic market. The demand price of wheat milling declines by −1.12 percent, and demand improves by 0.54 percent.

The effects on factor prices, which drive the result for household income, are presented in Table 5.17. The improvement in the value-added price results in higher factor prices, particularly for farm labor wages. While the increase in the average wage is only 0.97 percent, the wage effect varies across labor types. The labor wage for group L4 (medium farms in other Pakistan) registers the highest increase, at 6.03 percent. This translates into one of the highest increases in income for farmers in the corresponding group—h6 in Table 5.14. In addition, since the improvement in labor wages in non-agricultural sectors is much lower than for agricultural labor wages,

Table 5.17   Effects on factor prices (percent)

| Group | Factor price | Change (%) |
| --- | --- | --- |
| | Average wage | 0.97 |
| L1 | Labor wage, large farm | 2.86 |
| L2 | Labor wage, medium farm, Sindh | 2.13 |
| L3 | Labor wage, medium farm, Punjab | 1.97 |
| L4 | Labor wage, medium farm, other Pakistan | 6.03 |
| L5 | Labor wage, small farm, Sindh | 2.39 |
| L6 | Labor wage, small farm, Punjab | 2.86 |
| L7 | Labor wage, small farm, other Pakistan | 1.93 |
| L8 | Labor wage, agricultural wage | 2.05 |
| L9 | Labor wage, non-agricultural, unskilled | 0.88 |
| L10 | Labor wage, non-agricultural, skilled | 0.71 |
| K | Average return to capital | 0.92 |
| LD | Average return to land | 1.00 |
| WA | Average return to water | 1.00 |

Source: Authors' calculations.

**Table 5.18    Sectoral output and price effects**

| Sector | Change (%) in Output | Change (%) in Price | Sector | Change (%) in Output | Change (%) in Price |
|--------|--------|-------|--------|--------|-------|
| Wheat irrigated | 8.07 | –5.14 | Sugar | 0.09 | 0.97 |
| Wheat nonirrigated | 0.63 | 0.75 | Other food | –0.35 | 0.26 |
| Paddy IRRI | –0.33 | 0.76 | Cotton lint, yarn | –0.72 | 0.12 |
| Paddy basmati | –0.37 | 0.84 | Textiles | –0.54 | 0.30 |
| Cotton | –0.63 | 0.72 | Leather | –1.74 | 0.76 |
| Sugarcane | 0.07 | 0.81 | Wood products | –0.52 | 0.31 |
| Other major crops | 0.21 | 0.87 | Chemicals | –0.21 | 0.11 |
| Fruits, vegetables | –0.10 | 0.86 | Cement bricks | –0.39 | –0.92 |
| Livestock, cattle, dairy | 0.10 | 1.07 | Petroleum refining | –0.27 | 0.17 |
| Poultry | 0.10 | 1.07 | Other manufacturing | –0.68 | 0.02 |
| Forestry | –1.78 | 0.80 | Energy | 0.04 | 0.82 |
| Fishing industry | –0.18 | 0.81 | Construction | –0.81 | 0.02 |
| Mining | –0.48 | 0.01 | Commerce | 0.03 | 0.96 |
| Vegetable oil | –0.26 | 0.38 | Transport | 0.08 | 0.84 |
| Wheat milling | 0.87 | –1.12 | Housing | 0.00 | 1.49 |
| Rice milling, IRRI | –0.57 | 0.28 | Private services | 0.01 | 0.82 |
| Rice milling, basmati | –0.49 | 0.44 | Public services | 0.14 | 0.86 |

Source: Authors' calculations.

the improvement in income of non-agricultural household groups is lower than for agricultural households.

The general equilibrium effects of the removal of distortions in the wheat sector are presented in Table 5.18, which clearly indicates reallocation effects toward wheat and wheat-related sectors. The output of these sectors improves, while other sectors generally contract. Removing the producer tax on wheat improves the price received by farmers, who increase output. This, coupled with the removal of the consumption subsidy, results in a drop in consumer prices. The opposite effects occur in the rest of the sectors.

The share of wheat in the consumption basket of households varies widely, from 4 percent (household group h18) to 11.7 percent (household group h15). Thus, while wheat prices drop, the increase in the prices of other commodities (Table 5.18) results in higher expenditure-weighted prices for certain of the household groups in Table 5.14.

## Conclusions

The economy of Pakistan is dominated by agriculture, and the livelihood of a majority of the people depends on it. This sector directly employs nearly 42 percent of the country's total labor force; export earnings are largely based on the surplus generated in the agriculture sector. The performance of this sector over the past four decades has remained satisfactory, with an average growth rate of 3.4 percent per annum—higher than the population growth rate. Still, the country is far behind in its efforts to provide an acceptable level of dietary requirements for its people, even at the aggregate level: the daily average availability of calories per person in the country is substantially lower—by about 10 and 26 percent, respectively—than that in other developing and developed nations.

The change in diet composition over time (based on calories consumed) shows a declining share of wheat (and other cereals) and an increasing share of foods of animal origin. However, wheat remains the primary source of calories and thus plays a vital role in food security and human nutrition in the country. Despite the fact that the daily average availability of calories per person from all sources was considerably lower during the 1970s and the 1980s than during the 1990s, the incidence of poverty was also lower during those earlier decades. This demonstrates that enhanced food availability at the national level does not necessarily indicate actual increased food consumption at the regional or household level; not every individual enjoys improved access to food. Regardless of the reasonable rate of growth in the agriculture sector, calorie-based poverty increased during the 1990s—highlighting the fact that other factors, apart from national income growth, have been much stronger in pushing a greater proportion of people below the poverty line. A major reason for this shift could be the worsening inequality in income and landholdings. Disparities in access to education and health may also be crucial factors leading to widespread income inequality. Despite significant improvement in food supply in the aggregate, malnutrition is still a widespread phenomenon in Pakistan.

Food and agricultural prices are the major determinants of producers' incentives and of real income in developing countries. The government of Pakistan has accordingly pursued actively interventionist policies in the markets for both agricultural inputs and outputs, as a way of ensuring food security. Most of these interventions have now been abolished. However, some market distortions still continue—specifically, interventions in fixing agricultural prices and involvement of state-owned enterprises in trading. In particular, wheat marketing is dominated by the public sector. A distortion-free and competitive private food marketing system remains a distant goal.

In trade policy the government of Pakistan has also been pursuing the objective of greater openness through liberalization, maintaining minimal tariff and nontariff barriers and instituting a market-based exchange rate system. The difference between the official exchange rate and that in the open market has declined to a negligible level, 1.45 percent in 2000/01. The customs tariff (average applied rate) fell from 56 percent in 1993/94 to 20.4 percent in 2000/01. The maximum rate of customs duty has been reduced from 70 percent in 1995 to 25 percent in 2002, and the government has completely dismantled quantitative restrictions. Furthermore Pakistan has removed all textile products from its negative list, despite the fact that many of them are key export products. However, imports and exports of wheat and wheat flour are still to a large extent restricted by the government, which also largely controls domestic wheat marketing.

The comparison between domestic prices and parity prices for different crops shows that basmati rice growers—followed by wheat growers—are the groups most adversely affected by policy disincentives. IRRI rice and cotton growers are relatively better off, as are sugarcane growers. The net result of the interventions has been an immense resource transfer from the agriculture sector to non-agriculture sectors. The major beneficiaries have been processors and consumers, at the expense of producers and the government exchequer.

A comparison of the incidental marketing costs incurred by government-owned departments with those of private traders shows higher costs for the state-owned enterprises. Moreover corruption is pervasive in commodity marketing, particularly in the public sector. Rent-seeking activities increase transaction costs and uncertainty, discourage marketing investment and participation, and ultimately lead to a negative fiscal impact for the government.

The modeling study shows that removing these distortions in the wheat market would be welfare improving in general and across household groups. Overall welfare improves by 0.29 percent of the total disposable income of households. Across household groups, the net positive effects come from income effects that dominate price effects. The positive effects for farm households are relatively higher than those for nonfarm households.

The effects on the wheat grain sector indicate a large drop in imports of wheat, which is expected as the distortions are removed. Production improves as taxes are eliminated. The price received by farmers improves as well.

The result is a decreasing demand price of wheat, showing that the supply effect dominates the price increase of the removal of subsidy. As a result demand for wheat improves. The impact on wheat milling is generally similar but lower, because not all wheat grain is processed in wheat milling. Thus the price of wheat flour (which accounts for about 10 percent of the consumption expenditure of households) drops.

As the distortions are removed, there is a clear reallocation effect toward the wheat sector. Prices for other commodities increase, but this increase is offset by the improvement in income. Thus overall welfare improves. The general price increase is not very sensitive to large changes in the trade elasticities in the wheat sector.

Moreover, our simplified partial equilibrium analysis shows that the gain from removing production taxes would not entirely compensate for the loss in consumer welfare caused by eliminating consumer subsidies. However, the government would save the expenditures that would otherwise go into the wheat procurement and distribution system (and that ultimately benefit millers).

Based on these results and conclusions, what are the options in wheat marketing? The existing system of procurement and distribution, enforced through movement restrictions on wheat grains, creates disincentives for the private sector to invest in wheat trade. However, in light of the importance of wheat in household consumption and production, it may not be advisable to leave the wheat economy completely in the hands of the markets.

The policy prescription is that the government slowly step out of the food market and allow the market to function. However, to avoid extreme fluctuations in food prices, the government needs to monitor wheat production and availability. It has to maintain a buffer stock of optimal size, either purchased on the domestic market or through imports, with interventions based on market prices during normal times. To guard against an extreme fall in prices that could bankrupt farmers, the government may also consider interventions at a support price that is linked to variable (material) costs of production.

The government must develop food insecurity maps and target the extremely and moderately food-insecure regions through food stamps. The huge amount of subsidies provided by the government can be redirected to developing physical infrastructure and to agricultural research. Expenditures on research aimed at developing high-yielding varieties of crops that are resistant to biotic and abiotic stresses, and that have higher nutritional value, may prove a cheaper and more effective option to ensure food security.

## Notes

1. Registered flour mills, like other mills, also purchase wheat on the open market to meet their requirements.

2. Average calorie availability per person per day is 2,700 in Asia, 2,663 in developing countries, and 3,246 in developed countries, while the world average is 2,792 (FAO 2004) (August).

3. For example, in Hyderabad contaminated water took 10 lives, with 1,000 people hospitalized, over the course of two months in 2004. Khan et al. (2002) reported that 51 percent of the vegetable produce was unsuitable for human consumption due to excess chemical residues.

4. This section benefits heavily from Khan and Ahmad (2004).

5. Recently the government of Pakistan has decided to discourage the sowing of those crops that show no comparative advantage and that consume significant water resources, for example, sugarcane and IRRI rice.

6. Nonetheless Hamid, Nabi, and Nasim (1990) also show that there was price protection for wheat during most of the 1960s; that finding does not agree with this result regarding underproduction of wheat.

7. The detailed specifications of the model—including the equations, values of the various parameters, and the underlying SAM database—are available in Ahmad et al. (2006).

8. The elasticities used in our analysis are at half the level of the estimated parameters of the Global Trade Analysis Project model (Hertel et al. 2003).

9. The drop in imports is significantly larger than the improvement in production because imported wheat accounts for only 10 percent of total supply.


# References

Abedullah, A., and M. Ali. 2001. Wheat self-sufficiency in different policy scenarios and their likely impacts on producers, consumers, and the public exchequer. *Pakistan Development Review* 40 (3): 202–223.

Ahmad M., C. Cororaton, A. Qayyum, M. Iqbal, and P. Dorosh. 2006. Impact of domestic policies towards agricultural trade liberalization and market reform on food security in Pakistan. Unpublished project report. Washington, D.C.: International Food Policy Research Institute.

Amjad, R., and A. R. Kemal. 1997. Macroeconomic policies and their impact on poverty alleviation in Pakistan. *Pakistan Development Review* 36 (1): 87–97.

Appleyard, D. R. 1987. *Report on comparative advantage.* Islamabad: Agricultural Prices Commission, Government of Pakistan.

Ashfaq, M., G. Griffith, and K. Parton. 2001. Welfare effects of government interventions in the wheat economy of Pakistan. *Pakistan Journal of Agricultural Economics* 4 (1): 99–113.

Barkley, A. P. 1992. Wheat price policy in Pakistan: A welfare economics approach. *Pakistan Development Review* 31 (4): 1157–1171.

Central Bureau of Revenue (CBR). Various years. *Pakistan customs and tariffs.* Islamabad.

Chaudhry, M. G. 1995. Recent input-output price policy in Pakistan's agriculture: Effects on producers and consumers. *Pakistan Development Review* 34 (1): 1–24.

———. 2001. *Taxation of agriculture: Current practice, recommended policies and optimal tax system for Pakistan.* VRF Series 35. Chiba City, Japan: Institute of Developing Economies.

Cororaton, C. B. 2005. *Rice reforms and poverty in the Philippines: A CGE analysis.* Research Paper 57. Tokyo: Asian Development Bank Institute.

Deomampo, N. R. 1997. Agricultural marketing systems in Asia and the pacific region. In *Marketing systems for agricultural products.* Seminar report. Tokyo: Asian Productivity Organisation.

Dorosh, P. 2004. *Wheat policy and food subsidies in Pakistan: Recent developments.* Memo. Washington, D.C.: World Bank.

Dorosh, P., M. K. Niazi, and H. Nazli. 2004. *A social accounting matrix for Pakistan, 2001–02: Methodology and results. Background research paper for the Pakistan Rural Factor Markets Study,* South Asia Rural Development Unit. Washington, D.C.: World Bank.

Dorosh, P., and A. Valdes. 1990. *Effect of exchange rate and trade policies on agriculture in Pakistan.* Research Report 84. Washington, D.C.: International Food Policy Research Institute.

Food and Agriculture Organization of the United Nations (FAO). 1998. *Poverty alleviation and food security in Asia: Lessons and challenges.* Rome.

———. 2000. Pakistan. In *Agriculture, trade and food security issues and options in the WTO negotiations from the perspective of developing countries,* Volume 2: *Country case studies.* Rome.

———. 2002. *The state of food insecurity in the world 2001.* Rome.

———. 2003. Food security: Concepts and measurement. In *Trade reforms and food security: Conceptualizing the linkages.* Rome.

———. 2004. FAOstat. Food balance sheets. http://faostat.fao.org/.

Faruqee, R. 2005. Reforming the wheat policy in Pakistan. Draft paper. Washington, D.C.: World Bank.

Gotsch, G. H., and G. T. Brown. 1980. *Prices, taxes, and subsidies in Pakistan's agriculture, 1960–76.* World Bank Staff Working Paper 387. Washington, D.C.: World Bank.

Government of Pakistan. 2008. *Economic survey 2007–08.* Islamabad: Finance Division.

———. Various years. *Agricultural statistics of Pakistan.* Islamabad: Economic Wing, Food, Agriculture and Livestock Division.

Hamid, N., E. Nabi, and A. Nasim. 1990. *Trade, exchange rate, and agricultural pricing policies in Pakistan.* Washington, D.C.: World Bank.

Hertel, T., D. Hummels, M. Ivanic, and R. Keeney. 2003. *How confident can we be in CGE-based assessments of free trade agreements?* GTAP Working Paper 26. West Lafayette, Ind., U.S.A.: Center for Global Trade Analysis, Purdue University.

Jafri, S. M. Y. 1999. Assessing poverty in Pakistan. In *A profile of poverty in Pakistan.* Islamabad: Mahbub-ul-Haq Centre for Human Development.

Kemal, A. R. 2005. Pakistan's prospects for achieving the Millennium Development Goals on poverty and hunger. In *The role of agriculture in poverty reduction in Pakistan.* Proceedings of the seminar organized by IFPRI, BNU, and IDS, held March 12, 2005, in Lahore, Pakistan.

Khan, A. A., and Q. M. Ahmad. 2004. Agricultural terms of trade in Pakistan: Issues of profitability and standard of living of the farmers. *Pakistan Development Review* 43 (4): 515–537.

Khan, M. 2003. Nutrition: A factor for poverty eradication and human development. In *Pakistan Human Condition Report 2003.* Islamabad: Center for Research on Poverty Reduction and Income Distribution, Planning Commission of Pakistan.

Khan, M. A., A. M. Iqbal, I. Ahmand, and M. H. Soomro. 2002. Economic evaluation of pesticide use externalities in the cotton zone of Punjab, Pakistan. *Pakistan Development Review* 41 (4): 683–698.

Khushk, A. M., and L. E. D. Smith. 1996. A preliminary analysis of the marketing of mango in Sindh Province, Pakistan. *Pakistan Development Review* 35 (3): 241–255.

Khushk, A. M., M. S. Chaudhry, M. I. Lashari, and A. Memon. n.d. *Production and marketing of selected fruits in Pakistan: Constraints and opportunities.* Islamabad: Social Sciences Division, Pakistan Agriculture Research Council.

Kurosaki, T. 1996. Government interventions, market integration, and price risk in Pakistan's Punjab. *Pakistan Development Review* 35 (2): 129–144.

Lashari, M. I., J. A. Lund, A. M. Khuskh, and M. A. Memon. 2002. Production and marketing of onion in Sindh. In *Socioeconomic research studies 2001–2002,* ed. K. M. Aujla, W. Malik, and M. Sharif. Islamabad: Pakistan Agriculture Research Council.

Lofgren, H., and S. Robinson. 1997. *The mixed-complementarity approach to agricultural supply in computable general equilibrium models.* TMD Discussion Paper 20. Washington, D.C.: International Food Policy Research Institute.

Malik, S. J. 2003. *Agricultural growth and rural poverty in Pakistan.* Manila: Asian Development Bank.

Ministry of Finance. 2008. *Pakistan Economic Survey, 2007/2008.* Islamabad, Pakistan.

Mohammad, F. 1977. *Pricing efficiency in agricultural markets in Pakistan.* Research Report 106. Islamabad: Pakistan Institute of Development Economics.

Mohy-ud-Din, Q. 1992. Improving marketing of citrus fruit in the Punjab Province. In *Proceedings of the First International Seminar on Citriculture in Pakistan,* ed. I. A. Khan. Faisalabad: University of Agriculture.

Mustafa, U., and M. Iqbal. 1996. Inter-provincial trade of fruits in Pakistan. Paper presented at the national workshop on agricultural marketing, held August 27–29 in Quetta, Pakistan.

Orden, D., A. Salam, R. Dewina, H. Nazli, and N. Minot. 2006. The impact of global cotton and wheat prices on rural poverty in Pakistan. *Pakistan Development Review* 45 (4, Part II): 601–617.

Planning Commission and UNICEF. 2004. *National nutrition survey 2001–2002.* Islamabad: Planning Commission, Government of Pakistan.

Qureshi, S. K. 1974. The performance of village markets for agricultural produce: A case study of Pakistan. *Pakistan Development Review* 13 (3): 280–307.

Qureshi, S. K., and G. M. Arif. 1999. *Profile of poverty in Pakistan, 1998–99.* Islamabad: Pakistan Institute of Development Economics.

Robinson, S., and C. Gehlhar. 1995. *Land, water, and agriculture in Egypt: The economywide impact of policy reform.* TMD Discussion Paper 1. Washington, D.C.: International Food Policy Research Institute.

Siddiqui, S. A. 1979. *Marketing of agricultural products in Sindh.* Tando Jam, Pakistan: Department of Agricultural Economics and Rural Sociology, Sindh Agriculture University.

Slam, A. 2003. Country paper on Pakistan. Prepared for the workshop Agribusiness: From parastatals to private trade, held December 15–16 in New Delhi, India.

Tahir, Z., and K. Riaz. 1997. Integration of agricultural commodity markets in Punjab. *Pakistan Development Review* 36 (3): 241–262.

Turvey, R., and E. Cook. 1976. Government procurement and price support of agricultural commodities: A case study of Pakistan. *Oxford Economic Papers* 28 (1): 102–117.

Zahid, N. S., and Hyder, S. S. 1986. Pakistan's agricultural terms of trade: 1973–74 to 1983–84. *Pakistan Journal of Applied Economics* 5 (2): 91–141.

# Chapter 6

# Impacts of Trade Liberalization and Market Reforms on the Paddy-Rice Sector in Sri Lanka

Jeevika Weerahewa

Sri Lanka, classified as a lower middle-income country, has a rich experience in pursuing a variety of strategies to achieve food security. The Universal Food Subsidy Scheme was initiated in 1942 as a wartime necessity to ensure food security: basic food items were provided to all individuals at subsidized prices. The pressure on the treasury was enormous, and it turned out that the neediest could not always benefit from the policy. Between 1970 and 1977 several changes were made to reduce the fiscal burden, but without altering the fundamental nature of the program. These included cutting back on subsidies (by adjusting prices of rationed food, reducing food rations, removing taxpayers from the ration scheme, and controlling food costs), restricting imports, channeling food imports through a state monopoly, distributing food through cooperatives, and imposing price controls.

The year 1977 saw landmark changes, with the country moving toward liberal economic policies. On the supply side, the policy was to increase the availability of food through liberalizing imports, allowing the private sector to import and distribute, abolishing the quota and ration system, and removing distortions in food prices through the elimination of subsidies and price controls. Nevertheless, in the case of the paddy-rice sector, the government continues to restrict imports to avoid adverse impacts on poverty, although paddy procurement, milling, and distribution are mainly handled by the private sector. In 1979 the government implemented a food stamp program targeted only at the poor, for purchasing specified food items and kerosene. In 1994 the food stamp program was modified and renamed Janasaviya, with separate income transfers provided for consumption and investment. The Janasaviya program was later converted into a similar program, called Samurdhi, with broadened coverage.

This study focuses on the impacts on food security of different types of policies implemented by successive governments in Sri Lanka, with special emphasis on paddy-rice. An extensive literature relates to the issue of food security in Sri Lanka, including several studies at the national level (Kelegama 2000; Sanderatne 2001). Herath and Weerahewa (2005) provide an account of the status of food security in Sri Lanka at the national, household, and individual levels. Various poverty assessment reports provide information on the basic needs of different types of households, classified by region, employment, education, ethnicity, irrigation, and so forth (World Bank 2000; Department of Census and Statistics 2008a). The Dietary and Health Survey (Department of Census and Statistics 2008b) provides some statistics on individual food security.

Other studies assess the production efficiency of rice farming (Amarasinghe 1974; Karunaratne and Herath 1989; Abeyratne et al. 1990; Shilpi 1995; Kikuchi et al. 2000, 2002; Rafeek and Samarathunga 2000). The broad conclusion of these studies is that rice farming is inefficient and income from paddy farming is very low (Ranaweera, Samarathunga, and Hafi 1990; Weerahewa, Gunatilake, and Pitigala 2003). Studies relating to consumption find that the rural sector is less price responsive than the urban sector, but more responsive to expenditure than the urban sector (Tudawe 2002); there are significant differences in individual elasticity estimates between recipients of food aid and others (Bogahawatte 1992).

Though paddy and rice marketing is crucial, relatively few studies have assessed marketing efficiency. While some argue that it is competitive (Harrison 1995; Ellis, Senanayake, and Smith 1997), others find that it is characterized by oligopolistic buyers (Dharmaratne and Hathurusinghe 1999; Rupasena 2002). The degree of protection afforded the rice industry was evaluated by Epaarachchi, Jayanetti, and Weliwita (2002), using nominal and effective rates of protection, and by Ekanayake (2003), using a partial equilibrium model. They find that producers are protected at the expense of consumers.

Against this background, the broad objective of this study is to investigate the effects of domestic agricultural trade liberalization and market reforms on national- and household-level food security in Sri Lanka, focusing on the paddy-rice sector. The study has several specific objectives:

1. Document the evolution of domestic and trade policies, to assess the implications of the World Trade Organization (WTO) Agreement on Agriculture for the paddy-rice sector.

2. Describe the present system of paddy production, procurement, and distribution, detailing the involvement of government agencies and the private sector.

3. Investigate the impact of rice trade liberalization and the privatization of the paddy procurement system on prices, supply of paddy, demand for rice, imports of rice, and calorie intake at the national level.

4. Investigate the impact of rice trade liberalization at the household level and for different segments of the population, to understand the implications for poverty.

5. Analyze the potential impacts of elimination of the oligopsony power of the paddy collectors on the well-being of paddy farmers.

The chapter is organized as follows. The next section begins by discussing the importance of the paddy-rice sector in the Sri Lankan economy, especially its significance for the rural economy and rural poverty. It also discusses the structure of the paddy market in Sri Lanka, focusing on the role of government and the private sector in the procurement and distribution of paddy-rice. The third section discusses the evolution of trade policies and market reform as they affect the paddy sector. It also briefly assesses the implications of Sri Lanka's WTO commitments to further liberalize agricultural markets. The fourth section evaluates the impacts of rice trade liberalization and market reforms on calorie intake at the national level. The following section assesses the impacts of rice trade liberalization on poverty at the regional level. The sixth section assesses the impacts of oligopsony power on income from paddy farming at the national level. The final section summarizes the findings of the study and provides suggestions for further research.

## The Paddy Sector in Sri Lanka

The paddy sector occupies a key position in the economy of Sri Lanka. During 1996–2000 this sector contributed on average 22 percent to agricultural gross domestic product (GDP). (The agricultural sector as a whole contributed 20 percent to national GDP.) Paddy accounts for the largest share of cultivated land among all crops (about 850,000 hectares or 45 percent). Paddy is cultivated during two seasons, maha and yala. Maha (October–March) usually accounts for about 65 percent of the annual production, with the remaining 35 percent coming from the yala crop (April to September). Paddy is grown in almost all districts, but most comes from the districts of Anuradhapura, Hambantota, Kurunagala, Monaragala, Polonnaruwa, and Ratnapura. Two-thirds of the paddy is grown under irrigated conditions, and the paddy crop is heavily dependent on rainfall.

Rice is the staple food and the main source of calories in the Sri Lankan diet. Average per capita daily consumption is about 300 grams of rice, providing about 1,050 kcal and 45 percent of the protein requirement—the major source of calories as well as a source of protein for both rich and poor Sri Lankans. The average daily calorie intakes of the lowest and highest income deciles are 1,964 and 2,097 kcal, respectively (Department of Census and Statistics 2002).

Given the significance of the paddy sector, governments over the years have placed great emphasis on increasing paddy production in order to achieve self-sufficiency. Substantial government resources have been directed toward improving the paddy sector, implementing large-scale irrigation projects, land development and settlement schemes, free provision of irrigation water, fertilizer subsidies, and guaranteed prices. These initiatives improved paddy yields and output over time; as a result, Sri Lanka is at present 98 percent self-sufficient in rice (Table 6.1).

Paddy is the principal contributor to the rural economy; the majority of rural households engage in not only production but also marketing of rice as their source of livelihood. A majority of paddy farmers (70 percent) are smallholders, with a land area of less than 1 hectare, and only 5 percent of farmers have holdings greater than 2 hectares. Only 22 percent of the population own any paddy land (Gunawardena 2000). Though shrinking, the agricultural sector still absorbs 32.6 percent of the labor force (Central Bank 2001), of which the paddy sector employs nearly 50 percent.

The income from paddy is not sufficient, however, to meet the basic needs of a family. According to Ranaweera, Samarathunga, and Hafi (1990), real income from paddy farming has been declining over time. A more recent study by Weerahewa, Gunatilake, and Pitigala (2003) finds the same pattern. They evaluated income from

Table 6.1    Rice production and imports, selected years, 1970–2008

| Year | Gross area sown (thousands of ha) | Production (thousands of MT) | Yield (kg/ha) | Imports (thousands of MT) | Self-sufficiency ratio (%) |
|---|---|---|---|---|---|
| 1970 | 759 | 969.6 | 677.4 | 526 | 64.83 |
| 1975 | 696 | 692.4 | 1,362 | 457 | 60.24 |
| 1980 | 845 | 1,279.8 | 1,756.2 | 167 | 88.46 |
| 1985 | 882 | 1,596.6 | 2,079 | 182 | 89.77 |
| 1990 | 857 | 1,522.8 | 2,071.8 | 172 | 89.85 |
| 1995 | 915 | 1,686 | 2,121 | 9 | 99.47 |
| 2000 | 878 | 1,716.0 | 2,313.6 | 15 | 99.13 |
| 2005 | 937 | 3,246 | 3,963 | 52 | 98.42 |
| 2006 | 910 | 3,342 | 4,137 | 12 | 99.64 |
| 2007 | 817 | 3,129 | 4,385 | 88 | 97.26 |
| 2008 | 1053 | 3,875 | 4,184 | 84 | 97.88 |

Source: Central Bank of Sri Lanka (various years).

paddy farming over the past two decades, using data for maha, the major cultivation season, for three benchmark years: 1980/81, 1990/91, and 2000/01. Income from paddy farming per year was compared with the income of an average Sri Lankan family. Table 6.2 shows the income from paddy farming as a percentage of average per capita income for those years, in nominal and real terms. Their analysis suggests that the income of the average paddy farmer, with 4 acres, was 21 percent of the average income of the country in 1980/81, and that it declined to 10 percent in 1990/91 and to only 5 percent in 2000/01. This suggests that the economic status of paddy farmers with 4 acres of lowland has deteriorated over the past two decades.

Table 6.3 shows the profitability of irrigated paddy farming in different districts, including and excluding family labor. (Note that irrigated paddy is the most profitable form of rice farming.) On average, excluding the imputed cost of family labor, the income of a paddy farmer is Rs 8,781.95 per acre *per season*. If this outcome can be

**Table 6.2    Comparison of income from paddy farming, selected years, 1980–2001**

| Variable | 1980/81 | 1990/91 | 2000/01 |
|---|---|---|---|
| Nominal income from irrigated paddy (Rs/acre per season) | 2,371.91 | 4,706.50 | 8,781.95 |
| Colombo Consumers Price Index | 318.20 | 1,008.60 | 2,539.80 |
| Real income from irrigated paddy (Rs/acre per season) | 18,932.03 | 11,851.64 | 8,781.95 |
| Real income from irrigated paddy (Rs/acre per year) | 37,864.05 | 23,703.29 | 17,563.90 |
| Gross domestic product in market prices (millions of Rs) | 66,527.00 | 321,784.00 | 1,255,535.00 |
| Population (millions) | 14.747 | 17.015 | 19.36 |
| Per capita income in market prices (Rs) | 4,511.22 | 18,911.78 | 64,855.36 |
| Real per capita income (Rs) | 36,007.55 | 47,622.59 | 64,855.36 |
| Average income per household (Rs) | 180,037.76 | 238,112.97 | 324,276.82 |
| Ratio of paddy income to per capita income of a household | 0.21 | 0.10 | 0.05 |

Source: Adapted from data in Weerahewa, Gunatilake, and Pitigala (2003).

**Table 6.3    Profitability per acre per season of paddy farming, selected years, 1980–2001 (Rs)**

| District | 1980/81 | | 1990/91 | | 2000/01 | |
|---|---|---|---|---|---|---|
| | Including imputed cost[a] | Excluding imputed cost | Excluding imputed cost | Including imputed cost | Including imputed cost | Excluding imputed cost |
| Anuradhapura | 1,496.94 | 2,042.26 | 4,709.00 | 2,522.00 | 2,570.16 | 7,767.11 |
| Polonnaruwa | 1,304.84 | 2,113.81 | 2,167.00 | 635.00 | 5,275.29 | 10,005.65 |
| Kurunagala | 1,908.71 | 2,533.55 | 7,779.00 | 5,257.00 | 3,815.80 | 9,507.26 |
| Hambanthota | 2,483.47 | 2,798.01 | 4,171.00 | 2,427.00 | 2,786.11 | 7,847.77 |
| Average | 1,798.49 | 2,371.91 | 2,710.25 | 4,706.50 | 3,611.84 | 8,781.94 |

Sources: Department of Agriculture (1980/81, 1990/91, 2000/01 maha).

[a]Imputed cost consists only of family labor.

duplicated each season, annual income for a farmer with 1 acre will be Rs 17,563.90. A farmer with 4 acres would have an annual income of Rs 70,255.60—just above the poverty line—if all labor is still supplied by the family. The majority of paddy farmers in Sri Lanka cultivate fewer than 2 acres, implying an annual income from paddy of less than Rs 35,127.80. Thus cultivating paddy alone does not allow a farm family to overcome poverty.

Sri Lanka had a poverty level of 25.17 percent (head count ratio) in 1995/96, assuming a poverty line of Rs 791.61 per person per month (Gunawardena 2000). The rural sector, in which paddy farming is concentrated, invariably exceeds the national poverty level on all three widely used poverty measures, according to surveys conducted in 1985/86, 1990/91, and 1995/96. Table 6.4 presents the status of poverty by sector in 1995/96 using various indicators.

Gunawardena (2000) has analyzed the poverty level with respect to type of income and size of paddy landholding. The poor are more likely to have wage or agricultural income; less likely to receive income from nonfarm self-employment; less likely to receive pensions and foreign remittances; and more likely to receive income from government payments (Janasaviya and Samurdhi). Table 6.5 shows poverty level by source of household income; Table 6.6 shows poverty level by size of paddy landholdings.

**Table 6.4    Poverty by sector and by province, 1995/96**

|  | Indicator[a] | | | | | |
|  | Incidence | | Depth | | Severity | |
| Sector or province | Index | Contribution (%) | Index | Contribution (%) | Index | Contribution (%) |
|---|---|---|---|---|---|---|
| Sector |  |  |  |  |  |  |
| Urban | 14.67 | 8.11 | 2.95 | 7.64 | 0.91 | 7.31 |
| Rural | 26.95 | 88.20 | 5.79 | 88.97 | 1.88 | 89.35 |
| Estates[b] | 24.92 | 3.69 | 4.88 | 3.39 | 1.55 | 3.33 |
| All | 25.17 | 100.00 | 5.36 | 100.00 | 1.73 | 100.00 |
| Province[c] |  |  |  |  |  |  |
| Western (15.6) | 14 | 17 | 3 | 15 | 1 | 14 |
| Central (45.3) | 28 | 17 | 6 | 18 | 2 | 19 |
| Southern (42.4) | 26 | 16 | 6 | 16 | 2 | 16 |
| Northwestern (48.0) | 34 | 18 | 7 | 17 | 2 | 16 |
| North central (82.6) | 31 | 8 | 6 | 7 | 2 | 7 |
| Uva (75.9) | 37 | 11 | 9 | 13 | 3 | 15 |
| Sabaragamuwa (51.1) | 32 | 14 | 7 | 14 | 2 | 14 |

Sources: Gunawardena (2000) and World Bank (2000).

[a]Based on the reference poverty line of Rs 791.67 per person per month.

[b]Estate in this context means a plantation.

[c]Figures in parentheses are agricultural households as a percentage of rural households.

Table 6.5    Poverty by source of household income

| Household type | Incidence of poverty (%)[a] | Gini coefficient | Average consumption expenditure (Rs) |
|---|---|---|---|
| Wage income only | 23.86 | 0.334 | 1,436.77 |
| Agricultural self-employment only | 26.73 | 0.282 | 1,221.19 |
| Non-agricultural self-employment income only | 13.56 | 0.346 | 1,715.99 |
| Agricultural and non-agricultural self-employment income only | 22.17 | 0.310 | 1,380.53 |
| Wage and self-employment income | 28.09 | 0.316 | 1,289.85 |
| No earned income | 18.58 | 0.359 | 1,794.28 |

Source: Gunawardena (2000).

[a]Based on the reference poverty line of Rs 791.67 per person per month.

Table 6.6    Poverty in Sri Lanka by size of paddy landholding, 1995

| Landholding size (acres) | Incidence of poverty (%)[a] | Mean consumption (Rs) |
|---|---|---|
| Landless | 27.47 | 1,280.04 |
| 0 to <0.125 | 24.86 | 1,125.23 |
| 0.125 to <0.25 | 24.85 | 1,185.09 |
| 0.25 to <0.5 | 24.11 | 1,234.53 |
| 0.5 to <1 | 28.66 | 1,269.58 |
| 1 to <2 | 24.08 | 1,328.82 |
| 2 to <3 | 24.72 | 1,311.11 |
| 3 to <4 | 18.74 | 1,413.68 |
| 4 to <5 | 10.86 | 1,940.08 |
| 5 to <10 | 11.65 | 1,964.52 |
| 10 to <20 | 15.62 | 1,934.07 |
| >20 | 33.47 | 1,701.19 |

Source: Gunawardena (2000).

[a]Based on the reference poverty line of Rs 791.67 per person per month.

## Policy Regime

### Policies to Promote Food Production

The government's strategy for promoting food production has been to focus on developing the dry zone of the country. The wet zone has high population densities, with much of the arable land area in commercial plantation or in small fragmented wet rice holdings; in contrast, the dry zone has abundant land and is relatively sparsely populated. Traditionally agriculture in the dry zone—primarily rice—was supported by small irrigation tanks and shifting cultivation. Government investment in restoring large irrigation systems, along with other improvements in the quality of life, provided the impetus for voluntary migration from the wet zone to the dry zone. As a result of these successful production promotion policies, rice production has increased substantially in Sri Lanka: imports of rice accounted for less than 5 percent of the country's requirements in 2001.

### Government Policy toward the Provision of Basic Needs

The onset of World War II disrupted normal imports of rice. To overcome the resulting food shortage, a universal Rice Rationing Scheme (RSS) was initiated in 1942 by the colonial government to ensure equitable distribution of food. Consumer cooperative societies with an islandwide network of retail shops provided the base for implementing the rationing system. After independence in 1948, the government continued the RSS until 1979. The Food Stamp Scheme (FSS) was the successor to the RSS; it differed mainly in targeting the poorest households of the economy.

### Domestic Marketing

The history of government intervention in domestic procurement dates from 1942, when the government introduced the Internal Purchase System (IPS) as a tool to supply RSS rice stocks (Table 6.7). After independence in 1948, the government introduced the Guaranteed Price Scheme (GPS) for paddy and a number of other food crops. The objectives of the GPS were to assure producers fair prices and a ready market, stimulate the production of food crops, and achieve the long-term goal of self-sufficiency.

In 1961 the government enacted the Domestic Produce Purchasing and Storage Act to promote cooperative societies in marketing. Existing consumer and producer cooperative societies were reorganized into Multipurpose Cooperative Societies (MPCSs) during the 1960s, to enhance operational efficiency through vertical integration.[1] The newly established People's Bank, a government agency, offered loans to the MPCS. Financing of new paddy-rice stores and paddy mills was supported through long-term credit facilities. The government lifted restrictions on private-sector procurement and marketing: several small-scale enterprises entered into paddy procurement and processing as well as marketing of rice.

In 1971, as the demand for rice continued to increase, the government—faced with foreign exchange constraints and record-high international rice prices—established the Paddy Marketing Board (PMB) to procure rice from the domestic market. This spelled the end of open-market operations and the dawn of a new era. The PMB assumed monopoly powers in the procurement and sale of paddy.[2] MPCSs now functioned as subagents of the PMB for procurement. Milling was done by the private sector, and rice was handed over to the Food Commissioner for distribution through the MPCSs. The government's objective in establishing the PMB was to purchase more paddy through domestic channels. However, despite the GPS's monopoly powers, the percentage of its paddy purchases declined after the inception of the PMB (Table 6.8).

This decline can partly be explained by the price differential between the open market price, GPS price, and ration price. Farmers chose to substitute their own rice

**Table 6.7    Chronology of policies and programs implemented in the paddy-rice sector**

| Year | Major policy milestone |
| --- | --- |
| 1942 | Universal RSS established. IPS introduced as a tool to meet demand for rice for RSS. |
| 1948 | IPS replaced by "Marketing of Home Grown Foods." GPS for paddy and some other food crops established. |
| 1958 | Paddy Land Act enacted to bring security to tenant farmers. |
| 1960 | Subsidies for fertilizer, seed paddy, and other inputs implemented. |
| 1961 | Domestic Product Purchasing and Storage Act enacted. |
| 1971 | Paddy Marketing Board established. |
| 1986 | NCRCS introduced to provide credit to smallholders. |
| 1995–2002 | Government progressively privatizes the management of paddy, sugar, and seed farms. |
| 1996 | Two new irrigation programs instituted: agri wells and the Micro Irrigation program. |
| 1997 | Fertilizer Subsidy Scheme limited to urea. |
| 1999 | Forward sales contract system introduced to reduce the volatility of farmer incomes and to promote agribusiness enterprises. Crop insurance market liberalized. |
| 2002 | Fertilizer Subsidy Scheme provides a fixed subsidy of Rs 6,000 per ton of urea, irrespective of the international market price. |

Note: GPS, Guaranteed Price Scheme; IPS, Internal Purchase System; NCRCS, New Comprehensive Rural Credit Scheme; RSS, Rice Rationing Scheme.

**Table 6.8    Purchases under the Guaranteed Price Scheme, 1965–74**

| Year | Total production (millions of bushels) | GPS purchases (millions of bushels) | GPS purchases as percent of total production |
| --- | --- | --- | --- |
| 1965 | 36.2 | 21.4 | 58.95 |
| 1966[a] | 45.7 | 28.0 | 61.26 |
| 1967 | 54.9 | 13.4 | 24.40 |
| 1968 | 64.6 | 15.1 | 23.37 |
| 1969 | 65.9 | 13.9 | 21.09 |
| 1970 | 77.4 | 26.5 | 34.23 |
| 1971[b] | 66.9 | 32.3 | 48.28 |
| 1972 | 62.7 | 26.3 | 41.90 |
| 1973 | 62.9 | 22.9 | 36.40 |
| 1974 | 76.8 | 20.9 | 27.21 |

Source: Yoshimura, Perera, and Gunawardana (1975).

Note: GPS, Guaranteed Price Scheme.

[a]This year witnessed a reduction of ration quantity.

[b]Establishment of the PMB.

for the paid ration and to receive only the free portion of the rice ration, leaving a smaller amount of surplus production to be sold. Failing to procure enough rice, the government was compelled to adopt other measures, including prohibiting storage and transport of paddy in bulk. However, none of these measures proved effective in persuading farmers to sell paddy to the government.

The abolition of the RSS in 1979 and its replacement with the FSS marked the end of an era of extensive government involvement in paddy procurement and distribution. This can be seen as part of a general policy trend toward liberalization and promotion of the private sector that began in 1977 and encompassed several elements: reducing protection and subsidies, reducing tariffs, and relaxing quota restrictions.[3]

Changing the government's policy on rationing greatly reduced its procurement needs. Although the PMB continued to operate, its purchases accounted on average for less than 5 percent of the total production (in normal years) during 1980–90. Annual average PMB purchases were only 1.3 percent for the period 1991–93. After the government began to transfer PMB facilities for other activities, around 1991, the PMB lacked the essential infrastructure to scale up its operations. PMB purchases increased after the change in government in 1994, but paddy sales incurred heavy financial losses, and PMB operations were terminated in 1996.

Nevertheless the government continued to intervene in the paddy market, ostensibly to stabilize prices; it used such channels as the Cooperative Wholesale Establishment (CWE) and the cooperatives, while providing funding to farmer organizations through government agents. In 2007 the government re-established the PMB to strengthen its interventions in the paddy market.

### International Trade

The Food Commissioner's Department (FCD) had the monopoly in rice imports until 1990, when it was given to the CWE. (The FCD had handed over the import of paddy in 1988 to three offshore companies that functioned as bondsmen.) The government monopoly in importing rice continued until 1993, when the private sector was allowed to import rice under licenses. Rice trade policy since then has suffered from instability. In 1996 licensing was abandoned: anyone was allowed to import rice at a specified duty (Rupasena and Ravichandran 2000). The period since 1997 has seen frequent changes in tariffs, which at times prevented the private sector from importing rice despite domestic shortages (Central Bank of Sri Lanka 1999). In July 2000 licensing was reimposed on the import of rice, and it continued until November 22, 2001.

Under licensing the price of rice reflected high levels of protection, in both the nominal rate of protection (NRP; the ratio of the domestic price to the border-equivalent price) and the effective rate of protection (ERP; the ratio of the value added under intervention to the value added at the border price). The NRP and ERP in 2000 stood at 25.1 percent and 25.8 percent, respectively. This indicates that import restrictions were more important than input subsidies in providing protection to farmers (Epaarachchi, Jayanetti, and Weliwita 2002). The caveat is that international prices in 2000 were abnormally low, and domestic prices in many countries (including India and Thailand) were found to be 25 percent above the world price. NRP and ERP values greater than one would imply a noncompetitive price.

## Structure of the Paddy Market in Sri Lanka

The concept of marketing covers the entire flow of activities from farm production to the point of purchase by the consumer. In Sri Lanka more than half of paddy production comes to the market as a surplus (small-farmer production in excess of consumption needs). In marketing this surplus, both the private and government sectors play a role, but the level of their operations has changed significantly over the years.

Paddy has been purchased by the government under the GPS since 1948; it was marketed initially by the Department of Agrarian Services. In January 1972 marketing functions were taken over by the PMB as the sole marketing outlet for paddy in Sri Lanka. Through the 1970s rice was marketed principally through government agencies. The MPCSs collected paddy from farmers for the PMB. Private millers were hired to process the paddy, and they handed over the rice to the FCD, which in turn issued it to the cooperatives for distribution to consumers on ration. Apart from its marketing functions (collection, milling, and distribution of paddy-rice), the PMB also implemented a "Buffer-Stock Scheme" for rice, using regional warehouses.

The government's role in marketing paddy-rice changed as part of the liberalization of 1977. In 1978 the PMB act was amended to allow private-sector marketing of rice. The resulting intense competition dramatically reduced the government's market share in purchasing paddy (Table 6.9). Government involvement was now mainly confined to farm and retail. As in the past, the Agrarian Service Centers, PMB centers, and MPCSs continued to purchase paddy from farmers under the GPS, and the FCD distributed rice milled by the PMB. The public-sector marketing channels for rice in the mid-1980s are shown in Figure 6.1.

After liberalization the private sector began to handle nearly 80 percent of rice marketing in Sri Lanka. At the farm level, paddy purchases were made by assembly agents, brokers, small traders, and rice millers. Assembly agents, or assemblers, are the first buyers of paddy, often referred to as collectors. Some assemblers are paddy producers, input suppliers, and grocery traders. Many are located in the paddy-producing areas; only a very few have the storage facilities and financial capability to hold stocks. The assembly agents distribute the stocks to millers, located in different

Table 6.9    Market share of the Paddy Marketing Board, selected years, 1972–95

| Year | Total paddy production (thousands of MT) | Paddy purchases by the PMB (thousands of MT) | Market share of the PMB (%) |
|---|---|---|---|
| 1972 | 1,305 | 551 | 42 |
| 1975 | 1,158 | 242 | 21 |
| 1977 | 1,681 | 513 | 31 |
| 1980 | 2,137 | 212 | 10 |
| 1985 | 2,487 | 324 | 13 |
| 1990 | 2,538 | 31 | 1.2 |
| 1995 | 2,810 | 282 | 10 |

Source: Central Bank of Sri Lanka (various years).
Note: PMB, Paddy Marketing Board.

Figure 6.1    Market flow of the Paddy Marketing Board

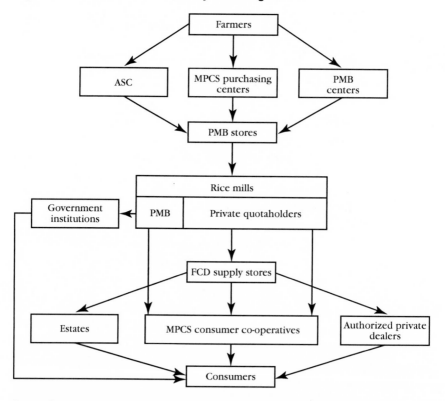

Source: Somaratne (1987).
Note: ASC, Agrarian Service Centers; FCD, Food Commissioner's Department; MPCS, Multi-purpose Cooperative Societies; PMB, Paddy Marketing Board.

parts of the country. The millers may stock paddy, to be milled at a later date. The amount of paddy milled at a given time usually depends on the price of rice.

The wholesalers in the Colombo market play a major role in the distribution channel. They operate on a commission basis and also buy outright from millers. In addition to distribution, wholesalers also make advance payments to suppliers, break up bulk quantities to match demand, inform suppliers and distributors about prices, and finance trade (Somaratne, 1987). The Colombo wholesalers handle about 60 percent of total rice production and sell to retailers in every part of the country. The private-sector marketing channel that developed following liberalization is shown in Figure 6.2.

The literature does not provide a definitive picture of the market structure for paddy in Sri Lanka. According to Rupasena (2002) the major reason for low farm prices is that buyers do not compete in pricing: as the number of paddy collectors and millers is smaller than the number of paddy suppliers, they may enjoy oligopsony power. Harrison (1995) points to the number of rice millers to argue that Sri Lanka has a competitive rice processing sector. However, the number of firms is a weak indicator of market power; it is the strategic interactions among firms that determine the degree of market power. According to Rupasena (2002) competition in farm markets in Sri Lanka is limited due to the dominance of a few traders.

**Figure 6.2   Private-sector marketing channels**

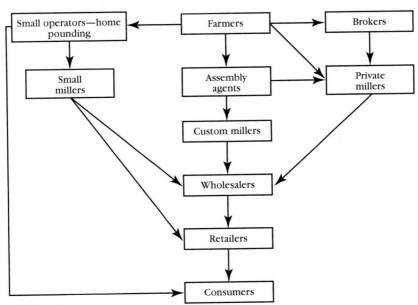

Source: Somaratne (1987).

Ubaldulah (1999) and Wicramasinghe (1999) report that the number of millers declined during 1997 as a result of liberalization of the rice trade. More than 100 mills stopped operations, while 20 large-scale mills continued operations in the Polonnaruwa area—reflecting the inability of small millers to survive (Wicramasinghe 1999). Ubaldulah (1999) attributes monopoly power to the Colombo rice commission agents. Ellis, Senanayake, and Smith (1997) nevertheless argue that the paddy market is efficient, as marketing margins have been stable over the years, particularly when PMB operations contracted. Again the qualification applies: the market could have stable margins over a given length of time despite the existence of one-sided bargaining power.

## Government and Private-Sector Interface in Paddy Marketing in Sri Lanka: The Impact of Trade Liberalization on Price and Consumption

The rice sector in Sri Lanka has been protected by successive governments through import restrictions; involvement in imports, procurement, and distribution; and input subsidies. In 1977 the rice trade was liberalized by allowing the private sector to participate in imports, procurement, and distribution. Currently the private sector is heavily involved in purchasing and importing paddy (subject to duties).

### Conceptual Model

This study uses a partial equilibrium model, treating Sri Lanka as a small net importer of rice, to investigate the impact of rice trade liberalization on prices, supply and demand of rice and paddy, and rice imports and calorie intake, and to investigate the impact of the government paddy procurement program on supply, demand, and prices.

Conceptually the model involves a demand system for cereals (rice, wheat, and millet); a paddy supply function; and marketing functions linking prices of paddy and rice. Government procurement is treated as exogenous. Tariff and other border charges link the retail price of rice with the world price. The demand system, paddy supply function, and marketing function are considered stochastic and are estimated econometrically.

Few identities are required to close the model. A constant proportion technology between paddy and rice is considered. Demand is met from domestic supply as well as imports. The level of rice imports is the difference between domestic rice consumption and domestic production, adjusted for buffer stocks. The calorie contents of rice, wheat, and millet are used to obtain the total calorie intake.

Changes in trade policy are simulated by changing tariff levels and by eliminating other border charges that affect the retail price. Paddy procurement policy is simu-

lated by changing the government involvement in procurement, which affects producer prices of paddy. An algebraic description of the model follows.

*Stochastic equations.*    1. Demand functions. The per capita demands for rice
$(D^r)$, wheat $(D^w)$, and millet $(D^m)$ are functions of the price of rice $(P^r)$, price of wheat
$(P^w)$, and price of millet $(P^m)$ and the expenditure on rice, wheat, and millet $(M)$:

$$D^r = D^r(P^r, \overline{P^w}, \overline{M})$$

$$D^w = D^w(P^r, \overline{P^w}, \overline{P^m}, \overline{M})$$

$$D^m = D^m(P^r, \overline{P^w}, \overline{P^m}, \overline{M}).$$

2. Paddy supply function. The supply of paddy $(S^p)$ is a function of the lagged
paddy price $(P^p_{t-i})$, price of seed paddy $(P^s)$, price of fertilizer $(P^f)$, and time trend $(T)$:

$$S^p = S^p(P^p_{t-i}, \overline{P^s}, \overline{P^f}, \overline{T}).$$

3. Price linkage equation. The price of paddy is a function of the price of rice
and the ratio of paddy purchased by government agencies to total paddy output $(G)$,
a proxy for government intervention:

$$P^p = f(P^r, G).$$

*Identities.*    4. Paddy-rice conversion. The supply of rice $(S^r)$ is a constant proportion (cf) of rice production:

$$S^r = cf \cdot S^p.$$

5. Rice imports. The total imported quantity of rice $(Imp)$ is obtained by subtracting the supply of rice and change in stocks $(STOCK)$ from the total demand.
The total demand for rice is obtained by multiplying the per capita demand by the
population $(pop)$:

$$Imp = (D^r \cdot \overline{pop} - S^r - \overline{STOCK}).$$

6. Tariff. The domestic price of rice is determined by the world market price of
rice $(P^{rw})$, the tariff rate $(Tariff)$, and other border charges $(Other)$:

$$P^r = P^{rw}(1 + \overline{Tariff} + \overline{Other}).$$

7. Cereal intake. Total calorie intake (*Totcal*) is obtained using the calorie contents of rice, wheat, and millet (*ccr, ccw,* and *ccm,* respectively) and the per capita demand for rice, wheat, and millet:

$$Totcal = ccr \cdot D^r + ccw \cdot D^w + ccm \cdot D^m.$$

The endogenous variables are $D^r$, $D^w$, $D^m$, $P^r$, $S^p$, $P^p$, $S^r$, $Imp$, $Totcal$. The exogenous variables are $\overline{M}$, $\overline{P^w}$, $\overline{P^m}$, $\overline{P^s}$, $\overline{P^j}$, $\overline{T}$, $\overline{G}$, $\overline{cf}$, $\overline{pop}$, $\overline{STOCK}$, $\overline{P^{rw}}$, $\overline{Tariff}$, $\overline{Other}$, $\overline{ccr}$, $\overline{ccw}$ and $\overline{ccm}$. The policy variables are $\overline{G}$, $\overline{Tariff}$, $\overline{Other}$.

### Empirical Specification

Following Strotz (1957), the consumer is assumed to allocate expenditure among commodities in stages. In the first stage the consumer allocates expenditure to a broad group of commodities such as food and nonfood items. In the second stage the consumer allocates expenditures within each broad group to smaller subgroups (cereals, meat, vegetables, and so on). This process continues through the various stages.

This study focuses on the allocation of expenditure among cereals. The demand system includes three commodities—rice, wheat, and millet—the three major cereals in the Sri Lankan diet. The utility of cereal consumption is assumed to be weakly separable from the utility of other commodities. Accordingly an almost ideal demand system (AIDS) is developed for rice, wheat, and millet. The algebraic form of the AIDS follows Deaton and Muellbauer (1980). The AIDS in budget form is expressed as

$$w_i = a_i + c_i \cdot \ln(E/\overline{P}) + b_{1i} \cdot \ln P_{1i} + b_{2i} \cdot \ln P_{2i} + d \cdot t, \tag{1}$$

where $w_i$ is the budget share of the *i*th commodity; $E$ is total consumption expenditure on rice, wheat, and millet; $P_i$ is the price of the *i*th commodity; $\overline{P}$ is the price index defined by

$$\ln \overline{P} = a_0 + \Sigma_k \cdot a_k \cdot \ln P_i + 0.5\Sigma_k\Sigma_j b_{ij} \cdot \ln P_i \cdot \ln P_j; \tag{2}$$

and $a_o$, $a_i$, $c_i$, and $b_{ij}$ are parameters to be estimated.

Deaton and Muellbauer (1980) suggest approximating the price index $\overline{P}$ by the Stone geometric price index:

$$\ln \overline{P} = \Sigma_i w_i \cdot \ln P_i. \tag{3}$$

Adding up restrictions for the demand system requires

$$\Sigma_i a_i = 1, \Sigma_i c_i = 0, \Sigma_j b_{ij} = 0, \text{ and } \Sigma_j d_i = 0.$$

The homogeneity restriction is $\Sigma_j b_{ij} = 0$, and the cross-equation symmetry restrictions can be imposed as $b_{ij} = b_{ji}$ for $i \neq j$.

The demand model presented here is a nonlinear system. This system has three equations to be estimated. However, due to theoretical restrictions, it is sufficient to estimate only two of them. The expenditure $(e_{iy})$, own-price $(\eta_{ii})$, and cross-price $(e_{ij})$ elasticity values are derived as follows (Sadoulet and de Janvry 1995):

$$\eta_i = 1 + c_i/w_i; \; e_{ii} = -1 - c_i + b_{ii}/w_i; \; e_{ij} = b_{ii}/w_i - c_i/w_i \cdot w_j.$$

The parameters are estimated using the two-stage least square estimation. Per capita consumption levels of rice, wheat, and millet are from the Food Balance Sheets published by the Food and Agriculture Organization of the United Nations. Retail prices of rice and wheat and farmgate prices of paddy are from the Statistical Abstracts published by the Central Bank of Sri Lanka. The retail price of millet is from the Hector Kobbakaduwa Agrarian Service Centre. Prices have been deflated using the Colombo Consumers Price Index, published by the Central Bank of Sri Lanka. Figures for total paddy production, imports of rice, price of seed paddy, price of fertilizer, purchases of paddy under the GPS, and population have been obtained from the annual reports of the Central Bank of Sri Lanka. The price of fertilizer was obtained from A. Bours and Company (a major private-sector supplier of fertilizer). Descriptive statistics for the data are presented in Table 6.10.

**Results**

*Model estimates.*    The parameter estimates of the AIDS demand system and the elasticity estimate of demand using 1990 values are presented in Tables 6.11 and 6.12, respectively. All the elasticity estimates with respect to own prices have the expected negative sign and are statistically significant at the 1 percent level. The estimated paddy supply function is given by the following inverse equation:

$$PDN = 0.014 - 806{,}283.0/FGP_{-1} + 0.231E8/SP + 0.800E8/FP + 55{,}980.6/t$$
$$\phantom{PDN = }(3.17) \qquad (-2.77) \qquad\qquad (2.18) \qquad\qquad (0.61) \qquad\qquad (6.22)$$
$$R^2 = 0.75 \qquad n = 29$$

where $PDN$ is paddy production, $FGP$ is the farmgate price of paddy (lagged by one year), $SP$ is the price of paddy seed, $FP$ is the price of fertilizer, and $t$ is the time trend.

**Table 6.10    Per capita calorie consumption**

| Variable | Mean | Standard deviation |
|---|---|---|
| Consumption of rice (kg/year per capita) | 95.6828 | 6.2319 |
| Consumption of wheat (kg/year per capita) | 43.9452 | 5.8325 |
| Consumption of millet (kg/year per capita) | 0.5190 | 0.2262 |
| Imports of rice (thousands of MT) | 156.87 | 84.03 |
| Paddy production (thousands of MT) | 2,122.13 | 505.10 |
| Retail price of rice (Rs/kg) | 13.54 | 7.01 |
| Retail price of wheat (Rs/kg) | 10.34 | 4.74 |
| Retail price of millet (Rs/kg) | 24.99 | 18.04 |
| Farm-gate price of paddy (Rs/kg) | 4.79 | 3.39 |
| Price of seed paddy (Rs/kg) | 139.48 | 108.90 |
| Price of fertilizer (Rs/kg) | 4.948 | 4,788.61 |
| Colombo Consumers Price Index | 801.65 | 356.49 |
| Purchases under GPS (thousands of MT) | 225.20 | 221.90 |
| Population (thousands) | 15,863.80 | 2,098.07 |

Sources: As detailed in the text.

**Table 6.11    Parameter estimates and standard errors of the almost ideal demand system model, 1979–2000**

| Dependent variable | Parameter | Estimate | Standard error | _p_-value |
|---|---|---|---|---|
| Rice share | Intercept | 0.8269 | 0.6807 | 0.22 |
| | Rice price | 0.0474 | 0.0267 | 0.07 |
| | Wheat price | −0.0452 | 0.0265 | 0.08 |
| | Expenditure | −0.0216 | 0.1376 | 0.87 |
| Wheat share | Intercept | 0.1307 | 0.6779 | 0.84 |
| | Wheat price | 0.0414 | 0.0264 | 0.11 |
| | Expenditure | 0.0257 | 0.1370 | 0.85 |

Source: Author's calculations.

The figures in parentheses are _t_-statistics. The time period used in the estimation is 1971–99. This supply function implies that current production is determined by the product price that prevailed during the previous year—the implication being that policy influences production with a lag. Estimates of the supply elasticity of paddy with respect to paddy price and input prices are also presented in Table 6.12. The own-price elasticity has the expected positive sign and is statistically significant. The supply elasticities with respect to input prices are negative, and seed price elasticity is statistically significant.

Table 6.12    Elasticity estimates: Demand, supply, and price linkage

| Type | Variable | Elasticity | $p$-value |
|------|----------|-----------:|----------:|
| Rice demand | Rice price | −0.9126 | 0.00 |
| | Wheat price | −0.0543 | 0.44 |
| | Millet price | −0.1279 | 0.08 |
| | Expenditure | 0.9700 | 0.00 |
| Wheat demand | Rice price | −0.2355 | 0.00 |
| | Wheat price | −0.8728 | 0.00 |
| | Millet price | −0.0145 | 0.01 |
| | Expenditure | 1.0949 | 0.03 |
| Millet demand | Rice price | 0.1114 | 0.98 |
| | Wheat price | 0.8390 | 0.00 |
| | Millet price | −1.2573 | 0.00 |
| | Expenditure | 0.3068 | 0.82 |
| Paddy price | Rice price | 1.004 | 0.00 |
| Paddy supply | Paddy price | 0.609 | 0.01 |
| | Seed paddy price | −0.063 | 0.04 |
| | Fertilizer price | −0.074 | 0.54 |

Source: Author's calculations.

The estimated price linkage equation is given by the following log-linear equation:

$$FGP = -0.776 + 0.982 \cdot RP + 0.004 \cdot Govt$$
$$(33.85) \qquad (10.88) \qquad\quad (2.44)$$
$$R^2 = 0.90 \qquad n = 23$$

where *FGP* is the log of the farmgate price of paddy, *RP* is the log of the retail price of rice, and *Govt* is paddy purchased by the government as a percentage of the total output. All the coefficients are statistically significant. The equation was estimated for the period 1978–2000. These results imply that the farmgate price of paddy increases with an increase in rice price, and that the price of paddy increases with an increase in government purchases of paddy. These results suggest that, in the absence of government intervention, private buyers would be able to purchase paddy at lower prices, implying scope for welfare improvement.

*Simulation results.*    Econometrically estimated equations were combined with the identities discussed in the conceptual model to develop a model to be used in the simulation. Data availability determined the period for the simulation to be 1979–99.[4] The validity of the model is tested by comparing actual data with the model predictions for each endogenous variable. Validation statistics are shown in Table 6.13. High correlation coefficients, low percentage root mean square errors,

Table 6.13    Validation statistics

| Variable | Mean | Correlation coefficient | Root mean square error | Bias |
|---|---|---|---|---|
| Calorie intake | 50,422 | 0.98 | 317.67 (0.628) | 0.0001 |
| Rice demand | 95.68 | 0.88 | 2.79 (2.915) | 0.0000 |
| Wheat demand | 43.94 | 0.80 | 3.41 (7.760) | 0.0000 |
| Rice imports | 168,047 | 0.24 | 130,303 (77.53) | 0.0002 |
| Rice supply | 1,681,600 | 0.64 | 140,836 (8.37) | 0.0002 |
| Paddy supply | 2,402,285 | 0.64 | 164,882 (6.86) | 0.0002 |
| Paddy price | 6.21 | 0.93 | 0.04 (0.644) | 0.0009 |

Source: Author's calculations.

Note: Figures in parentheses are root mean square error as a percentage of the mean of the variable.

and small bias are observed for all the variables except imports, which show a lower correlation coefficient and a higher percentage root mean square error.

Three simulations were carried out to assess the impacts of liberalization. In the first simulation all border charges were removed. The second simulation was based on removing only import duties. Paddy procurement policy was simulated next, by allowing only private-sector milling. Results are shown in Table 6.14.

As expected, trade liberalization would increase the demand for rice as well as calorie intake. It would also decrease the price of paddy for the producers, and therefore paddy and rice production levels should also drop. As a result imports would increase. Removal of all border charges would lead to an increase of calorie intake by 33.15 percent. If import duties only were removed, the increase in calorie intake would be 23.22 percent. Figure 6.3 shows predicted and simulated values of calorie intake for the period 1979–99.

Table 6.14    Impacts of trade liberalization on prices, calorie intake, demand, production, and trade

| | | Policy experiment | | |
|---|---|---|---|---|
| Variable | Baseline value | Removal of all border charges | Removal of import duties | No government purchases |
| Calorie intake per day | 138.15 | 183.95 (33.15) | 170.24 (23.22) | 138.15 (0.00) |
| Rice demand (kg/year per capita) | 95.67 | 139.17 (45.47) | 126.03 (31.74) | 95.67 (0.00) |
| Wheat demand (kg/year per capita) | 43.96 | 47.10 (7.11) | 46.27 (5.23) | 43.96 (0.00) |
| Rice imports (MT) | 188,540 | 1,016,823 (704.21) | 1,027,466 (490.31) | 208,365 (5.43) |
| Rice supply (MT) | 1,661,242 | 1,185,158 (−28.28) | 1,331,016 (−19.62) | 1,641,417 (−1.28) |
| Paddy supply (MT) | 2,373,203 | 1,693,084 (−28.28) | 1,901,451 (−19.62) | 2,344,882 (−1.28) |
| Paddy price (Rs/kg) | 0.59 | 0.39 (−34.03) | 0.43 (−26.36) | 0.57 (−2.15) |

Notes: Impacts evaluated at the mean of the sample. Figures in parentheses are percentage changes from the baseline value.

**Figure 6.3   Predicted and simulated levels of calorie intake, 1979–99
(thousands of kcal/yr per capita)**

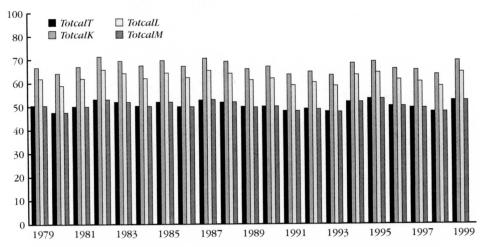

Source: Author's calculations.
Notes: *TotcalK*, total calorie intake simulated with removal of all border charges; *TotcalL*, total calorie intake simulated with removal of import tariffs; *TotcalM*, total calorie intake simulated with no government purchases; *TotcalT*, total calorie intake predicted by the model.

If the government had no involvement in purchases, the producer price of paddy would decrease by 2.15 percent, leading to a drop in paddy production by 1.28 percent. Importantly, in this simulation government purchases are set to equal zero and the mean value of the government purchases during this period is rather small. As a result, the impacts are small. Such a policy would not influence the demand-side variables, on the assumption that Sri Lanka can import any amount of rice at the world price, subject to trade restrictions. Figures 6.4 and 6.5 show predicted and simulated values of price and production of paddy for the period 1979–99.

This analysis clearly shows that if lower prices had prevailed due to removal of trade restrictions, calorie intake would have been higher. This suggests that trade liberalization can be used as a direct policy intervention to increase calorie intake. Yet producer prices—and therefore the income of the paddy producers—would be lower. That reduction in incomes would lower the capacity of the farming community to purchase food and might offset some of the gains made by net consumers of food. Furthermore if the price drops inefficient producers would be the first to exit the industry. In Sri Lanka small paddy farmers are among the poorest segments of the

**Figure 6.4  Prices of paddy: Predicted and simulated, 1979–99 (Rs/ton)**

Price (Rs/ton)

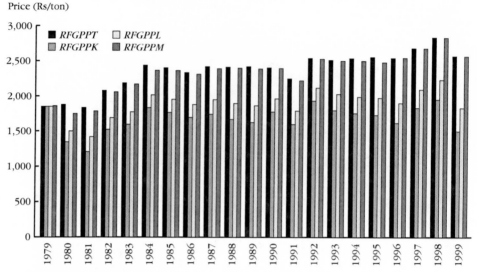

Source: Author's calculations.
Notes: *RFGPPK,* real farmgate price of paddy simulated with removal of all border charges;
*RFGPPL,* real farmgate price of paddy simulated with removal of import tariffs; *RFGPPM,* real
farmgate price of paddy simulated with no government purchases; *RFGPPT,* real farmgate price
of paddy predicted by the model.

**Figure 6.5  Production of paddy: Predicted and simulated, 1979–99
(thousands of MT)**

Production (thousands of MT)

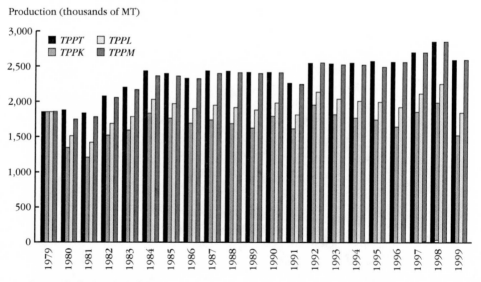

Source: Author's calculations.
Note: *TPPK,* total paddy production simulated with removal of all border charges; *TPPL,* total
paddy production simulated with removal of import tariffs; *TPPM,* total paddy production
simulated with no government purchases; *TPPT,* total paddy production predicted by the model.

population, and their exit would have serious repercussions on poverty in the short term. Do the gains to consumers outweigh losses to producers?

According to the underlying assumptions of the model, gains can indeed compensate for the losses. Using similar models, Rafeek and Samarathunga (2000) and Ekanayake (2003) show that rice trade liberalization improves economic efficiency at the national level. Although the earlier studies on rice trade liberalization did mention poverty impacts, no formal attempt was made to quantify those impacts. The next section assesses the impact of trade liberalization on poverty.

## Rice Trade Liberalization and Its Impact on Poverty in Sri Lanka

### The Model

This study uses the method proposed by Nicita, Olarreaga, and Soloaga (2002) to assess the poverty impacts of liberalization; the model was later used by McCulloch (2002) to assess the impacts of rice trade liberalization at the provincial level. The model calculates the impacts of rice trade liberalization, which lowers paddy and rice prices, according to the relative importance of paddy-rice in the expenditures and income of a household. If a particular group depends more on paddy as an income source, it is likely to experience losses due to rice trade liberalization. A group with substantial expenditures for rice will experience gains from rice trade liberalization. Overall group gains or losses due to rice trade liberalization are determined by the relative difference between the income and expenditure shares of that group. It is generally believed that poor people, especially in urban areas and on plantations (known as estates), spend more on rice compared to other groups, while rural (non-estate) households depend heavily on paddy as an income source. Whether rice trade liberalization helps the poor is thus an empirical issue.

The income $Y$ of a household is given in the model as

$$Y = \left(\sum_j p_j^O q_j^O - \sum_k p_k^I q_k^I\right) + \sum_f w_f L_f + \sum_m \sum_n T_{mn},\qquad(4)$$

where $p_j^O$ is the price of output $j$; $q_j^O$ is the quantity of output $j$; $p_k^I$ and $q_k^I$ are the corresponding input prices and quantities; $w_f$ is the wage rate for factor $f$; $L_f$ is the net sale of factor $f$ by the household; and $T_{mn}$ is the net transfer received by household member $n$ from source $m$.

The first term in equation (4) is the value added from all production (including farming and nonfarming enterprises). This includes marketed production as well as own consumption. The second term is the value of net factor sales by the household. In the case of most poor households, this is simply the net labor sales (employment income minus payments for hired labor), since the only factor that most poor households sell is their own labor. The final term represents the net transfers received by the household.

Similarly we can write the consumption of the household as

$$C = \sum_i p_i^C q_i^C, \tag{5}$$

where $p_i^C$ is the price of good $i$ and $q_i^C$ is the quantity consumed of good $i$. Note that $q_i^C$ includes own consumption as well as goods purchased from the market.

It is possible to simulate the impact of price changes on household incomes induced by structural reforms. In the short run we can assume that all quantities remain fixed, so that

$$\Delta Y = \left( \sum_j \Delta p_j^O q_j^O - \sum_k \Delta p_k^I q_k^I \right) + \sum_f \Delta w_f L_f + \sum_m \sum_n \Delta T_{mn}. \tag{6}$$

Similarly the change in consumption (assuming that quantities remain fixed) is written as

$$\Delta C = \sum_i \Delta p_i^C q_i^C. \tag{7}$$

A first-order approximation of the change in money metric utility resulting from a change in the price of a commodity can be given by[5]

$$\Delta MMU = \Delta Y - \Delta C. \tag{8}$$

The intuition for the expression in (8) is as follows. An increase in the price of a good that is both produced and consumed both increases income and increases the cost of achieving the original level of consumption. The difference between the two is therefore an approximation to the net welfare change.

Combining equations (4)–(7) gives

$$\frac{\Delta MMU}{Y} = \left( \sum_j BS_j^O \frac{\Delta p_j^O}{p_j^O} - \sum_k BS_k^I \frac{\Delta p_k^I}{p_k^I} \right) + \sum_f BS_f^w \frac{\Delta w_f}{w_f} + \frac{\sum_m \sum_n \Delta T_{mn}}{Y} - \sum_i BS_j^C \frac{\Delta p_j^C}{p_j^C}, \tag{9}$$

where $BS_j^O$ indicates the budget (or income) share of the output revenue in total income, $BS_j^I$ is the budget share of the input costs, $BS_j^W$ is the income share of the net factor income from factor $f$, and $BS_j^C$ is the budget share of good $j$ in consumption. The first-order percentage change in net income can be approximated by multiplying the budget shares of income and expenditure for each item times the percentage change in prices.[6]

### Data

The data required for the model are the income and expenditure shares among different groups in Sri Lanka. Following Gunawardena (2000), households were classified by the level of consumption expenditures. The poor are defined as households below the higher poverty line (Rs 950.00 per person per month). The very poor are defined as households below the reference poverty line (Rs 791.67 per person per month). The nonpoor are households above the higher poverty line. Food expenditure is a larger share of the budget for the poor and very poor. Rice accounts for the largest share and shows a decreasing share with increasing consumption expenditures (Gunawardena 2000). Table 6.15 shows the expenditure shares.

Data on income from rice is not available, hence income from all agriculture is presented. Agricultural income, which includes income from cultivation of paddy, tobacco, chilies, onions, vegetables, and fruits, is more important for the poor and the very poor (Table 6.15). For the poor the share of income from government transfer programs (Janasaviya and Samurdhi) exceeds earnings from agriculture.

Consumption patterns among sectors show that households in estates have the biggest expenditure share for rice; the urban sector has the lowest (Table 6.16). Rural households have the highest income share from agriculture among all sectors. Except for the rural sector, the share of income from transfer programs is much higher than from agriculture.

Expenditure and income shares at the provincial level were obtained from the Consumer Finance and Socio-economic Survey of the Central Bank and the Sri Lanka

**Table 6.15  Share of items in total income and total expenditure by income group, 1995/96**

| Group | Income share | | | Expenditure share | | |
|---|---|---|---|---|---|---|
| | Agriculture | Samurdhi/ Janasaviya | Other sources | Rice | Other food | Nonfood |
| Poor (below the higher poverty line) | 7.7 | 9.85 | 82.45 | 20.51 | 54.53 | 24.96 |
| Very poor (below the reference poverty line) | 7.57 | 11.23 | 81.20 | 21.77 | 54.44 | 23.79 |
| Poor excluding very poor | 7.9 | 7.64 | 84.46 | 18.90 | 54.64 | 26.46 |
| Nonpoor | 4.97 | 3.27 | 91.76 | 10.11 | 46.95 | 42.94 |

Source: Calculated using the shares provided by Gunawardena (2000).

Table 6.16    Share of items in total income and total expenditure by sector, 1995/96

| Sector | Income share | | | Expenditure share | | |
|---|---|---|---|---|---|---|
| | Agriculture | Samurdhi/Janasaviya | Other sources | Rice | Other food | Nonfood |
| Urban | 0.20 | 1.43 | 98.37 | 5.18 | 32.33 | 62.50 |
| Rural | 6.97 | 6.31 | 86.72 | 10.89 | 39.51 | 49.60 |
| Estates[a] | 1.39 | 1.28 | 97.33 | 14.87 | 52.13 | 33.00 |

Sources: Income shares calculated using the shares provided by Gunawardena (2000). Expenditure shares calculated using data from the Consumer Finances and Socio-economic Survey (1996/97) of the Central Bank of Sri Lanka.
[a]Estate in this context means a plantation.

Integrated Survey (1999/2000), respectively. According to Gunawardena (2000), the highest incidence of poverty is observed in Uva province (55 percent) and the lowest incidence in the Western province (23 percent). These incidences are reflected in the pattern of income and expenditures. Share of food expenditure and share of rice expenditure as a percentage of total expenditure are 56.2 and 14.1 percent, respectively, in Uva province—the highest among all provinces. These values are 41.8 percent and 6.5 percent in the Western province—the lowest among all provinces (Table 6.17). Similarly the percentage of farm income is highest in Uva province (41.4 percent) and lowest in the Western province (6.5 percent).

The percentage of land under rice cultivation is used to approximate the income from rice. Though the area under rice is highest as a percentage of total area, income from rice is merely 2.66 percent in the Western province. Income from rice is nearly 7 percent in Uva and Sabaragamuwa provinces (Table 6.18).

### Results

In order to assess the impacts of rice trade liberalization, prices of rice and paddy after liberalization must be estimated. The current duty on rice (Rs 5.00/kilogram) is

Table 6.17    Consumer expenditure shares, 1996/97

| Province | Rice | Other food | Nonfood |
|---|---|---|---|
| Western | 6.50 | 35.30 | 58.20 |
| Central | 10.90 | 39.60 | 49.50 |
| Southern | 11.80 | 42.40 | 45.80 |
| Northwestern | 13.20 | 42.60 | 44.20 |
| Northcentral | 13.00 | 41.70 | 45.30 |
| Uva | 14.10 | 42.10 | 43.80 |
| Sabaragamuwa | 12.30 | 39.00 | 48.70 |
| All | 9.90 | 38.50 | 51.60 |

Source: Consumer Finances and Socio-economic Survey 1996/97 of the Central Bank of Sri Lanka.

**Table 6.18    Average percentage share of different sources of income, rural households**

| Province | Area under rice | Agriculture | | Samurdhi | Sources other than rice and samurdhi |
|---|---|---|---|---|---|
| | | Farm | Rice | | |
| Western | 41.0 | 6.50 | 2.66 | 1.90 | 95.43 |
| Central | 31.0 | 13.80 | 4.27 | 5.30 | 90.42 |
| Southern | 33.5 | 20.80 | 6.96 | 3.70 | 89.33 |
| Northeastern | 44.0 | 29.00 | 12.76 | 2.30 | 84.94 |
| Northwestern | 22.4 | 10.50 | 2.35 | 4.70 | 92.94 |
| Northcentral | 22.3 | 26.40 | 5.88 | 6.90 | 87.21 |
| Uva | 18.6 | 41.40 | 7.70 | 6.80 | 85.49 |
| Sabaragamuwa | 25.3 | 29.40 | 7.44 | 4.30 | 88.26 |
| All | 28.3 | 17.80 | 5.11 | 3.60 | 91.29 |

Source: World Bank (2000).

equivalent to a 25 percent tariff, as the cost insurance freight of rice is approximately Rs 18/kilogram. Trade liberalization is therefore modeled as a drop in prices of rice and paddy by 25 percent, assuming perfect passthrough of savings. Epaarachchi, Jayanetti, and Weliwita (2002) provide an NRP of 25 percent for rice in 2000.

Since the simulations here consider a drop in price, the model outcome would show a negative value for changes in income and expenditure. Change in welfare is obtained by subtracting change in expenditure from change in income. If it is positive, it indicates that on average, loss in income can be compensated by the drop in expenditure, and there is a net gain from rice trade liberalization. The higher the change in welfare, the higher the benefits of trade liberalization.

While all income groups gain, the very poor obtain the highest welfare gain as well as the highest reduction in expenditure. Hence rice trade liberalization can to that extent be called pro-poor. The lowest gain accrues to the nonpoor, as they spend only a small portion of their income on rice and derive a very small share of their income from agriculture (Table 6.19).[7] The poor (excluding the very poor) incur the highest losses and show a moderate gain in welfare.

While all sectors gain from rice trade liberalization, the housing-development sector gains the most (Table 6.20). This sector has the second highest incidence of poverty; hence trade liberalization should alleviate poverty to some degree. Although paddy is one of the key income-generating crops, on average a considerable portion of expenditure on rice is incurred in the rural sector. Thus the rural sector has a net gain from rice trade liberalization—though on average it incurs the highest income loss among the sectors (Table 6.20).

Regionally all the provinces show a gain from rice trade liberalization (Table 6.21).[8] The Northwestern province gains the most; as that province has a higher incidence of poverty, rice trade liberalization can be called pro-poor in this context

Table 6.19    Impacts of rice trade liberalization by income group (percent)

| Income group | Change in income | Change in expenditure | Change in welfare |
|---|---|---|---|
| Poor (below the higher poverty line) | −1.93 | −5.13 | 3.20 |
| Very poor (below the reference poverty line) | −1.89 | −5.44 | 3.55 |
| Poor excluding very poor | −1.98 | −4.73 | 2.75 |
| Nonpoor | −1.24 | −2.53 | 1.29 |

Table 6.20    Impacts of rice trade liberalization by sector (percent)

| Income group | Change in income | Change in expenditure | Change in welfare |
|---|---|---|---|
| Urban | −0.05 | −1.29 | 1.24 |
| Rural | −1.74 | −2.72 | 0.98 |
| Estates[a] | −0.35 | −3.72 | 3.37 |

[a]Estate in this context means a plantation.

Table 6.21    Impacts of rice trade liberalization by province (percent)

| Province | Change in income | Change in expenditure | Change in welfare |
|---|---|---|---|
| Western | −0.67 | −1.63 | 0.96 |
| Central | −1.07 | −2.73 | 1.66 |
| Southern | −1.74 | −2.95 | 1.21 |
| Northwestern | −0.59 | −3.30 | 2.71 |
| Northcentral | −1.47 | −3.25 | 1.78 |
| Uva | −1.93 | −3.53 | 1.60 |
| Sabaragamuwa | −1.86 | −3.08 | 1.22 |
| All | −1.28 | −2.48 | 1.20 |

as well. On average a 1 percent drop in the price of rice reduces the income of households by 1.28 percent. The reduction varies with the share of income from rice, from 1.93 percent in Uva province to only 0.59 percent in the Northwestern province (where only a small proportion of land is under rice). The producers in Uva and Sabaragamuwa incur the biggest losses. The impact of the price drop on expenditure also differs among provinces. The average reduction in expenditure is 2.48 percent, with the highest reduction occurring in Uva province (3.53 percent) and the lowest in the Western province (1.63 percent).

To estimate impacts by size of paddyholding would require detailed data on farmers' income shares from paddy and expenditure shares for rice. In the absence of such data, impacts by size of holdings were inferred based on the estimated size of paddyholding required to meet the rice requirement of an average household.

Assuming that an average household comprises five members and the annual rice requirement per person is 96 kilograms (FAO various years), then the household's rice requirement is 475 kilograms/year. This is equivalent to 679 kilograms of paddy per year (assuming a conversion ratio of 0.7). The average yield of paddy is approximately 3.856 metric tons (MT)/hectare (1,560 kilograms/acre), hence a 0.217-acre plot is sufficient to meet household needs if two seasons are cultivated with paddy. Farmers who cultivate more than 0.217 acre are assumed to be net sellers of paddy.

The distribution of landholdings indicates that approximately 7.5 percent of the paddy farmers possess holdings of less than 0.217 acre (Gunawardena 2000). The rest of the farmers, who sell surplus production, are expected to incur net losses from rice trade liberalization, and the less efficient farmers will incur higher losses. According to Weerahewa, Gunatilake, and Pitigala (2003), farming less than 2 acres is inefficient. Therefore the most adverse impact of trade liberalization will fall on small farmers with more than 0.217 acre but less than 2 acres of land.

The results reveal that rice trade liberalization would not only improve overall economic efficiency but also reduce poverty in certain categories. Among sectors, the highest gains accrue to the housing-development sector; among income groups, to the very poor; and among provinces, to the poverty-afflicted Northwestern province. Based on the efficiency and poverty-reduction gains, it could be concluded that rice trade liberalization is a desirable strategy. However, at least in the short run there are adverse impacts on the poor (*not* the very poor), especially farmers in the rural areas of Uva and Sabaragamuwa (mainly small-scale farmers).

The estimated gains from rice trade liberalization for consumers reflect the assumption of a perfect (domestic) market. Consumers may not reap the gains from rice trade liberalization if domestic markets are imperfect. The next section analyzes the impact of imperfections in the structure of the domestic market for paddy.

## Trade Impacts in Oligopsony Markets: The Case of Paddy in Sri Lanka

Paddy production in Sri Lanka is mainly carried out by small farmers, with about 70 percent of them farming less than 2.5 acres. These farmers have little bargaining power in dealing with the buyers of paddy. With prices effectively determined among a relatively few buyers (oligopsony), producers get a lower price than a simple supply-and-demand model might suggest. In this section the impact of rice trade liberalization on the oligopsonistic paddy market in Sri Lanka is assessed using a static simulation model.

### Conceptual Model

A partial equilibrium model under imperfect competition (with perfect competition and monopsony as special cases) is applied to the paddy market.[9] In this model the paddy demand function is the derived demand of the paddy buyers (collectors and millers, in the domestic market). The paddy supply function is the farmgate supply by the primary producers. The market clears when paddy demand equals supply. Due

**Figure 6.6    Equilibrium in the paddy market before and after tariff liberalization, and with and without oligopsony power**

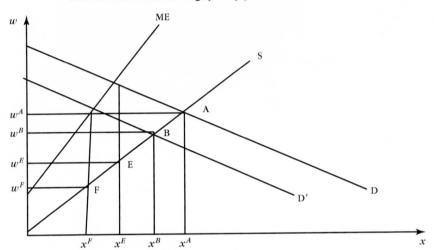

Note: D, demand; ME, marginal expenditure; S, supply; $w$, price of paddy; $x$, quantity supplied.
A, with tariff and competition; B, no tariff with competition; D, no tariff with oligopsony.

to trade liberalization—the elimination of tariffs—the price of rice drops and the demand for paddy shifts to the left (decreases). Figure 6.6 shows the equilibrium of the paddy market before and after trade liberalization and with and without oligopsony power.

From the figure it is clear that the *direction* of the impact of trade liberalization on paddy prices and quantities (negative) does not depend on the oligopsony power. However, depending on the position of the demand and supply curves, the magnitude of trade liberalization shocks, and the degree of the oligopsony power, it is possible to have positive impacts from trade liberalization. This occurs if trade liberalization is coupled with reforms to reduce the oligopsony power of the buyers. The market structure is captured by the values of the conjectural variation elasticity $\theta$ (see the description in the next section). When conjectural variation elasticity is zero, the market is perfectly competitive. The market power of the buyers increases with increasing conjectural variation elasticity; the highest possible market power occurs when the elasticity equals unity.

### Algebraic Model

Suppose that paddy collectors and millers are competitive in the output market and possess oligopsony power in the input market.[10] Oligopsony power in the input market is captured based on the conjectural variation approach, which considers the strategic interactions among firms. The conjectural variation approach measures market power on the assumption that firms simultaneously and independently choose input levels based on their beliefs about their rivals' reactions to their choice. Following Azzam and Pagoulatos (1990), the model is specified as follows.

The objective of the $j$th paddy buyer is to maximize profit $\pi_j$:

$$\text{Max}\pi_j = Pq_j - Wx_j, \tag{10}$$

subject to

$$q_j = f(x_j) \tag{11}$$

$$X = \sum_{j=1}^{n} x_j \tag{12}$$

$$W = g(X, Zs_s), \tag{13}$$

where $P$ is the price of rice, $q_j$ is the quantity of rice produced, $W$ is the price of paddy, $x_j$ is the quantity of paddy, $X$ is the supply of the paddy, and $z_s$ is the set of exogenous factors affecting paddy supply.

First-order conditions of the above problem are

$$\frac{\partial \pi_j}{\partial x_j} = P \cdot \frac{\partial q_j}{\partial x_j} - \frac{\partial w}{\partial X} \cdot \frac{\partial X}{\partial x_j} \cdot x_j - w = 0 \tag{14}$$

$$P \cdot MP_j = P \cdot \frac{\partial w}{\partial X} \cdot \frac{X}{w} \cdot \frac{\partial X}{\partial x_j} \cdot \frac{x_j}{X} \cdot w + w \tag{15}$$

$$P \cdot MP_j = \left(\frac{\theta}{\varepsilon} + 1\right) \cdot w, \tag{16}$$

where $\theta = \frac{\partial X}{\partial x_j} \cdot \frac{x_j}{X}$ is the conjectural variation elasticity and $\varepsilon$ is the paddy supply elasticity with respect to own price. If the market is perfectly competitive, then $\theta = 0$, as $\frac{\partial X}{\partial x_j} = 0$ by definition. If $\theta = 1$ the market is monopsonistic, and for $0 < \theta < 1$ it is an oligopsony. Let

$$w_d = w\left(\frac{\theta}{\varepsilon} + 1\right). \tag{17}$$

$MP_j$ is a function of $x_j$ for a well-behaved production function. Hence demand for $x_j$ can be written as

$$x_j = f(P, W_d, Z_d), \tag{18}$$

where $Z_d$ is a vector of other factors affecting demand.

Assuming that the aggregation conditions hold, demand for $x$ by the industry is given by

$$X = f(P, W_d, Z_d) \quad \text{where} \quad X = \sum_{j=1}^{n} x_j. \tag{19}$$

Equilibrium in the input market is given by equations (13), (17), and (18). The exogenous variables in the system are $P$, $Z_d$, and $Z$. The endogenous variables are $W_d$, $X$, and $W_s$.

### Data
The model is calibrated using quantities and prices from 2001. The quantity of paddy supplied and demanded is 2,700 MT. The prices of paddy and rice considered are Rs 12/kilogram and 32.50 Rs/kilogram, respectively. A range of elasticity values for supply and demand ($|0.5|$, $|1.0|$, and $|1.5|$) has been used, showing inelastic, unitary elastic, and elastic functions, respectively. Similarly a range of conjectural variation elasticity values (0.0, 0.5, and 1.0) is used in the sensitivity analysis.

### Simulation Results
Three policy experiments have been conducted: trade liberalization, elimination of market power, and trade liberalization along with elimination of market power. Trade liberalization is modeled as a reduction in the retail price of rice by 30 percent. Elimination of market power is modeled by setting conjectural variation elasticity to zero. Impacts are assessed under different assumptions regarding the elasticities of demand and supply.

The results show that rice trade liberalization has negative impacts on paddy production and paddy prices. Under alternative assumptions about the degree of oligopsony power and price elasticities, a drop in the price of rice by 30 percent decreases paddy price from 12 to 10.20 Rs/kilogram—that is, by 15 percent. Depending on the elasticity assumption, the drop in paddy production could range from 7.5 to 15 percent.

In contrast the elimination of oligopsony market power has positive impacts on production and prices under all scenarios. When the supply is inelastic (and the degree of oligopsony power is therefore high), the impact of eliminating oligopsony power is also high. Table 6.22 shows the impacts under various scenarios. If the demand and supply functions are elastic and conjectural variation elasticity is 0.5 (oligopsony), elimination of oligopsony power could increase the paddy price from Rs 12 to Rs 13.71/kilogram—that is, by 14.28 percent. If demand and supply are inelastic and conjectural elasticity is 1.0 (monopsony), the impact on price can be as high as 50 percent.

If the degree of market power is small—that is, when conjectural variation is 0.5 (oligopsony)—trade liberalization still has negative impacts on production and prices even with the elimination of oligopsony power. When the conjectural variation elasticity is close to 1 (monopsony), we see a positive impact of trade liberalization on production and price if oligopsony power can be eliminated. The direction of impact also depends on the elasticities of supply and demand. With inelastic demand and supply functions, liberalization combined with reforms to eliminate market power leads to higher gains, as the initial condition is characterized by high oligopsony power.

The results of this analysis show that losses to the paddy producers due to trade liberalization can be minimized if oligopsony power can be eliminated at the same time. Further research to estimate the degree of oligopsony power is therefore worthwhile. Effective measures to eliminate oligopsony power would take the form of domestic market reforms aimed at removing the existing market imperfections.

**Table 6.22    Impacts of trade liberalization on the paddy market**

| Elasticity | Market structure | No market power | | Trade liberalization and no market power | |
|---|---|---|---|---|---|
| | | Price | Quantity | Price | Quantity |
| Base | | 12.00 | 2700.00 | 12.00 | 2700.00 |
| Elastic \|1.5\| | Oligopsony | 13.71 | 3278.57 | 11.66 | 2504.28 |
| | | (14.28) | (21.42) | (−2.86) | (−4.29) |
| | Monopsony | 15.00 | 3712.50 | 12.75 | 2953.12 |
| | | (25.00) | (37.50) | (6.25) | (9.38) |
| Unitary elastic \|1.0\| | Oligopsony | 14.40 | 3240.00 | 12.24 | 2754.00 |
| | | (20.00) | (20.00) | (2.00) | (2.00) |
| | Monopsony | 16.00 | 3600.00 | 13.6 | 3060.00 |
| | | (33.00) | (33.00) | (13.00) | (13.00) |
| Inelastic \|0.5\| | Oligopsony | 16.00 | 3150.00 | 13.60 | 2880.00 |
| | | (33.33) | (16.67) | (13.33) | (6.67) |
| | Monopsony | 18.00 | 3375.00 | 15.30 | 3071.25 |
| | | (50.00) | (25.00) | (27.5) | (13.75) |

Note: Numbers in parentheses are percentage changes from the bases.

In order to maximize efficiency, levels of price support should be adjusted to reflect market conditions, whether due to policy changes (trade liberalization) or natural factors (bumper harvests). For example, if trade is liberalized, the support price should be reduced, to avoid an adverse impact on the milling sector. Similarly, if there is a bumper crop, lowering the support price of paddy would be necessary, to allow consumers to benefit from lower rice prices.

## Conclusion

The rice sector in Sri Lanka has been protected by successive governments through various input subsidies and import restrictions, as well as government involvement in import, procurement, and distribution. In 1977 the policy framework started to shift toward more liberal policies, by allowing the private sector to participate in the import, procurement, and distribution of rice. However, the rice trade continues to be restricted, reflecting policymakers' concerns that trade liberalization may have adverse impacts on poverty.

Analysis of the marketing channels for paddy-rice indicates that they are mainly associated with the private sector. State involvement in procurement, storage, and distribution has been minimal. Import restrictions on rice have been ad hoc, imposed during glut seasons and relaxed during shortage periods.

In this study the impacts of rice trade liberalization and privatization of the government procurement program were simulated using an econometrically estimated partial equilibrium model. The results reveal that with the drop in retail prices due to trade liberalization, calorie intake would increase; hence trade liberalization would be a step toward increasing food security. At the same time trade liberalization depresses producer prices, reducing the income of paddy producers. Such a reduction may offset some of the gains to the net consumers of food.

At present the legal framework in Sri Lanka does not allow conversion of paddy lands into nonpaddy lands. Furthermore when paddy lands are converted to other uses, waterlogging can occur in those located in the wet zone. As a result lands released from paddy may not be demanded by other sectors in the short run. This implies adverse impacts of rice trade liberalization on paddy landowners as well. The model treats wage rates as exogenous, considered to be determined by supply and demand conditions in the nonfarm sector. However, if the wage rate is depressed due to changes in the rice market, there will be adverse impacts on the labor force as well.

Results of the analysis of the poverty impacts of rice trade liberalization indicate a net gain to all income groups, provinces, and sectors. The biggest gainers are the very poor (those who earn less than Rs 791.67 per person per month), the Northwestern province, and the housing-development sector, where the incidences of poverty are the highest. Paddy farmers with relatively bigger holdings (greater than 0.217 acre and less than 2 acres) would be negatively affected, however.

To a close approximation, rice trade liberalization appears to be a pro-poor policy. However, the losses to the net producers of paddy have only been partially incorporated into the analysis due to the unavailability of data. Moreover in this analysis it has been assumed that quantities do not adjust due to price changes, and the results show only the impacts in the short run. Further analysis is required to reveal medium- and long-term impacts.

Another aspect of the study was the analysis of the effect of the elimination of the oligopsony power of middlemen. This can be considered as one possible strategy to mitigate the adverse impacts of rice trade liberalization on the farming community. Results reveal that losses to the paddy producers due to trade liberalization can be minimized if oligopsony power is eliminated simultaneously. Further research is necessary to reveal the actual degree of oligopsony power and therefore the extent of potential gains.

The overall policy recommendation emerging from the study is support of rice trade liberalization to secure efficiency gains. To minimize the losses to the farming community, it is recommended that well-designed complementary reforms be implemented to eliminate the oligopsony power exercised by middlemen.

## Notes

1. The 1960s saw the emergence of several state enterprises to promote nonpaddy agricultural activities in the country, such as the National Milk Board and the Ceylon Fisheries Corporation and Fishery Harbour Corporation.

2. The government also used the PMB to intervene in the market for other field crops, such as vegetables and eggs.

3. In 1977 the multiple exchange rate system was converted into a unified system. In addition many state-owned enterprises were subjected to liquidation or conversion into public companies, in which the state initially retained the majority shareholding. These controlling stakes were later sold to the private sector through competitive bidding.

4. The AIDS demand system was estimated for the period 1979–2000 and the paddy supply formula was estimated for 1971–99. These two equations determined the period for the simulation experiments to be 1979–99.

5. See Chen and Ravallion (2002) for an exposition of the theory.

6. See Minot and Goletti (1999), Appendix 2, for a full derivation.

7. Note that the share of income from agriculture was used in the analysis because the share of income from rice was not available. This must have overestimated the losses and underestimated the net gains from rice trade liberalization.

8. Due to the unavailability of data, the Northeastern province was not included in the analysis.

9. See Azzam and Pagoulatoes (1990) for a model adapted to either oligopoly or oligopsony—that is, market domination by a few sellers or a few buyers.

10.  The output market is assumed to be competitive as it is open to the world market, subject to an import tariff.

## References

Abeyratne, F., E. Neville, W. G. Somaratne, and P. Wickramaarachchi. 1990. Efficiency of rice production and issues relating to protection. *Sri Lanka Journal of Agricultural Economics* 1 (1): 16–25.

Amarasinghe, N. 1974. Efficiency of resource utilization in paddy production on settlement farms in Sri Lanka. *Modern Ceylon Studies* 5 (1): 77–91.

Azzam, A., and E. Pagoulatoes. 1990. Oligopolistic and oligopsonistic behaviour: An application to the U.S. meat packing industry. *Journal of Agricultural Economics* 41: 362–370.

Bogahawatte, C. 1992. Impact of food aid on consumption behavior of rural sector households in semi-arid districts of Sri Lanka. *Sri Lankan Journal of Agricultural Sciences* 29: 46–56.

Central Bank of Sri Lanka. 1999. *Report on consumer finances and socio-economic survey, Sri Lanka 1996/97.* Colombo.

——. 2001. *Annual report, 2000.* Colombo.

——. Various issues. *Annual report.* Colombo.

Chen, S., and M. Ravallion. 2002. *Household welfare impacts of trade reform in China.* Washington, D.C.: World Bank.

Deaton, A., and J. Muellbauer. 1980. An almost ideal demand system. *American Economic Review* 70 (3): 312–326.

Department of Agriculture. Various issues. *Cost of cultivation of agricultural crops, 1980/81, 1990/91 and 2000/01.* Colombo.

Department of Census and Statistics. 2002. *Household income and expenditure survey, 2002.* Colombo.

——. 2008a. *Household income and expenditure survey, 2006/07.* Colombo. http://www.statistics .gov.lk/HIES/HIES2006_07Website/index.htm.

——. 2008b. *Sri Lanka Demographic and Health Survey, 2006/7: Preliminary Report.* Colombo. http://www.statistics.gov.lk/DHS/DHS%20Sri%20Lanka%20Preliminary%20Report.pdf.

Dharmaratne, T. A., and C. P. Hathurusinghe. 1999. Paddy/rice marketing: Perspectives and prospects in 90's. *Economic Review* (January–March): 6–11.

Ekanayake, S. 2003. Impact of rice trade liberalization in Sri Lanka. Unpublished project report. Peradeniya: Department of Agricultural Economics, University of Peradeniya.

Ellis, F., P. Senanayake, and M. Smith. 1997. Food price policy in Sri Lanka. *Food Policy* 22 (1): 81–96.

Epaarachchi, R., S. Jayanetti, and A. Weliwita. 2002. *Policies and their implications for the domestic agricultural sector of Sri Lanka: 1995–2002.* Agricultural Policy Series 5. Colombo: Institute of Policy Studies.

Gunawardena, D. 2000. *Consumption poverty in Sri Lanka, 1985–1996: A profile of poverty based on household survey data.* Washington, D.C.: World Bank.

Harrison, P. 1995. Domestic marketing in the non-plantation crop sector in Sri Lanka. In *Sri Lanka: Non-plantation crop sector policy alternatives.* Working Paper 1. Washington, D.C.: World Bank.

Herath, D., and J. Weerahewa. 2005. Food security in Sri Lanka. Paper presented at the South Asia regional conference on globalization of agriculture in South Asia: Has it made a difference to rural livelihoods?, held March 23–25 in Hyderabad, India.

Karunaratne, M. A. K. H. S. S., and H. M. G. Herath. 1989. Efficiency of rice production under major irrigation conditions: A frontier production function approach. *Tropical Agricultural Research* 1: 142–157.

Kelegama, S. 2000. Food security issues in Sri Lanka. In *Hector Kobbakaduwa felicitation volume,* ed. S. G. Samarasinghe. Colombo: Hector Kobbakaduwa Trust.

Kikuchi, M., R. Barker, M. Samad, and P. Weligamage. 2000. Comparative advantage of rice production in an ex-rice importing country: The case of Sri Lanka. Paper presented at the third conference of the Asian Society of Agricultural Economists, held October 18–20 in Jaipur, India.

———. 2002. Comparative advantage of rice production in an ex-rice importing country: The case of Sri Lanka. In *Sustainable agriculture, poverty and food security,* Volume 1, ed. S. S. Acharya, S. Singh, and V. Sagar. Jaipur, India: Rawat.

McCulloch, N. 2002. The impact of structural reform on poverty: A simple methodology with extensions. Paper presented at the Organisation for Economic Co-operation and Development seminar How are globalization and poverty interacting and what can governments do about it?, held December 9–10 in Paris.

Minot, N., and F. Goletti. 1999. *Rice market liberalization and poverty in Viet Nam.* Research Report 114. Washington, D.C.: International Food Policy Research Institute.

Nicita, A., M. Olarreaga, and I. Soloaga. 2002. *A simple methodology to assess the poverty impact of economic policies using household data: An application to Cambodia.* Washington, D.C.: World Bank.

Rafeek, M. I. M., and P. A. Samarathunga. 2000. Trade liberalization and its impact on the rice sector of Sri Lanka. *Sri Lankan Journal of Agricultural Economics* 3: 143–154.

Ranaweera, N. F. C., P. A. Samarathunga, and A. A. B. Hafi. 1990. Economics of paddy production: Past, present and future. In *Proceedings of the Rice Congress, Department of Agriculture,* ed. S. L Amarasiri, S. Nagarajah, and B. M. K. Perera, 147–68. Peradeniya, Sri Lanka: Department of Agriculture.

Rupasena, L. P. 2002. Food marketing: Problems, constraints and solutions. *Economic Review* 28 (2–5): 22–27.

Rupasena, L. P., and T. Ravichandran. 2000. Marketing system for paddy and rice. Paper presented September 13–14 at Eastern University, Sri Lanka.

Sadoulet, E., and A. de Janvry. 1995. *Quantitative development policy analysis.* Baltimore, Md., U.S.A.: Johns Hopkins University Press.

Sanderatne, N. 2001. Food security: Concept, situation and policy perspectives. *Sri Lanka Economic Journal* 2 (2): 22–37.

Shilpi, F. 1995. Policy incentive, diversification and comparative advantage of non-plantation crops in Sri Lanka. Working Paper 2 (Sri Lanka). Washington, D.C.: World Bank.

Somaratne, W. G. 1987. Some aspects of paddy/rice marketing in Sri Lanka. Unpublished M.Sc. thesis, Wye College, Kent, U.K.

Strotz, R. H. 1957. The empirical implications of a utility tree. *Econometrica* 25: 269–280.

Tudawe, I. 2002. Food demand and energy adequacy: Implications for the poor. *Sri Lanka Economic Journal* 2 (2): 73–108.

Ubaldulah, S. A. M. 1999. Problems and challenges encountered by rice producers. *Economic Review* 24 (10–12): 26–28.

Weerahewa, J., H. M. Gunatilake, and H. Pitigala. 2003. Future of paddy farming in Sri Lanka: Scale, comparative advantage and rural poverty. *Sri Lanka Economic Journal* 3 (2): 104–144.

Wicramasinghe, W. D. 1999. Government intervention in rice market. *Economic Review* 25 (January–March): 12–13.

World Bank. 2000. Sri Lanka integrated survey of the World Bank. Produced in collaboration with the Sri Lanka Department of External Resources. Colombo, Sri Lanka. http://www.erd.gov.lk/publicweb/ERDDOCS.html. Accessed February 24, 2010.

Yoshimura H., M. P. Perera, and P. J. Gunawardana. 1975. *Some aspects of paddy and rice marketing in Sri Lanka: Based on a study done in four selected districts.* Colombo: Agrarian Research and Training Institute.

# Conclusion

A. Ganesh-Kumar, Devesh Roy, and Ashok Gulati

The availability of adequate sources of nutrition is an issue with serious implications for human and physical capital formation, and ultimately for overall economic growth. The relationship between food security and poverty follows a vicious circle, and food security is thus critical in achieving sustainable growth and development. In the past half century, the South Asian nations have come a long way in enhancing food availability to their citizens. India and Pakistan have emerged as food-surplus states, while food deficits in Bangladesh and Sri Lanka have declined. Nepal is the only country in the region that has moved the other way.

The countries all adopted similar policy measures soon after independence, though their policies diverged over time. New agricultural technology eventually brought about changes in food production and availability that would have been scarcely conceivable years earlier, in spite of the pro-industry bias of the initial phases of development. But policy reforms—adopted first by Sri Lanka, followed by Bangladesh, India, Nepal, and Pakistan—have had varying impacts on food production and availability. India and Pakistan have pursued a gradual approach toward liberalization, rewarded by a food surplus; Sri Lanka's relatively freer approach has not yielded a similar outcome. Nepal, in spite of significant reforms at the border, suffers from considerable market imperfections domestically due to its challenging topography.

The preceding chapters bring out many interesting analytical conclusions and policy implications related to food security in these nations. In this chapter we summarize the unified messages that emerge from the country studies and highlight the way forward for countries in South Asia to enhance their gains through further policy changes.

## Messages from the Country Studies

### Cost Effectiveness of Public Intervention in Domestic Grain Markets

Public-sector intervention in domestic grain markets through procurement and storage has been in vogue in all five countries, though it has been severely rolled back in Nepal and to a lesser extent also in Bangladesh and Sri Lanka. In India and Pakistan government intervention in this area continues to be significant. These interventions in the marketing of foodgrains are fraught with serious inefficiencies.

In Chapter 3 Jha, Srinivasan, and Ganesh-Kumar estimate the marketing costs of private traders at only 70 percent of the costs borne by the Food Corporation of India, the parastatal agency responsible for procurement and storage. Similarly in Chapter 5 Ahmad et al. show that the incidental costs of the parastatals in Pakistan—the provincial food departments and the Pakistan Agricultural Services and Storage Corporations—were 15–27 percent higher than those for private traders for the years 2000–03. For Nepal Chapter 4 provides evidence that the marketing costs of private traders were about 41 percent lower than those of the Nepal Food Corporation from the 1980s through the early 2000s. Bangladesh seems to be the only exception to this rule: private traders there have slightly higher costs than the government (by about 1 percent).

These large inefficiencies bring home the need for drastic reforms of the government machinery for procurement and storage. Such public intervention was perhaps necessary during the decades immediately following decolonization, which were marked by serious and recurring food shortages. More recently, however, the inefficient functioning of the procurement and storage systems raises fundamental questions about the rationale for intervention in the foodgrains market. A more basic objection centers on the significant price distortions that arise directly from government procurement and support price operations.

Ahmad et al. show that in Pakistan the real prices of commodities in cases in which the government does not intervene have remained more stable (with some of them even showing a small rise) compared to the prices of commodities in which the government intervenes. Indeed the market price of wheat has usually been *higher* than the government-announced support prices; coercive measures are therefore often required to achieve procurement targets. They also point to evidence suggesting widespread corruption and leakages in government procurement and storage operations. The benefits from procurement operations (if any), they argue, are reaped by only a few, while the majority of farmers, particularly small farmers, do not benefit at all from the system.

Several studies for India show that the situation is no different. In the past government procurement and stock operations operated at a price lower than the market price (Vyas 2003), in effect serving as a tax on farmers. The situation reversed briefly during the late 1990s and early 2000s when the government offered a higher-than-market price, resulting in large stocks being absorbed by the government—even as significant segments of the population are undernourished and remain hungry (Parikh, Ganesh-Kumar, and Darbha 2003). Dev et al. (2004) point out that in the late 1990s the Indian government increased both the procurement and the "offtake" price for its public distribution system (PDS), in order to keep the food subsidy bill in check. With the narrowing of the price differential between the PDS and the retail market, PDS distribution declined, highlighting the failure of the system to benefit consumers. The decline in the offtake through the PDS is indeed one of the reasons cited in the literature for the slowdown in India's reduction of poverty during the 1990s. The Indian experience highlights the problems with public procurement, stocking, and distribution at administratively fixed prices that conflict with market prices, especially within the context of a liberal trade regime. If it is to materially benefit consumers, such a system will either impose an implicit tax on farmers or else require enormous subsidies that may not be fiscally sustainable.

### Impact of Border Trade Reforms

Of foremost interest in this book is the impact of border reforms on food security—that is, the reduction or elimination of tariffs and subsidies and the removal of quantitative restrictions on imports and exports. The country case studies show that this impact depends on whether the country is a net importer or a net exporter of food. For net importing countries (such as Bangladesh, Nepal, Sri Lanka, and, until recently, Pakistan), trade liberalization would increase import competition, thus lowering domestic prices. Lower prices benefit consumers but harm producers. The studies for these four countries bear this out clearly with respect to the most important item in the food basket: rice in the case of Bangladesh, Nepal, and Sri Lanka and wheat in the case of Pakistan.

In Chapter 2 Chowdhury, Farid, and Roy show that the real price of rice has fallen in Bangladesh by 2.57 percent per annum during the period 1981–2003. (Trade restrictions were gradually liberalized during the 1990s.) Liberalization also helped by smoothing seasonal price fluctuations during those decades. They also demonstrate that competition among private traders forced them to source commodities from the cheapest (usually the closest) international suppliers. Since the mid-1990s India has replaced Thailand as the main supplier of rice imported into Bangladesh. The fall in rice prices clearly benefited poor consumers, as seen in the narrowing of the per capita consumption gap between the bottom 40 percent and the top 20 percent of the population. The Gini coefficient of foodgrain consumption halved, from 0.08 in 1992 to 0.04 in 2000. Trade liberalization seems to have improved food security in that country.

A similar outcome is seen in the case of Nepal. In Chapter 4 Pyakuryal, Thapa, and Roy show that almost 10 percent of the rice consumed in that country is sourced from India; cheap rice from India has likely benefited 60 percent of the landless households. (A large undocumented flow probably further raises the share of rice from India.) However, the benefit from trade liberalization seems to be limited to districts bordering India. The price in the terai region is on average 12 percent lower than that in the remote parts of Nepal (the hill and mountain regions)—approaching the difference in price between Indian and Nepalese rice. Simulation results using a computable general equilibrium (CGE) model for Nepal confirm that farm households suffer a loss in output and income, resulting in a welfare loss in the terai as well as in the hill and mountain regions. The welfare gains for consumers and income losses for farmers affect different segments of the population differently. The simulation results show that trade liberalization would produce a slight reduction in the depth of poverty in rural areas among the very poorest, but a rise in poverty among the moderately poor, while the very wealthy households would be the main beneficiaries.

In the Sri Lankan study in Chapter 6 simulation exercises by Weerahewa using a partial equilibrium model for rice show that, following trade liberalization, prices have fallen by 34 percent. The benefit to consumers is reflected in a 45 percent rise in demand and a 33 percent rise in calorie intake. However, the adverse incentive effect on farmers would result in a 28 percent fall in the rice supply. Trade liberalization would improve efficiency, however, and would also help in poverty alleviation in certain categories. The model outcomes show a gain in welfare that is highest for the very poor and lowest for the nonpoor, while the moderately poor incur the highest losses. Among Sri Lanka's geographic sectors, the estate sector—with the second highest incidence of poverty—gains the most, as net buyers of rice. Among regions, the Northwestern province, with the highest incidence of poverty, gains the most, as it is not a major rice-producing region.

In Chapter 5 Ahmad et al., using a CGE model, find a similar contrast in the impact on consumers and producers following wheat trade liberalization in Pakistan. Pakistan has recently become a net exporter of its main staple, wheat, a commodity that has been relatively untouched by trade reforms. To capture the effect of trade liberalization under conditions when Pakistan was a net importer of wheat, Ahmad et al. calibrate the model parameters to the 1990s. Using international wheat prices as reference prices, they find that the 1990s suffered market distortions in the form of a consumption subsidy (22 percent) and a production tax (23 percent). Their simulation results show that removing these distortions for wheat would on balance be welfare improving: the producers would gain somewhat more than the consumers would lose. Part of the net gain reflects a reduction in the rents paid to millers, who are the primary purchasers of wheat grains.

The findings for these four countries stand out in contrast to the findings of similar studies for India, a net exporter of cereals. In Chapter 3 Jha, Srinivasan, and Ganesh-Kumar report that for a net exporting country trade liberalization would result in a rise in domestic prices. The rise would benefit farmers but hurt consumers. Reviewing studies that have carried out simulations using CGE models, they show that agricultural trade liberalization benefits only *some* sections in rural areas and adversely affects *all* classes in the urban sector. Furthermore, within agriculture, liberalization of the rice sector would result in an increase in rice exports and rice prices, as the preliberalization domestic price is lower than the world market price. This would hurt the welfare of all sections of the population except the rural rich. The actual Indian experience in the 1990s, as analyzed here, confirms these findings.

### Spatial Integration of Domestic Markets

A major lesson that emerges from the country case studies is the importance of spatial integration of domestic markets for food security. Spatial integration refers to the degree of price uniformity between different regions within a country and depends on the ease with which goods can be moved from a surplus region to a deficit region. From the perspective of food security, spatially integrated markets ensure that local shortages in certain food items do not translate into a sharp rise in prices, forcing a reduction in food consumption and ultimately resulting in diminished food security.

Difficult physical terrain without transportation infrastructure is typically the main reason for lack of spatial integration. The case of Nepal exemplifies this scenario. However, as the cases of India and Pakistan show, government policies that regulate the movement of goods between districts or states also result in a lack of integration.

Difficulties relating to terrain require sustained investments in transport infrastructure to enable easy movement of goods across a country. The contrasting experiences of Bangladesh and Nepal stand testimony to this. Both countries face difficulties due to terrain—especially the hills and mountains in Nepal and, less dramatically, the river-crossed landmass of Bangladesh. While Bangladesh invested consistently in developing transport and communication infrastructure, Nepal's record on this front is abysmal.

Since the 1990s, road kilometerage in Bangladesh has grown by over 4 percent, the number of trucks by nearly 5 percent, and telephone connections by nearly 17 percent. This led to significant savings in time, reflected in a noticeable fall in transport and marketing costs. In Chapter 2 Chowdhury, Farid, and Roy point out that these improvements led to the emergence of new production centers and marketing channels, resulting in greater spatial integration of the food markets in Bangladesh.

In Nepal the situation in the hill and mountain regions presents a clear contrast to that in the terai region. The terai has relatively better transport and communication infrastructure, providing opportunities for private sectors to exploit price differentials. Significant price differentials prevail among the three regions. Pyakuryal, Thapa, and Roy refer to several studies that have pointed out the contrast between the terai on the one hand and the hills and mountains on the other.

Overcoming terrain and infrastructural bottlenecks to improve spatial integration requires sustained efforts over a long period of time—especially in hilly and mountainous terrain such as Nepal's. Policy-induced spatial isolation of markets (as in India and Pakistan) can be overcome more readily, given political determination. Removing the restrictions on intracountry movement of goods can fairly quickly result in large efficiency gains.

This is clear from the study by Jha, Srinivasan, and Ganesh-Kumar in Chapter 3, using a spatial equilibrium model for rice and wheat in India. That study shows that India's zoning policies systematically increase interstate food price dispersion. This leads to a worsening of food security for food-deficit households in food-deficit states. With the removal of these zoning restrictions, private trade would occur between neighboring states, driven by arbitrage possibilities rather than their deficit or surplus status. This is in contrast to the practice of government agencies, trading directly between surplus and deficit states over long distances. Significant savings in trade and transport costs can thus be realized, resulting in a fall in prices in the deficit states and greater price stability between states. The consequent rise in demand and welfare in the deficit states more than balances any producer loss in surplus states. Furthermore the government realizes savings on procurement and stocking. Another interesting finding is that removal of zoning laws combined with external trade liberalization opens up the possibility of some deficit states sourcing their food from international markets rather than from surplus states within the country, due to differences between the international and domestic transport costs.

While India has removed explicit zoning restrictions for foodgrains, interstate movement barriers continue to persist in several other forms. For example, the requirement that transport operators have interstate or national permits to move goods (of any kind, not just grains) represents a barrier, as it provides a rent to the few who have such permits. State- and local-level entry taxes (octroi) collected from transporters on the value of goods constitute other interstate movement barriers. Jha, Srinivasan, and Ganesh-Kumar also find that a reduction in domestic transport costs has a much larger impact on interregional price stability than the removal of zoning laws by itself. This again points to the critical importance of infrastructure investments in promoting spatial integration of markets.

## Role of Domestic Market Structures

One of the persistent complaints about private traders in agricultural markets, especially food markets, is that they have relatively more market power than either farmers or consumers. The market power of traders works in two directions. In their transactions with farmers, traders have oligopsony powers, while in their transactions with consumers they have oligopoly powers. This allows them to be price fixers and not price takers in both sides of the transaction. The large traders' margin is in fact often taken as justification for government intervention in agricultural markets. But, as already shown, government intervention in foodgrains market has not been the solution to the problem. Nevertheless the problem of traders' market power is real and must be addressed in most developing countries.

In Chapter 6 Weerahewa examines the impact of eliminating this market power on the prices faced by farmers, and the resulting impact on farm output and income. She develops a simple model in which the paddy collectors and millers are competitive in the output market but possess oligopsony powers in the input market, that is, in their transactions with farmers. The results show that the impact of eliminating the market power of the middlemen depends on the underlying demand and supply elasticities and on the degree of initial market power. If the demand and supply are relatively elastic, elimination of oligopsony powers is not sufficient to compensate for the negative impact of free trade on price and quantity of paddy. If the degree of market power is near unity (that is, a situation of near monopsony), then elimination of market power is more than sufficient to compensate for the negative impact of free trade on price and quantity. If the demand and supply are inelastic, elimination of oligopsony power has positive impacts on prices and quantities under both autarky and free trade, though the impact under free trade is less. These results suggest that losses to paddy producers from trade liberalization can certainly be minimized, if the oligopsony power can be restrained along with the implementation of border reforms.

Chowdhury, Farid, and Roy point to a situation in which growth in production and marketable surplus in Bangladesh led to the entry of a new breed of traders who did not indulge in loan gouging. The number of rice traders in Bangladesh increased twelvefold, from 4,000 in the 1960s to over 48,000 by the 1990s. Similarly the number of rice mills increased from about 6,000 to over 50,000 during this period. The resulting competition among traders and millers has led to a twofold increase in the radius of their marketing sphere over this period. The authors claim that this rise in competition among traders has ensured that farmers are able to avoid distress selling, hold a fairly high proportion of stocks on farm, and sell their produce at the farmgate rather than in distant markets, thereby avoiding transportation costs. The absence of large-scale government intervention in the output market in Bangladesh is a major reason for the increase in competition in trading services.

These findings clearly point out the importance of bringing greater competition to domestic markets even when they are being thrown open to international competition. Reduction in traders' margins will benefit both producers and consumers.

## The Way Forward

### Within-Country Policy Changes

An overarching message that emerges from the country studies is that government intervention in food markets in most of South Asia has had limited success but many failures. The successes have been mostly in promoting new agricultural technologies that have resulted in a rise in productivity levels in the region, making the region as a whole either self-sufficient or nearly so. But the path is littered with many policy failures that, if anything, stifle agriculture and prevent or slow down poverty reduction and hinder further improvements in food security.

Most of the failures are due either to excessive interventions by the government in the domestic markets for foodgrains or lack of policy initiatives to provide the necessary infrastructure to develop a competitive market. These failures have led to serious distortions in the price regime, prevented the development of spatially integrated domestic markets, and stifled internal competition, resulting in the concentration of market power in the hands of traders. As a result of these market failures, farmers in the region are subject to serious disincentives, which, if left uncorrected, threaten to reverse some of the gains in national-level food security achieved by these countries in the past.

Divergence in the evolution of policy measures over the past four decades in these countries indicates that each of them faces different tasks going forward. While Bangladesh has effectively liberalized its regime over the past few years, excessive governmental procurement of food is still a reality. Given the fiscal burden of such procurement schemes, it is imperative that the private sector be entrusted with increased participation, especially given that its involvement in food procurement and distribution has already yielded positive results in the postliberalization regime.

The landlocked country of Nepal, on the other hand, faces a unique topographical challenge, which has led to a stratified retail price structure for foodgrains within the country. Consequently people in the high-altitude mountain regions are being regressively taxed. The Nepalese government needs to concentrate on the development of adequate transport infrastructure; a smoother flow of supply from the plains to higher altitudes can decrease the price differential between the terai and the mountains.

As the contrasting experiences of Bangladesh and Nepal suggest, government's primary role in these countries should be investing in infrastructure—such as irrigation, storage, transport, and communication—that helps promote agricultural production and deepen agricultural markets. Furthermore government should move away from subsidizing inputs used primarily by only a few farmers and toward subsidizing general-purpose public goods, such as agricultural research and extension services.

In spite of liberalizing earlier than its neighbors, Sri Lanka has had a variable trade policy. Rather than following a procyclical tariff policy tied to the domestic availability of food, the government should maintain tariffs at a consistent level. Such policy stability will ensure better intertemporal smoothing of domestic consumption. Under such a regime effective measures to improve agricultural productivity will help Sri Lanka attain food security earlier than it will under the current policy.

Even the food-surplus countries, India and Pakistan, must undertake further measures to correct market imperfections and anomalies. Reeling from serious fiscal imbalances, these countries must look again at their elaborate public machinery for food procurement and distribution. It is time that government's role be restricted to facilitating private participation and maintaining orderly conditions in the food-grains markets. In their study on India, Jha, Srinivasan, and Ganesh-Kumar have highlighted the gains from trade liberalization, assuming an unchanged public distribution policy. But if government were to reduce or eliminate its unproductive expenses on food procurement and food stock maintenance, the social gains could be used to generate productive investments and employment. In fact, on theoretical grounds, this seems to be true for all the countries in the region. India must also do away with existing restrictions on within-country movement of foodgrains.

Overall the role of the government in each of these countries should ultimately be limited to promoting competition within the country, so that domestic price determination can be free of policy-induced distortions. This will help farmers to better allocate resources, as well as allow consumers to benefit from competitively priced food. Government must recognize the role of the private sector in all these activities. The private sector delivers best in a competitive environment, and, as the Bangladesh and Sri Lanka studies show, competition among traders can indeed deliver outcomes favorable for the food security of the poor. In Bangladesh competition among traders resulted in a decline in real food prices as well as reduced volatility of food prices—both outcomes favorable to food security.

But the role of the private sector need not be limited to trading activities. It can also deliver in other spheres that bear directly on agriculture and food security: agricultural extension services, value addition in agriculture, and the development of infrastructure. For the private sector to deliver, however, the policy regime governing the domestic markets is at least as important as border trade reforms.

### Intraregional Trade and Rationale for Policy Coordination

A theme that is implicit in the country case studies is the need for policy coordination among the countries of South Asia, especially in view of the rise in intraregional trade in rice and wheat in the region. Bangladesh and Nepal, unlike Pakistan and Sri Lanka, have relatively porous borders with India, and border trade protection measures can therefore have only a limited bite. The impact of policies pursued by India—the largest economy in the region—would be felt across the border in both Bangladesh and Nepal, and perhaps to a lesser extent in Sri Lanka. India's policies regarding farm output and input subsidies would have direct implications for the farmers of net importing countries. Output subsidies by India would dampen prices in Bangladesh, Nepal, and Sri Lanka even more than the country case studies suggest, with adverse consequences for farmers in those countries.

This clearly brings out the need for greater policy coordination among the countries of the region, and especially for greater policy discipline on the part of India. Recurring political differences, however, make it difficult to coordinate economic policies. The platform afforded by the South Asian Association for Regional Cooperation (SAARC) can be explored to promote policy coordination.

In August 2008 the 15th SAARC summit in Colombo was held against the backdrop of an unprecedented rise in food prices. The food price crisis produced a realization that there could be a collective benefit from regional cooperation in ensuring each country's food security. The summit thus adopted a declaration that reaffirmed SAARC's resolve to ensure regionwide food security and make South Asia the granary of the world. This was followed by a meeting of regional agriculture ministers in early November 2008, which adopted the SAARC Declaration on Food Security.

The food price crisis also brought out the stark consequences of uncoordinated actions aimed at achieving greater *national* food security. India's unilateralism in banning exports, for example—initially even to Bangladesh—compounded the impact of international food price hikes on that country. Recognizing that surplus and deficit countries are neighbors, the November 2008 declaration included a proposal for a regional granary to which all countries would contribute; any severe idiosyncratic shock would trigger outflow from the cumulative stocks to supply the affected country. The regional food bank is still under consideration, but its merits seem to be well recognized. In principle a regional physical food bank is akin to country-specific buffer stocks, but with an expanded supply base and a lower level of control by each government. Based on the analysis in this volume, however, a regional food bank would prove largely ineffective unless trade within the region were also liberalized— just as internal movement restrictions within a country impede government efforts to smooth prices. Hence free trade agreements, such as those provided for in the South Asian Free Trade Area, need to be adopted by the regional governments as a complementary and essential collective action.

A regional food bank and freer trade are expected to smooth price differentials across space and time by moving grains from surplus to deficit areas. Localized higher prices can generally be attributed, at least in part, to speculative bubbles: arbitrage opportunities from anticipated higher future prices create incentives to horde and thus create an artificial shortage in the markets. Physical stocks involve slow transactions as well as storage costs that could make the cost-benefit ratio higher for such stocks. As a complementary policy, von Braun and Torero (2008) propose the idea of a *virtual* reserve, backed by a financial fund, that could be a contingent supply of national food reserves. Such a mechanism could lower the incentive to speculate, as long as it is deemed credible that, when prices rise beyond a certain level, the virtual reserves would become real through government intervention. This would mitigate at least some price spikes.

The project of creating regional reserves, whether physical or virtual, would require third-party facilitation—not only financial but also political. In the case of South Asia, the design of such a project would be complicated less by economics than by the complex politics of the region.

A further avenue of regional cooperation, with direct implications for food security for the region as a whole, is the transport of food commodities, as many observers have noted. For example, it could be advantageous for India to transport goods to its northeastern states via Bangladesh.

Limited border trade reforms have ushered in a new era of food production and availability in the South Asian countries, but there remains scope for further improvement. Effective food policy measures have great potential for decreasing poverty and thus enhancing economic growth. The combined effect of correct policy reforms, good governance, and economic growth will ensure food security to current and future generations in the region.

## References

Dev, S. M., C. Ravi, B. Viswanathan, A. Gulati, and S. Ramachander. 2004. *Economic liberalisation, targeted programmes and household food security.* MTID Discussion Paper 68. Washington, D.C.: International Food Policy Research Institute.

Parikh, K. S., A. Ganesh-Kumar, and G. Darbha. 2003. Growth and welfare consequences of rise in MSP. *Economic and Political Weekly,* March 1, 891–895.

Von Braun, J., and M. Torero. 2008. *Physical and virtual global food reserves to protect the poor and prevent market failure.* Policy Brief 4. Washington, D.C.: International Food Policy Research Institute.

Vyas, V. S. 2003. Market reforms in Indian agriculture. Paper presented at the JNU-IFPRI workshop on the dragon and the elephant: A comparative study of economic and agricultural reforms in China and India, held March 25–26 in New Delhi.

# Contributors

**Munir Ahmad** is a professor at the Pakistan Institute of Development Economics, Islamabad, Pakistan.

**Nuimuddin Chowdhury** is an independent consultant for the Small and Medium Enterprise Foundation, Dhaka, Bangladesh.

**Caesar Cororaton** is a research fellow in the Global Issues Initiative of the Institute of Society, Culture, and the Environment at Virginia Polytechnic Institute and State University, Blacksburg, Va., U.S.A. He is also a consultant for the International Food Policy Research Institute and the World Bank, Washington, D.C.

**Paul Dorosh** is a senior research fellow in the Development Strategy and Governance Division of the International Food Policy Research Institute, Washington, D.C.

**Nasir Farid** is a doctoral student in economics at the University of Reading, United Kingdom.

**A. Ganesh-Kumar** is an associate professor at the Indira Gandhi Institute of Development Research, Mumbai, India.

**Ashok Gulati** is director in Asia for the International Food Policy Research Institute, Washington, D.C., and is based in New Delhi.

**Muhammad Iqbal** is head of the Department of Agricultural Production, Markets and Institutions Division, Pakistan Institute of Development Economics, Islamabad, Pakistan.

**Shikha Jha** is a senior economist in the Economics and Research Department, Asian Development Bank, Manila, Philippines.

**Bishwambher Pyakuryal** is a professor in the Central Department of Economics, Tribhuvan University, Kathmandu, Nepal.

**Abdul Qayyum** is head of the Department of Econometrics and Statistics, Pakistan Institute of Development Economics, Islamabad, Pakistan.

**Devesh Roy** is a research fellow in the Markets, Trade, and Institutions Division of the International Food Policy Research Institute, Washington, D.C.

**P. V. Srinivasan** is a professor at the Indira Gandhi Institute of Development Research, Mumbai, India

**Y. B. Thapa** is president of the Renaissance Society Nepal, Kathmandu, Nepal.

**Jeevika Weerahewa** is a senior lecturer in the Department of Agricultural Economics and Business Management, Faculty of Agriculture, University of Peradeniya, Peradeniya, Sri Lanka.

# Index

Page numbers for entries occurring in boxes are suffixed by *b*, those for entries occurring in figures by *f*, those for entries occurring in notes by *n*, and those for entries occurring in tables by *t*.